THE SHOCKING

THE SHOCKING

THE MESSAGE

CHARLES FLETCHER

ARPress
ILLUMINATING IDEAS
EMPOWERING VOICES

ARPress
45 Dan Road Suite 36
Canton MA 02021

Hotline: 1(888) 821-0229
Fax: 1(508) 545-7580

Ordering Information:
Quantity Sales. Special discounts are available on quantity purchases by corporations, associations, and others. For details, contact the publisher at the address above.

Printed in the United States of America.

ISBN-13   Paperback   979-8-89389-832-3
             eBook   979-8-89389-833-0

Library of Congress Control Number: 2024923526

The Shocking

If you have an open mind and are seeking a much higher level of truth and understanding this book is for you.

This book is for those who are *environmentally conscience.*

Charles Fletcher

This Book

Is dedicated to the two women I love the most, my beloved Mother who nourished me to become who I am today, my beautiful wife Vivian the one that really helps me to understand what I am today. And to all of my wonderful children and grandchildren and great grandchildren that gave me the courage, inspiration, and the light to find the path to where I am today.

Contents

Polluted Thoughts

By Torrance Holmes

Please lend me an ear to something you need to Hear, about hazardous
chemicals in the atmosphere

Certain elements are causing environmental change and got us Acting
strange, dangerous toxin chemicals are clogging our brains

These chemicals make it hard to stay focus, it seems the fight for fresh
air is hopeless, making violent behavior more explosive

Unlike formally, we're no longer breathing normally, our Children are
being born with larger numbers of deformity

The average citizens are blind or not paying attention,
The government is aware of this fact but want mention

Please listen and pay very close attention, we're Victims of modern day
slavery chemical lynching

Chemical miscarriages to unborn daughters and sons, Overtaken by
toxin chemicals in the mother's lungs

We're having trouble breathing and don't even know the reason, every
year it gets worst making it harder to adapt to change of season

This situation is massively harmful to our nation polluting

Our waters and vegetation. We have to rely on
environment education, or it's complete chemical malfunction we're facing

This work is a Non-Traditional approach to the effects of the elements in the Environment

This book contains information that will shock the consciousness of the reader and may change the way the individual think about life and the environment. This book is a **non-traditional** outlook on "the environment, what is the environment? What does the environment do? Why is it important to understand? What are the effects, how does it impact human behavior? What are the true effects? Where should you begin to look? First and foremost, it began within your human self, within your brain, your mind, your conscientious and sub-conscientious thinking. The **whole environment** is made of Atoms and many other elements that we point to below, we now look at the who, what, where, when and how of the environment as to what is the whole environment? We conclude that the earth, all planets, stars, galaxies, space are all part of the whole environment.

We call this the external workings of the environment. The human body was created from this same environment that is made up of flesh and bone. The skin or dermas is the outer layer of the human body and rightly so to cover the internal environment or the workings of the body that houses the organs, heart, kidneys, bladder, lungs, brain, blood, veins, vassals, plasma, brain tissue etc. How does the body function? It functions from the use of biological energy which is the same energy used to grow the many nutrients needed to support human life. It is the same energy that propels the planets to spin, the sun and stars to shin with high volumes of heat. This same energy that grows the food also supplies the food with the nutrients needed to energize the body once it is consumed.

This should have a profound effect on your health and understanding. What we know about the environment is very little but after reading this book you might not look at the environment the same way again. ***Had*** *we not written this book in the non—traditional style, it would not have the gravitas effect we wanted.* Many Scientists today is baffled by the little they do know. This work examines many separate environments, the elements, **Atoms**: All matter such as solids, liquids and gases are composed of atoms. Any material that composed of only one type of atom is called a chemical element. The atom is the smallest particle of any element also implies the characteristic of that element. For clarity these elements such as **Neutrons:** an elementary particle having no charge, mass slightly greater that of a Proton. A **Proton**: is a subatomic hadrons particle with a positive electric charge of one elementary charge, generally one or more protons are present in the nucleus of each atom, along with the neutron. Then there is the **Electron: a** subatomic particle carrying negative electric charge and the electron has a mass that is approximately 1/18.36 that of a proton. This imply that atoms are found within the human body as well as the external environment all around us at every second, then there is the earth's environment, the oxygen from trees and green foliage that we breath, the energy or air we inhale is to keep us alive, there is the environment above the earth, the atmosphere, ionosphere, stratosphere, troposphere, mesosphere, thermosphere, exosphere etc. The planets, stars, space, galaxies, the cosmos etc. As a connection to the whole of the environment. **Everything is the environment, and the environment is everything.**

Then there is **"Energy,"** this energy is created from *atoms, hydrogen, oxygen and helium*, energy is everything, everywhere and Omni-present, everything is energy, and energy is and will always be the controlling factor in the total environment. The intricate details of the elements in the environment begins with micro-organisms, they are always at work. *The whole of creation is nothing more than a science project in active motion*. The first is the internal environment of the human body, organisms this environment is totally separate from the external as mentioned above. The second is the external environment (see above), the third is the environment outside of the earth's atmosphere, out of space all mentioned above and there is a fourth environment.

The Fourth environment connects us with the next dimension and beyond or the afterlife, as it is called in religion, it may be called heaven or hell. The reader should beware that religion is not a science and could never become a science. All religions are unnatural from its original conception, religion was not created by the natural environment, such as atoms, neutrons, protons, electrons etc. It is an illusion and utterly impossible to take something from the natural environment and claim it as your own. To do this one must alter the elements from their natural inhabitant, meaning that they no longer function as they were intended, then we pretend to teach this unnatural behavior as a religion, it is no longer natural, it becomes unnatural and manmade. Energy is the teacher and provider of all knowledge and intelligence, like an alternating current, from energy we were created and to energy we will return.

Foot Note

In the practice of religion, a great percentage of believers have never ever question as to who God was, what God is and where God reside. The antiquated teachings in religion barred the believers from ever questioning the word or the source of the term called God, but why? Who is God and what is God? Why shouldn't the word of God be questioned? He or she who has an eye let them see. They who have an ear let them hear.

Our first focus should be the focus within the human anatomy that causes illness, disease, behavior, death, and the effects of magnetic energy fields. The process of thought through energy or the way one thinks or the process that develops thought are directly related to the environment that gives us the life we breathe. In no way have we tried or intended that this material should be the sole source of information that comes to a final conclusion. Much of the information contained in this book was taken from the many communications, newsletters we organized in Victory Heights West Pullman, the Hard-Times Newsletters written by the author. The reading flow may not be in the sequence of events, but the message is the same and very clear. It is the elements such as the atoms, electrons, neutrons, protons that creates and feeds the environment and this environment feeds into everything and everything feeds into the environment. All information is complex and fragmented to where we obtain a huge amount of information not truly understanding what is happening with the information we obtain around us. Many will never ever research their own individual minds to find the answers to their own thoughts.

We share this knowledge of the environment as it appears in the writer's eye, much of it is not taught in the public school, colleges, or universities. ***It is the energy in the environment that feeds into every single thing we do.*** There is not *one single thing* we can do that energy in the environment always produce the final outcome, ***NOT ONE.*** Many are born with intelligent insight on certain topics, in religion they say one is blessed. It is very true that you must be very careful as to what you wish for as it could be the very thing that will destroy you or elevate your thinking.

When one reads religious scriptures the reader general fines that the prophets had requested from their God to give them something that God had never gave to any other human being. Especially reading about King Solomon and his wisdom, this should give us more courage to search for knowledge. How is it that certain knowledge is given to certain individuals and not to others? We must search for it, and it is hidden in secret places in the deep recesses of the subconscious mind...

The Scripture states: "seek and you shall find". These are merely forms of expression that individuals had tested over the centuries of time, and they found that it help them to become what they wanted to become. It started out with *their own will power* to do what they wanted to do. Will power is *energy*, this energy provides the means of control, *energy levels* decrease it or expand it within one's own being to achieve the final outcome. A Prophet in religion only means to prophases on things to come or to take place in future times. What the environment does is not only tell you what is to come but also provides you with intelligence to show you the way as to **how** it will come.

Secret Societies

Like the Knight Templar's, Illuminati, Masonry, Skull and Bones just to name a few has been around for hundreds if not thousands of years and the more you read about them, the more conscious we become of their presents all around us. *These secret organizations are controlled by the Rich and Wealthy Slave Masters of the world today. They have systematically withheld certain knowledge from the masses as a control factor to instill fear into the minds of the people.* Let's get straight to the point. **I don't know about you but when we look at workings of these energies like Tornadoes, Hurricanes, Tsunami, Earthquakes, rain, snow heat in these disaster areas it always appears to happen in middle class and poor poverty-stricken communities.** You almost never see these disasters hitting rich wealthy communities, it almost never hit chateaus, mansions, the White House, the Pentagon, United Nations, The Queen of England's Castle, the Kremlin, etc. The United States must be prone for these disasters. I have never seen or heard of big city disasters, **they never hit prisons no matter where they are.** *We know that these systems are associated with energies that are produced by a mathematical system hidden from the eyes of the masses.* Climate change is real and a factor of creation, but **these things happen based upon human use of the elements in the environment.** They always say that this an act of "Mother Nature" to keep the masses from really looking at the root cause of these events. What is "Mother Nature"? **An action always causes a reaction.**

As a researcher and activist on the environmental question we merely want to awaken the conscientiousness of the reader so that they might understand the living environment that we now breathe. It was once said: **"Why should we believe in another person's facts"?** *"A history of all subjects is best qualified to reward research and study".* When we gather facts to support our change of thought, it should but not always agree with our common sense and understanding. We have more than five physical senses as we were taught in elementary school. We develop many other senses that may or may not confirm the truth of which we seek understanding. We in no way try to discourage anyone to stop believing in whatever it is that they believe to be true, we simply share this information so that you may decide for yourself what is true or false. If this material is against what you believe to be true or against the tenets of your faith, we urge strongly that you put this information down **now** and walk away from it.

Home is Where the Heartache Is

Mark Newman, NMA News Correspondent.
Location, location, location is the mantra used to describe prime real estate.

Unfortunately, it also refers to an underlying cause of why the health of so many African-Americans especially children is adversely affected. From the inner cities to the countryside, African Americans are far more likely to have illnesses impacted by their environment or in many instances, by what is located in proximity of their environment. In a 1983 study by the General Accounting Office, it was found that in the southeastern part of the U.S., 75% of all hazardous waste sites were located in or near predominantly African-American communities. "This is a historical problem, said "Dr. Jewel Crawford, Medical Officer in the Office of Urban Affairs at the Agency for Toxic Substances and Disease Registry. *"Anytime you have three-fourths of all dump sites near African-American communities, it's not coincidence or happenstance; it's racism".*

Dr. Crawford cited another study by the United Church of Christ, which found that in 1987, one in five of all African Americans lived within at least 1 mile of a hazardous waste site. "And these are just the sites that they know about", Dr. Crawford said. "There's no telling how many people live close to more than one dump site". Dump sites are not the only perils of living in rural or under populated areas, according to Daniel Schwartz, Executive Director of the Children's Environmental Health Network. "Rural areas have shutdown farms, and the pollutants are imported", he said. "Whereas in industrial areas of larger cities they are in close proximity. However, there is also the problem of factory farms that are so prevalent in rural areas, especially the southeast". Factory farms are where meat packagers grow their "crops', i.e., pigs, chickens, etc. In these factory farms there are hundreds of thousands of animals in a very concentrated area resulting in huge amounts of fertilizer and manure seeping into the ground water. Such seepage can greatly affect the amount of nitrates and nitrites found in the local water supply. These contaminants are of particular risk to infants as they interfere with the infant's ability to absorb oxygen, which can lead to methemoglobinemia (blue baby syndrome) and result in death.

Lead and the Environment

The most common of the environmental contaminants is lead. Lead levels were much higher in the environment before the advent of unleaded gasoline. Currently lead is most often found in paint and other construction materials. Lead is especially hazardous to young children where research has shown that 10 micrograms per deciliter of blood can result in lowered intelligence, reading and learning disabilities, reduced attention span, hyperactivity, and antisocial behavior. However, there is no "safe" level for lead in blood and lower concentrations can lead to other adverse health effects. For the years 1992 to 1994, the highest concentration of lead poisoning in children ages 1-5 were found among African American children regardless of poverty level. According to studies by the CDC, the National Center for Health Statistics, and the National Health and Nutrition Examination Survey, over 16% of African American children below the poverty level had elevated blood-lead levels compared to just over 6% of white children and almost 5% of Hispanic children. According to the March of dimes, 20 to 70% of all birth defects are related to the environment. "Compare race and infant mortality, "Dr. Crawford said. "Why is the infant mortality rate so much higher in black children? It's easy to say that the mothers simply don't have access to adequate prenatal care, but the impact of the environment is often overlooked.

When you have communities already impacted by racism, poverty, and lack of education, and those communities are often next to hazardous waste sites, it's easy to see how the problems can be exacerbated. It's hard to prove but the weight of evidence implicates the environment as a perpetrator".

Asthma and the Environment

Asthma also affects African Americans more adversely than other races, especially children. Almost 7% of all African American children under the age of 18 have some form of asthma according to the previously cited studies. When the study shifts to those children living below the poverty level, the percentage for African Americans rises to 8% with both white and Hispanic children's asthma levels just over 5%. "The death rate for asthma is on the rise and this is unconscionable, "Dr. Crawford said. "There is no reason why children should be dying from asthma". According to Asthma and the Role of Air Pollution published by physicians for Social Awareness, 5 million children in the United States have asthma. The death rate from asthma for children under the age of 19 has increased 78% from 1980 to 1983. Dr. Crawford cites the fact that so many African Americans who do not have health coverage do not seek treatment until their asthma has reached the critical stages, and by that point they often end up in the intensive care unit. Air pollution is an obvious link to asthma and is evidenced by the rise in emergency room visits for asthma-related causes when the outdoor air quality is lower. Children are especially susceptible because they tend to spend more time outside "absorbing" their environment. A study published in the September 2000 issue of the *American Journal of Respiratory and Critical Care Medicine* further reiterated the environmental link to asthma, but firmly established a link to urban environments rather than race alone. "Black populations living in Africa have very low prevalence, and the asthma that does occur is associated with environmental factors related to urbanization", according to Dr. Andrew C. Aligne lead author of the study.

Future Directions

The NMA is not oblivious to the effects of the environment on African American health, and it has taken the first step to investigate the situation further by establishing the Environmental Health Task Force. "One purpose of this task force is to educate and enlighten physicians in what to look for and how to treat and prevent exposure to environmental toxins. "He added that physicians are simply not trained in environmental health and that when a patient comes in with a certain ailment, seldom will a physician take that patient's environment into account. Dr. Crawford first saw the effects of the environment on patients' health while working in Oregon. "After 20 years as a family practitioner, I was not privy to information about the impact of the environment on health, and I'm no different from my colleagues", Dr. Crawford said. She noticed that several of her patients had thyroid problems, which she thought was odd. "At first I wondered if all these patients were related until one of them said that they were *'down winders'*—they lived downwind of a nearby nuclear power plant, "she said. "A patient gave me literature on the dangers of living near the nuclear power plant and that was my first exposure to environmental effects on health and its influence on illness". All physicians are inundated with information, Dr. Crawford added, but very little on the environment and health effects.

Physicians also need to be aware of what industries are in their practice area because many toxins are specific to certain communities, according to Dr. Morris. "The first is to determine what industries are in the community and use that industry as a guideline of sorts as to what to look for in the event that the environment plays a role in a patient's illness", he said.

"While dioxins may be a problem in one community, asbestos and lead may be a factor in another community simply based on what industries and manufacturing facilities are nearby". Dr. Crawford and Dr. Morris both agree that the impetus is not just on physicians-the public and industries themselves need to take part of the responsibility as well. "Doctors knowing what to look for and industry stopping these harmful practices are the answers", Dr. Crawford said. "But people have to be aware what's going on around them. All across the nation, advocacy groups are cropping up to fight back against the polluters while also getting the word out to the public". However, big business has not been so quick to get involved. "Acknowledging this problem is bad for business", Dr. Crawford said. "It will cut into their profit margins if they have to make their manufacturing processes more environmentally friendly. It's a lot easier to dump waste in a river or landfill than to dispose of waste responsibly. The technology is there as other countries have demonstrated". The CEHN's Schwartz also believes that communities need to be planned with the occupants' health in mind. "When you see low-income housing in urban areas, you see no places to walk; everyone drives which in turn creates even more pollution", he said. "These areas are 'urban canyons' in that the pollution rises to a certain level and stays there".

Schwartz added that these areas have very few parks and playgrounds, which can contribute to the occurrence of obesity and high blood pressure. "These areas need to include playgrounds, running tracks, and so on, but the sad truth is that most parks are in the wealthier areas. Aside from better civil engineering on the local level, the federal government needs to step up to the plate as well, according to Dr. Crawford. "The laws are there", said. "The EPA has been lax in enforcing the regulatory laws on big business, but people are using civil rights laws to their advantage by claiming that their civil rights have been violated by these polluters". People have gotten tired of being put upon by the government and big businesses and are successfully dragging these companies into court. One very high-profile example is the true story behind the Julia Roberts movie Erin Brockovich. Pacific Gas and Electric's wastewater was getting into the water supply of a California town. As a result, many residents had contracted various forms of cancer. However, they fought back against the utility giant and won a huge multimillion dollar settlement. Dr. Morris used an analogy to the Raiders of the Lost Ark when discussing the availability of the data on health effects related to the environment. "When the Ark of the Covenant was found, it was tagged and put on a shelf", he said. "that's what's being done with this information. The statistics are real, and the information is out there, but we have to make sure that it gets to the people who need it the most so lives can be saved, and illnesses prevented".

The Message

It is the environment that initiates and ignites the change for what we call a new world order. *If you never focus on the elements and energy that cause the change, then how can you ever know when the change will take place?* The message is real simple and clear, nor does it take a Harvard Scholar to understand this simplicity. Many scholars at institutions of higher learning has made environmental education a complex science, making it difficult for students and laymen to understand how the environment works. This is done so that institutions of higher learning can continue to control the curricula, financial programs and the flow of knowledge that's needed for change. When we study the environment we see that **every single thing** in creation is connected. The planetary system has never been separated from their orbit in space, meaning that they continue to orbit in their own atmosphere. It is energy and the elements that give space life.

All energy and elements in our solar system are connected to each and every galaxy, planet and everything that has life or death within the universe. Each planet has developed its own environment conducive to its atmosphere. Some planets are hotter than others and some are colder than others. There is some form of life on each and every planet because every planet cannot survived without energy nor function or operate without the power of energy. Scientist would argue, how do we know this? Because earth is a planet that was created like every other planet and have the same elements as other planets, each of the planets are endowed with the elements of life and are capable of producing life as we know it here on earth. Many of the elements and energy once pooled together form a far greater mass than the elements within the earth's atmosphere creating bigger galaxies and planets which suggest that life can be even greater or less on other galaxies and planets than life on earth.

The purpose of life on earth as on other planets is to study the planetary life and to note it. Because the environment is an ever changing system, we must observe the systematic changes in the way we *think* and how the brain makes us think differently. This is done by a chemistry within the brain. This chemistry can be controlled and manipulated by long distances. Energy is a chemistry, and the study of *Magnetic Energy Fields* gives us the knowledge as to how these energies work, it works the same on machines, household appliances and *human beings*. Too much energy will destroy you and not enough will cause docility and illness, this suggests a proper balance of energy. Uncontrolled energy can produce negative energy of which fear becomes a factor and can be induced. Like and automobile if you accelerate with control the faster you go, uncontrolled acceleration can cause accidents and death. *We were once connected to the cosmos in space, however, once we are disconnected from the cosmos in space we become candidates for* **SLAVERY.** This means that certain negative vibrate messages can be placed on a thought wave of energy in the brain and it will find its way to the weakest link. This can form deceptive thoughts even *violent behavior* in animals and humans.

Behavioral Science

Teaches us that mental patients sometimes are given **SHOCK** treatments. Physician that provide treatment such as electrical shock to the brain they do this as a means to stabilize patients with disruptive behavior and to silence them or quit them down. Shock treatments in hospitals are done with a machine that has Alternative {AC] current and Direct [DC] current, similar treatment for patients with heart failure the defibrillator is used. The point is clear that controlled energy can be an asset and a liability.

Thought Patterns In Behavior

There is a chemistry in the brain that causes us to think, talk, walk, eat, sleep, hear, see, breath, sex, smell, etc. Other than biology science, institutions of higher learning have never taught us about this chemistry or how this chemistry work within the brain, nor have science identified what this chemistry is or the combination of chemicals that cause these things to happen within the functions of the brain. *If the chemical was identified we could control the on— set of deception and violent behavior in the human being.* To allow it to run amuck is to support terrorism and other practice of deception. This same chemistry that is operative in the brain are developed from energy, these are the same elements in outer space as well as the elements within the earth's atmosphere. Absent of how this chemistry work or deprivation of this chemistry we can never really understand what or how this chemistry produce love, hate, deceptive thought, violent behavior in animals and humans.

If the Bible is correct in saying" As a man think, so is he". *What is the chemical and process by which he think?* We need to identify this chemistry in order to understand why violence and other deceptive thoughts have cause us to deceive one another and to save each other from deceptive behavior. *Massive control equal capital dollars.* America is the land of the free, yet we pay for water, light and gas of which each are forms of energy and are controlled by the elite power structure. So... why are there satellites and a space station two hundred miles above the earth's atmosphere? They say for better reception for radio/television... and human beings. What type of reception are we talking about and for who? Energy thought waves as well as telecommunications they all work on the same frequency.

Information and data can be extracted from these *same* lines of communication. Each has a direct and indirect affect on the thought process and behavior in humans. To give up this control would place equality between the rich and poor, between knowledge and ignorance, between love and hate. Environmental education should have been taught in grade school, however, we must consider rather our educators were just totally ignorant of the knowledge or was the greater population of educators deceived? In my judgment, I think the former rather than the latter.

In conclusion, when environmental hazards are released into the environment and absorbed by particulate matter or the microorganisms, this pattern is associated with the negative energies that can cause serious illness, disease, <u>behavior</u> and death.

Religion a Form of Superstitious Practice?

Has religion always been a cultural icon on the earth and if so, who really benefit from these many religious practices? We must go back to antiquity to see how these practices came into being. When we look at the two major religions Christianity and Islam, we can derive at other religions because these are the two initiators and from these religions, we must question first the ethnicity of these practices. Both of these practices developed a scriptural text, for Christianity it was the bible for Islam the Quran, Jewish the Torah etc. Man has always searched for something greater than himself, be it a man, inanimate objects, or just a power greater than himself. Did man need this as a measuring rod? When you study Christianity we see many prophets, in Islam only one prophet but they both have the same concept.

These prophets prophesied what was to come which laid the foundation for scriptural knowledge. In the content of each scripture, they all claim that the prophets talk with God or Allah and there were angels accompanying the Lord of Host. They both seem to believe that when a human being dies if they have been faithful to their God that they will enter heaven and see all their loved ones. If you are a mortar in Islam, Allah will give you seven virgins for your good deeds. While in Christianity you will walk on streets of gold and there will be no more suffering, everybody will be joyful. This type of teaching and preaching ignites joyful thoughts in the worshiper's mind, this gives the believer something greater to look for after his death. But let us take this one step at a time. First, when we die the first thing that happen to us is that the breath of life or all energy leaves the body. What is the breath of life? ENERGY & OXYGEN.

The breath of life is energy and other microorganisms and tiny elements, molecules, atoms, neutrons, electrons that forms the integral part of the breath of life, they are so small that when they are created, a high powered microscope is needed to capture their birth. Even then the lens **are not** great enough to as certain its originality or beginnings. Therefore, the breath of life returns from which it came and the human body returns from which it came, from the earth. What has puzzled man is **what is it** that brings the breath of life into the sperm and ovum that hopefully develops into a human fetus? The Scripture teaches that God breath into man's nostrils and man became a living soul. But they never state at what point the nostrils are developed? To be sure the statement should have read, God breath into the sperm and sperm became a living soul, because man does not know at what point life began in the spermatozoa and ovum.

Life is a progressive force that is entered into a creature by the will of Energy. Many religious factions equate Energy or Creator as God. The two are quite different in every respect. Energy is the bases for all creation and is far greater, more powerful than any God, Allah, Yawa combine or whatever name you wish to call Energy or the Creator. Energy is neither masculine or feminine and has no gender. Energy is self-contained *nothing* to its equal. We see Energy in the elements, the molecules, the atoms, neutrons, electrons the whole environment within this vast universal system of life. Therefore, when we breath we actually ingest energy and oxygen continuously until we die. Then the breath of life is released back into the environment. Where does the breath of life or energy go? In religion they say you return to your Maker. What all is in the breath of life? There is memory and knowledge, where does it go? It returns to the energy that created you and to all the other elements within our atmosphere and space we call air. It may travel upward and join other energies and living elements or it may linger in the same area until such time as the wind blows or moves it in other areas of the galaxy, or it might travel into outer space to other galaxies even planets, stars etc. Is all this memory or energy stored in one atom of life? Does it reincarnate itself or does it travel to the next dimension? **No** one has ever return from death to confirm that these things happen after death. Not even in ancient history, but scriptural knowledge has led us to believe that these things actually happens after your death. But theologians have no proof that this accrues they would hope that is does.

The Environment and the true meaning of worship?

First, we must define worship. *Webster* says that: "worship is to pay homage to God or deity, formal or ceremonial rendering, {Now used chiefly as a respectful epithet applied in Great Britain to certain magistrates, corporate bodies and employed in free masonry to indicate a certain official rank or dignity. The worship of financial success seems to be in every one's blood, the worship of *wealth and power.*] This appears to be a natural form for worship, but when you really look at it for what it means by definition it is to the contrary **unnatural.** Worship in a broader meaning implies to do things right in its natural order or sense, it is imperative that worship should be juxtapose to the natural order of creation. This is the way Energy created it to be.

Energy has never required that creatures should worship it as the Creator. Here again we must go back to antiquity to understand why this was ordained. Worship really began with emperors, kings, queens, the pope etc. these were people of power and they loved to be worshipped for things they had done or land they had conquered, so it was ordained that the masses should bow to them as their leader and ruler. This form of worship carried on until the Christian era, prayer seem to have been the order for worshippers who prayed to the many Gods of that time, once the Christian belief came into focus to worship the one God prayer became an institution. If Energy required the creatures to worship, it would be in accord with *the natural order in creation, it is the very nature of the human being to do the right thing and not worship energy just because it was energy that created the human being.*

[Providing that you were inherently taught to do the right thing]. We do a lot of things wrong in our nature, but the majority of things we do are right, it is clocked into our very nature to do right and consequently we are rewarded for the good things we do as well as the wrong things we do. Many of us now call these good things BLESSINGS. It is utterly impossible to do wrong without doing something right. When we are

breathing properly, this is the right thing to do, when the creature feeds itself this is the right thing to do, when the creature sleeps this is the right thing to do, when the creature urinates or defecates, this is the right thing to do. When the creature is able to use all of the body functions, mentally or physically the creature would in fact be worshipping its Creator.

Energy has never required that creature should bow down in worship. In religion, the Bible and other scriptures it reads: "And God said" I Command that ye worship me, I am your God, I am a jealous God". Dear reader, PLEASE tell me, why and how could or would Energy be jealous of the creature that was created by Energy? Energy has the power of life and death created all that you see and don't see but yet in religion, God is jealous? This doesn't make logical sense. The terminology of "God" is an invented ideology and has been linked or associated with the Creator. God and the Creator are two different entities that are so far apart in meaning, it is like measuring the distance from the earth to the black darkness in outer space. It is really strange that the things that are unnatural in life, we seem to think that they are natural and the things that are natural we seem to think they are unnatural.

Therefore, in religion there must be guidelines or steps that the believer must take to acquire these great blessings, one is that you must pray to your God continuously morning noon and night, from one or two prayers to five times daily. If you do not adhere to these practices you are considered a disbeliever and you might be labeled a hypocrite. Prayer was also instituted by emperors, kings and queens of antiquity as demand, this form of worship was done either when they took control of a land or a people or if someone was going to be put to death. They would then request mercy from the emperor of king who were considered Gods of their time because of their predictions, knowledge, wisdom, power and influence over the people.

The God concept came from the Greeks, from men with knowledge and a keen insight to predict the problems of that time. Until about ten thousand years ago when the Christian religious concept came on the scene. They discovered that there was a greater God than the God of Zeus, or Caesar, it was the God who created the heavens and earth and God of the universe. Thereby, the God concept became an institution. Then there was something call sin if you didn't pray often, otherwise you would go to hell this spark superstitious concepts in religion. Then there was the deity call Satin the Devil. If the individual did not agree with the high priest, you were considered evil and cursed. Then came witchcraft and sorcery which dealt with the psycho analyst of the mind and thought process of evil.

Witchcraft, voodoo, or devil worship is all psychological mind manipulations transposed through negative energies, in antiquity they were call [power]. Today these are call *[magnetic energy fields]* we call negative thinking or wrong thinking. This form of trickery of the mind has been known for millions of years by those who practice psychiatric thought analyses. Religion taught that the devil lived in hell, a place somewhere in the middle of the earth. *This place was hot with a burning perpetual fire that would torment the evil doers continuously they would never be consumed by this fire as does anything that comes in contact with it.* The problem with this scenario is that when a person dies, there is no more torment, as life has left the body and returned to the energy and all elements from which it came, as for the body it returns to the earth from which it came and in time it to will dissolve, disintegrate and return to dust and other elements of the earth. Today we also have what we call cremation another form of burial by which fire burns the remains or body into ashes. This is done for those who were good or bad.

It is true that the earth spends at 24,000 miles per hour which cause the core of the earth to become extremely hot by which we have volcanic eruptions that produce hot lava, that cause new land and vegetation to grow. So now what are we talking about? We are talking about {*behavior*}. Behavior as human beings comes from a source within the environment, especially the environment on the earth surface and beyond. There is another environment beneath the earth surface inhibited with human and animal creatures the world has never seen. We will talk more about this in depth later on.

Religion is not a true Science

Religion has never been a true science. There is no proof that any of the tails, stories, fables are true or that they actually happen. Many believers just accepted what was taught and never question the writer's motives for the work they wrote in the scriptures or bible. The bible is a work of art to those who believe its writings. In reality the authors of the original bible was very careful when they began planning this gigantic task. Once the bible was written there was mass murder afterward. Not much information has been said about King James and his version of the bible and those writers before him.

The King James Version of the bible was prepared by a special commission of scholars in England under King James and published in 1611. Then there was the Douay Version, an English translation of the bible from the Latin Vulgate that was prepared by Roman Catholic scholars, the Old Testament being published at Douay pronounced (Douai) in France in 1609-10 and the New Testament at Rheims, in 1582 some 28 years after the Old Testament. Then there was the revised version, a recession (methodical) of the authorized version of the bible prepared by a committee of British and American Protestant scholars, the New Testament being published in 1881, and the Old Testament in 1885.

For the mind that is wide awake, we can see that the New Testament was published first and the Old Testament was published four years afterwards, yet when you read the bible it is the Old Testament that is read first then the New Testament. History teaches us that once a land has been ceased the Rulers they would collect and confiscate all literature in opposition of the ruling party; they would burn literature and enforce laws that would prevent the masses from reading such propaganda. This form of book burning still exists in many parts of the world. In Ireland, the Catholics and Protestants are still fighting over beliefs in the year 2002. People especially Christian believers do not pay attention to little, small details that makes you go hum.

Here in America the First Amendment Right was guaranteed the right to free speech, assembly, and the practice of religion. It was obvious that the so-call Founding Fathers seen this was a serious problem in America and in England colony and that a constitution must be in place to insure freedom of religion as a right. However, the teaching of the bible had taken center stage to a mindless people. As we have said in previous issues of Hard-Times newsletter, deceptive thinking has always been a critical problem on the earth, but there has never been a challenge as to how deceptive thinking works and the cause or its process.

The Mind and the Environment

There was a Television commercial for the Negro College fund that said: ***"A mind is a terrible thing to waste".*** The mind is a very complex entity, to better understand this we must revert back to the spermatozoids and ask the question, at what point does life enter the sperm or ovum? We know that once the sperm is released from the male organ, it travels upward through the fallopian tube to the ovum, then it penetrates the female ovum and at that point it copulates with the ovum in total triple darkness and began to form the fetus. Physicians and Scientist are still baffled at how this is done, they know that this is done but they struggle and still don't know ***how*** it is done. This is one of the first seven wonders of the world.

Scientist can place the sperm in a test tube, transplant the sperm and it will clone into a human embryo or animal. But this still does not answer the question as to ***how*** does life enter the sperm and ovum at what point? First, we must look at the past, the present and future, the past dimension, the present dimension, and the future dimension. The past dimension is the dimension from which we came, we traveled through to this present dimension and when we die, we travel to another dimension. How is this possible? When we look at the sperm under a microscope, it appears to be a small organism moving like a little fish, there are millions released into the womb, but only one enters the ovum. In the case of triplets or quads, multiples they can all enter and develop in the ovum by these drops of sperm. Science know that sperm is created in the brain then travels down the spinal cord and rest within the male stratum. Like the blood cell, there are many small like animals working together to keep the blood alive so that each cell works together keeping the blood flow moving, there are billions of blood cells in one human body.

This same principle applies to the spermatozoa, they work together in mass to develop strength, these cells continue to produce and reproduce themselves in an effort to transform into human species, they work together in mass to give the human body the *impression* that the mind, spirit and soul is one organism. The life force energy within the sperm utilizes the sperm as the transport vehicle from the past dimension to the present dimension. When the energy or life force within the physical body departs from this dimension, it exits the body and advance forward into the next dimension. To be sure, once the energy or breath of life have past from the body, those elements that once gave your life returns to that energy, and the other elements that you were ingesting or breathing all the time you were alive. You inhaled energy and oxygen, you exhaled energy & oxygen, consisting of atoms, neutrons, electrons, particulate matter and other materials we call air. Not knowing that too much or not enough could destroy you, however, there was always the right balance of both to keep you alive.

Where is Heaven and Hell
in the Environment?

What is this thing we call heaven and hell? Brain washing is better yet a science, the whole idea is to trick the mind to believe and behave in the manner instructed. Ancient philosophers seen how easy the weaker mind responded to this tricknology.

Religion has taught that Jesus, Muhammad, Confucius, Buddha all have seen heaven and hell in their respective beliefs. Many worshipers believe that in times gone by there were some magical things done in the past that are not done in the present.

This is where brain washing is at best, Jesus walking on clouds or water, Muhammad seeing a giant silhouette of the Angel Gabriel. You would have to wonder were these people on drugs at the time, were they hallucinating? Surely wine and hallucinations were prevalent at that time. No one in that lifetime or this lifetime has ever died came back from the dead and told anyone that there was a heaven or hell, nevertheless, it has been made to appear that such thinking really exist. Not even the so-called devil who supposed to reside in hell can tell us what hell is like, this too is a fallacy. *But people that are living in this day and time can surely tell you what hell is like and the rich can surely tell you what heaven is like.* In religion however, the poor people will get theirs in heaven when they are dead. **What an assault on the psychic mind.** The only heaven or hell you will ever see, is the heaven or hell you design in your mind, spirit and soul.

This present dimension is a dimension of *physical vision*. What you see and experience in this physical life, you come to love. This life give the appearance that you don't know or want anything else other that what you have seen or experienced in your life time. Much of your travels as a mind spirit, soul from dimension to dimension has been in total triple darkness. This is where you origin, this is where you do your best work and there is plenty of light in darkness. Many of us have maintained knowledge from previous dimensions, some do not, why is this?

When we look at how knowledge is acquired, we see discipline and sacrifice. Isn't this what the sperm and blood cells do? They are discipline and they sacrifice for each other, they die off so that others may live. Many are afraid of dying because they just can't imagine anything better than this present life or dimension. This is all done to keep control over the mind, spirit and soul. But even in darkness there is vision, just look at entertainers like Stevie Wonder, Ray Charles. These men are physically blind, but each has remarkable vision.

Where is the Spirit in the Environment?

The spirit is the vehicle of inspiration and motivation, most people in religion will say that God is their inspiration and motivator and there are some that believe the devil is their inspiration and motivator. Let's look at these two entities, the word God spelled backward is dog (DOG). In broader terms this suggests that God is related to the dog as was in Egyptian hieroglyphics Rah as well as human, and that God is also an animal or beast. It would seem logical that God would be anything other than an animal since the Bible teaches that God was created in the image of a man.

In ancient Egypt, the dog was the symbol of a God (Rah) these deities were worshipped on a daily bases. Man has always sought after a savior greater that himself. He needed something greater than himself to clean him from his wrong doing; he never thought that once he corrects his thinking his wrong doing would vanish. Man began to love his personal life more than anything in creation; he began to love the power so much until this very day he is still looking for more ways and means to prolong his life just a little while longer. He began to clone animals to reproduce body parts not realizing that the environment must ultimately destroy him. He believed especially after he discovered that he could acquire lots more stuff and control the masses, he didn't want to leave this dimension so soon.

Kings and Queens went so far as to kill their slave servants when they died because they believed that they would need them to be serving them in the life after death.

To this very day, man has not figured out that the more he pollutes the environment with unnecessary toxin, the less likely he will live and the shorter the human life span will be. The Africans knew this thousands of years ago. Now let us look at the word Devil, when spelled backwards is LIVED, [past tense] **lived would seem more appropriate for the terminology of God than the Devil.** *God meaning should be the devils meaning {**when spelled backwards**} and the Devils meaning should be Gods meaning.* When you drop the (d) you have LIVE meaning life.

Where does the so-call God or the so- call Devil live? Since no one has ever return from the dead to tell us what heaven or hell is like. We must conclude that both of these entities live in the mind, spirit and soul of man. These are only words that formulate images of deception.

When you spell Creator backwards you get rotaerc pronounced ro-tae-rc, or (rhetoric) when you drop the rc you get rotae or add the (t) before the (e—you have rotate, rotary, rotation or rotating all meaning the same thing, revolution, gyration, circulation, spinning, circle around, whirl, they all have the same meaning. The bigger question is; "*who decide what or how a word should be spelled and what the meaning of that word should be*"? Computer technology has a new massage system call text massaging which will eventually revolutionize the English language as we know it today. Rap music has also established a new way of communicating with its rhymes and syllabus The English language is very complex, as stated above many of the same spelled words or words sounding the same have a different meaning, as does different people have different thoughts through expression the thought can mean the same. This is applicable to the spirit in creation, this is what's happening in this dimension, the spirit helps to absorb knowledge, the spirit help circulate wisdom, it helps to whirl understanding. The spirit is revolving continuously like the earth and all planetary systems, stars, galaxies they all spin. Everything within this universal orbit *rotates.*

Where is the Soul in the Environment

The soul of the human being is the intelligence by which one acquires through educational research study and life experiences. The intelligence, or knowledge, wisdom are things that travels with each given life. For example, the telephone and computer are manifestations of the brain. The brain is the home for the mind, spirit, soul, intelligence, knowledge, wisdom and understanding.

The brain has always had the computer and telephone as a means of communication at long distances, it has always been the vehicle of communication for the human being, it travels with energy and the life force and forms and activate the communications within the mind, spirit and soul of the individual. It holds in memory all things observed and acted upon by the individual and all universal creatures from one dimension to the next. Because of a denial of certain knowledge, many people black and white have been deprived of high intellectual and technical knowledge. This high-tech knowledge [was replaced by religion]. For the African-Americans as a people it has all but placed them in a state of ephemeral slavery.

Environment and The Life Force

When making the transition from one dimension to the next, the energy or the life force has to enter the organism, atom of life or whatever element that is needed within creation. These elements must be activated and placed in living motion. Therefore prior to entering the life force there is a barrier created, nothing can enter this barrier unless the Energy provide the entry. It is the same with death, nothing dies until the Energy commands entry, this is done by natural mathematical systems timing process clocked into the immune system. The Energy creates a situation every fraction of a second and sooner, this is what Energy does as creator. Out of the created situation that situation produces all that you can see and not see. When the energy life force enters the sperm it only enters by a natural force (a law) of creation and when the life force leave the creature, again it must past through a barrier. A tremendous life force pushes through to one dimension to the next continuously traveling stage by stage for *eternity*.

Environmental Education and Slavery

Dr. Brown newly appointed President of Smith University once said that education was never design to get an individual a better job. Education was design to expand the intelligence. Much of education has nothing to do with a person's job at all but has much to do with his past experience, qualifications and how well he comprehends. Most wealthy executive does not even have a high school diploma, never went to college and can't even read, but they encourage others under their watch to attend school, go to college so that they can acquire a better job. Why is it that politicians encourage good education? Because when you look back in history especially here in the United States. Many politicians never graduated from college or high school.

Yet those controlling the economy controls the curricula that teaches the student to become the source of this growing economy. Many still dropped out of high schools and colleges and still become the controlling source for the world. Even most student who parents literally paid for their degree but did not graduate with the college credits needed, end up with a degree holding an A+ average sitting in a political hot seat as a Senator, Governor even as President. It was never declared that a person should have a college degree to hold political office. Let's talk about traditional education for a minute, tradition means to continue the same practice, to mimic the previous format, to do the same thing the same way. This form of continuing education is a process of enslavement at a much higher level. Because we learn how to read, does not mean we are advancing our own cause, especially when someone else is writing the curricula for you. The curricula dictates what the knowledge is, what the individual should know, the method by which one should teach it, and to enforce the laws that dictates this curricula to the educators who teach it.

This is to stimulate the learning process so that the individuals will obey the educational laws by which controls his or her destiny. This type of education needs drastic reform, this is a system that still has the power to direct the flow of knowledge. Who are these people that control the educational system? Federal Health education and Welfare, State Board of Education and the Superintendent of Public Schools. All races fall into this same category. The practice of racism and discrimination only applies when it benefits the Rich and powerful. These are the cards held by the Rich to play whenever they feel the need.

Much of the wealthy rich obtained their wealth from inheritance off the backs of slaves. America, Britain, Arabia which is in Africa, Israel all are guilty of the slave trade. Did you know that {NAFTA} knew about slaves being traded as part of the Free Trade Agreement and stood by allowing Saudi Arabia to continue the slave trading that's been going on as a tradition for hundreds of years? America sets back and allow these kind of dealing to go on just as they allow Israel to continue their assault on the Palestinians.

Slavery was never targeted at one particular race, because history teaches us that every race of people have been utilized as slaves for the elite class. Even today the elite is always at the top of the pyramid and all those underneath serve those on top. You never hear about Trillionaires, but it is the Trillionaires that control the billionaires and the billionaires control the millionaires and it's the millionaires that control the so-call middle class and it is those that controls the poor and the have not's. The most illogical defeat for the slave was never question the knowledge of the slave master. To this very day many races still have not questioned the knowledge and motives of the slave master.

Many white slave owners condemned and hated chattel slavery, yet they supported subliminal slavery a mental form of deception and is prominent in today's lifestyle. Although African-Americans were chattel slaves, there were also white slaves right here in America. But you never hear any one talk about the white slave unless you hear someone talk about "Pimping" and are arrested under the white slavery Act [a form of prostitution]. Negroes were used more frequent and abundantly than white slaves, one reason was that Negroes cost much less than white slaves and the labor was cheap blacks would be forced to work much harder than white slaves through fear and punishment.

The Black slave was always threaten with death. During the early life of the Klu Klux Klan the white sheets and the burning crosses struck fear into the hearts of many Negroes at that time. The Klan was design to inject fear into the slaves and free Negroes who's only plight was to work, make a living for their families and educate their children. But the Klu Klux Klan wanted more, not only did they want to ensure that Blacks stayed in their place, but they wanted them to continue to work for the slave masters for free.

The elite knew of negative energy years before the Klan came on the scene and they utilized and capitalized on this negative energy as a means to instill fear into the slaves.

In reality, the Klu Klux Klan were slaves themselves they were being used by the powerful elite to maintain corruption and political control. This same mentality still exist today just look at the George W. Bush Administration who took the election in the year 2000 as a Republican, through political maneuvers, utilizing the Supreme Court to rule over the voting ballots in the State of Florida. Knowing that the Supreme Court is a neutral body and must stay out of political scandals, but again it was powerful elite Brotherhood that prevailed. We will talk more about the Brotherhood in a later Chapter. Many of the votes in the Florida election were never counted and the Bush Administration used clandestine tactics to maintain political corruption and control.

In January 2002, the Enron fiasco was another Bush run amuck, where millions of dollars were used to pay for political favors for corporate executives who sold Enron stock at top dollar for millions leaving the poor employees without a pension plan, and took all of the poor workers saving leaving them penniless. Racial profiling in the police departments was nationwide, these types of fiasco's were used to line the pockets of political leaders so that legislation could not past unless it fits the agenda of the rich and powerful.

In March of 1999 We wrote a letter to then President William Jefferson Clinton, we knew he would never respond because of the thousands of letter he get every day and the content of this letter was totally out of character from the traditional fan mail letters. The President had been found guilty of impropriety in the oval office with a young intern named Monica Lewinsky. Here is what we implied:

Dear Mr. President:

*It should be crystal clear to you what "hell" really is, that it is not a place to go but a place of actual participation such as what you have experienced in the last year. When you talk about the republican parties or the democratic parties it always remind me of something someone told me many years ago, they said; "**there*** *is no difference between a wolf and a fox".* He said; "the wolf however is and outright animal, he doesn't stalk his prey he attacks with viscous aggression". On the other hand, the fox is keen, slick and smooth, not only does the fox stalk his prey but he will wait until the right time to attack. But as you know both animals have a common thread, they are both members of the dog family and they both like the taste of lamb meat". This same phrase is applicable to the republicans and democrats, one mascot is the elephant and the other is a mule they both are cattle, both are vegetarians.

On Saturday February 27, 1999 on NBC News, Fredericka Woodsfield aired a small segment of a former slave named Fredrick Hughes that lived to be one hundred and one years old, he died in 1959. Prior to his death someone was nice enough to record some of the events of Mr. Hughes life as a slave, the thing that stuck out in my mind was the fact that Mr. Hughes stated that the slaves during his time were treated like dogs and they were not permitted to read. As a little boy, he was compelled to wear a girls dress and if he wanted to talk to the slave that lived next door he had to get permission from the slave master.

What's the difference between your situation as President and the scandals that continue to forever hunt you and that of Mr. Hughes? You are white, the slave was black. One can become a slave to his own passionate desires and like the former slave your soul begs to be free from this insidious behavior and the consequences that comes with it. This brings us to my next point of reference.

On Sunday February 28, 1999, on C-Span, members of the Black Caucus, ACLU requested that your administration must take a more aggressive stand on police brutality and race relations. This was on the heels of the young African-American that lived in New York that was shot 41 times, then there was Mr. Byrd in Jasper, Texas who was dragged to his death by young white males with racial insensitivity, then there was the young black woman in California that was shot in the back 27 times. Mr. President, hell is not a place to go, but you are actually living in it. The small pleasures you have are only reprieves of the consuming everyday hellfire.

The Implications of Slavery

*First off, we want to look at the whole idea of slavery and its implications. At a time in history the slave master did not allow the slave to read, not even the bible, it was prohibited. The slave master would threaten the slave and told him that if he was caught reading the bible the slave would be put to death. Therefore, for many years slaves were not permitted to read and only the very fortunate had the luxury of reading, such slaves as the **house nigger**. Many years later the slave master seen that it would be more profitable if the slave could read and there could be even more benefits for the master. After centuries of denying the slave this privilege, the master told the slave that he was allowed to read this great book and it was like an epidemic, slaves began to learn to read, and the slave master told the slave that they could now read the white man bible that was written by the hands of God. The slave master told the slave he could read this book, but only on one condition, the slave master told the slave that this book was a holy book and that this book contains the words of the most High God of the white man and the slave master told the slave that if he ever allowed the slave to read this book, he must never question the word of God.*

*T**he slaves were so excited they told other slaves that the master has allowed them to read. And that they should never question the word of God. From that day to this very day the slaves have never questioned the contents of the bible or as the slave master put it; **"the word of God".** But who was the God? When the slave was introduced to the Jesus hanging on the cross the slave could identify with that because the slave master had done the same thing to the slave. The slave master told the slave that this white man hanging from the cross was the son of God and the Savior for the slaves and the slaves believed it to this very day. But in reality it was the white man that was and still is the God of his time. It is the white man that loves to be worshipped as a master of deception. The broader question is where did this ideology come from? This is an old ancient concept used to enslave and control the masses. It was first practiced on the woman long before religion and Christianity became popular. When you read the parable of Adam and Eve in the bible you can see how the masterful tricknology works, a talking reptile (or was it* a reptilian?) convinced the woman to eat of the tree of knowledge she would then have the knowledge of good and evil.

Then God said: that the woman was an abomination because she had convinced Adam to eat the fruit from this forbidden tree of good and evil. First of all, why would God condemn the woman when it was Adam who violated God's order?

"Did the talking snake tell a lie"? No, the snake told the truth, so why was Eve punished with Adam? Secondly, if Eve influence Adam to eat of the tree (**influence in this instance is suggesting power**) then who had the most influence or power over Adam? "God or Eve"? The question is, why was the woman hated by men? Why was she targeted? At one time she had the power and control on the planet, Women were considered witches in ancient times because of their power. Men had made the woman a target and had to figure out a way to relinquish this power from her.

There had to be a mechanism by which to topple this female power, she had never shared this power with any other creature, she had power and control for millions of years and still until this very day she has power over the male. It is the male that THINKS he has power over the female, but the female in her most powerful manipulation of male senses controls his every destiny. Man ceased the opportunity by putting in place a convincing working knowledge that would one day give the male dominant **physical** power on the earth and this is not to say that the woman did not possess physical strength as the male developed physical strength from the female. Then there had to be established safeguards to enhance this ideology of man. Power in creation is established by a long natural process.

"Study Creation"

It took thousands of years to cultivate this revolution in power. When we look at the many forms of life in creation, we see the male serving the female, look at the vegetation, the female copulates with the male and it is the female that produce the off-spring. This same principle applies to the insect, the animals and the human being, in childbirth it is the female that go through the labor for the birth of the child. This takes power and strength. The woman in ancient terminology "FEMALE OF THE FIRST POWER IN HUMAN CREATION". This is applicable to all forms of life in creation. This issue is much more broader than you might think, in the female we see more of the "X" & "Y" chromosome. This is because during a woman's pregnancy the male fetus in the womb will first develop as a female prior to becoming a male, a natural process in creation.

It is the female that carries the child for nine months or less and after it is delivered, it is the mother that feeds it, teaches it and cares for it until it can become self [productive]. Note; for the exception of the {sea horse amphibian} a mammal is a male creature found in the ocean and it is the only male creature that carries a pregnancy. This process has always been the fact of life. Thereby, man did not like the woman controlling the planet, she was dominant with this control for millions of years. Man served the woman for centuries on end. There has always been more females on the earth than males and it will continue as this is the law of creation. The female lives longer, learns faster, her mental and physical strength is astronomically more powerful than men. She is the only creature that bleeds but do not die. Her beauty is created to enhance the lust in man, compelling him to hunt for her pleasures, every male species are created to serve the female. "Study Creation".

Observe the First Lady [Your wife] Hillary Clinton, take a closer look at the woman's demeanor. When the White Water affair was made public, do you remember the first person they pointed to in that political upheaval scandal? Your wife, Hillary Clinton. They tried desperately to break her but they couldn't because of her intelligence as a woman and as a female that has control of her man. Having sex with females other than your wife has never been a crime, the adulterous acts comes from the practice in religion as it is known in Christian analogy and philosophy. It comes from biblical version of the so-call ten commandments. These writings and documents such as the U.S. Constitution all written by men who wanted control and power over the masses. The document calls the constitution, and the founding fathers were not considering the African-Americans as citizens at the time of its writings. **NOT ONE** slave participated in the writings of the Declaration of Independence or the Bill of Rights, the slave was not even considered a human being, the slave was considered (3/5) three-fifth of a human being. Thereby, a system of government was formed. Religion was also practice as a means to deceive and control the masses; every word was generally in name of God. When conquerors and leaders took control of the land and its occupants, they first taken control of all forms of media and communications, in ancient times not only books in print or written documents but the philosophers were considered the media and communicators for their time.

All ancient Rulers knew of the practice of taking control of all media or all communications, King James, Shakespeare all knew it very well, Buddha, Jesus? Well there is a problem with Jesus concept, we will talk more about this in a later in the chapter. All those who wrote the Torah, Bible, Quran and religious scriptures knew it very well. The writers of these scriptures such as the Holy Quran and other scriptural teachings has made it appear convincing that these writings were the thoughts of their God. For example, in the Islamic religion thoughts of God was transmitted from Allah ("The God") to the Holy Prophet Muhammad and that Prophet Muhammad committed to memory the whole of the Quran. Traditional teachings of this practice makes it crystal clear that the followers has never question this form of religious teachings. They merely except it as true and fall within the preview of superstitious belief, they believe if they do not adhere to the strict tenets of the religion they will become hypocrites.

This is what most Muslims believe at least some of them. It is very strange that many can commit to memory the whole of the Quran but can't commit to memory the history of the woman when she had the power over the man and the planet. But when you just look at the Muslim woman who practices Islam she has become comfortable in her role as subservient to man. This comes from years and centuries of deception or brain washing. They say in the Islamic teachings, that the Quran raises the stature of the woman but yet in many third world countries such as Iraq, Iran, Arabia, and other Islamic countries the woman is forbidden to exercise the same privileges as men. Even right here in America the so-call Christians, Catholics, Buddhist, Mormons has prohibited women to exercise the same rights as men.

Yet the first writings of the Quran was written 200 years after the death of Prophet Muhammad, the problem with this is that this suggest that men can keep the whole of the Quran in perfect text and they never committed error. But when you read and study Islamic teachings you find that even Prophet Muhammad committed errors. Note that there were always a reason that things changed, either the people were corrupt or the men of power and influence were corrupt and wanted more control. The scheme has always been the same a philosophy design for the masses, to except as true and believable. The Quran speaks of those who practice schemes and secret arts. In the same breath the writers of the Quran are the same ones practicing a scheme and secret arts. To have control over the people one most obviously know that they are practicing a scheme, but wouldn't it be logical to tell those who are followers to beware of others who practice the same art?

Of course it would, this same principle is practiced in the Christian Church and other religions to maintain control of its parishioners. All religions practice the same thing, only in a different format. There is much good in all scriptural knowledge because the knowledge is borrowed from other generations gone by. There has never been a monopoly on knowledge rather we except this or not. As the earth evolves it diminish knowledge reproduce it and replenishes, it is utterly impossible to trace the history of the earth. The earth is older than quadrillion years in age. Nothing last forever on the earth, not even the pyramids, even the stars changes their shapes into other shapes and forms and they burn out as it was designed this way by Energy. The only thing in this creation that does last forever is the **darkness** in space. All forms of writings that would otherwise tell us the earth's history at one point must parish in time whereas other generations must seek and search for the earth's secrets that we might understand the meaning of human existence.

Nothing in creation is ever lost, the problem is, you cannot find it. Once certain knowledge have been lost or misplaced by memory, it is very hard to find and it is up to the individual or people of that generation to seek out the knowledge or hidden meanings of their existence. Much knowledge have been hidden or lost because of the thirst of power and control. Let us turn our attention to the word "God" and the word "Devil". Theatrics are something to take serious note, the theater help teaches what is in thought and mind of men. Motion pictures like "Inherit the Wind", "The Devil's Advocate" something you must see Mr. President. The cinema demonstrates the true power of the motion picture industry with all its factual research as its animated ideas and new technology. When studying history we see that the Greeks had referred to people of high intelligence as Gods, Greek history teaches that Zeus was a Greek God and he had a son that was later called the son of Zeus or [the Son of God]. This was a Christian concept that was borrowed from the Zeus philosophy however, Zeus never really existed he was only in the mind of men. The terminology of God, Jehovah, Allah, Yahweh all have the same implications and like most historians they have always equated these names with Energy the Creator of all life. Ninety nine percent of the people of the world population have been tricked, hoodwinked and bamboozled on the name for the God. They claim and believe that the words are one and the same. No one has ever questioned who made this assumption. They have excepted this as truth and just assumed that passed historian have researched this fact and came up with this conclusion. There is nothing in creation that can be compared to Energy "NOTHING" not even a name could ever be identified as the "Creator".

*T*hese are Biblical fables written by men like King James. The word create has been used very loosely by educators thinking that they can create, in reality man cannot create anything, everything that man has **discovered** he thinks he has created it. In reality he has borrowed something from what have already been created. He discovers that he can utilize this discovery and claim that he has created it. There is a parable in the Quran that stated: "Man cannot create a fly even if they all met for the purpose". To create is to start with nothing, however in this creation we are forced to barrow from what is already created to produce the end results. Why was this written? The writers knew that there was only one Creator who had no gender but yet we refer to the Creator as "He", why not "She"? The Creator is not masculine nor feminine. This was design to make the people believe that God is also the Creator. The true knowledge has always been hidden to make you believe such traditional none sense. The Creator is more than a God, Far Greater than a God and much more higher than anything in Creation of which there is no equal, ENERGY!

It is Energy that creates, this is what the Energy does, it is Energy that creates **situations** every fraction of a second and sooner this is all that Energy does, this is all that the Energy **has** to do. Once Energy creates an object of life it feeds into the rest of created matter or things just like the domino effect. It is Energy that creates consistently, at this very moment, life moving forward and backward. It is Energy creates laws to keep the creation in a check and balance. **Nothing** in creation or any of the created things can destroy any part of this creation. Energy works through the environment by which intelligence *is formed and used in the minds of men so that when man thinks that he is in control, Energy proves him otherwise. Energy creates different situations to show man the true "Will" power. The laws of creation keeps every living thing in proper check. This is all the more reason why we as human beings must understand and study the environment in which we live. If we don't understand the environment that causes anti-social behavior then we want ever understand the true nature of the Office of the President that appears to be a form of imprisonment. It is the duty of the Secret Service to shield the President from the aggressions of the world.*

*The Office of the President is design to ward off those who practice recidivism. (**"A tendency to relapse into anti-social behavior"**) This is what happen to you Mr. President, you relapsed. The reason for your relapse is because of your environment.*

You are surrounded by females and you are no different from the animals in the wild, the very sight of the females ignite the passion in your loins. Intelligent life suggest control of your desires but there are many triggers that perpetuate the sexual urges in men, much of this has to do with the way we think and the very sight of the female when they are in our presents.

The female has more control of her sexual desires than men, more often than not she is aroused by touch rather than sight unless her hormones forces her to become the aggressor. It is the environment that causes these emotional sexual gratification the "E" stand for energy in motion. During the sex act, it is truly energy in motion we are sharing our energy. Environmental hazards are the true cause of social behavior problems, such as post traumatic stress disorder (PTSD), post menstrual syndrome{PMS}, disruptive behavior, sexual harassment, gang violence and many more deviant personalities. Environmental contamination exist in many forms Mr. President and we urge that you take a closer look at your own environment and what it consist of. We believe Mr. President that you were caught up in your environment and relapsed. On Capitol Hill the Senate and House of Representative are all part of the same environment you live, you breath the same air that they breath and are subject to the same atrocities as they are.

Keep in mind Mr. President, that the woman has a natural ability to lead and she must be given the opportunity. As you can see, she has been leading the male all the time rather you except it or reject it the facts are there. If she is not given the opportunity she will aggressively take it by any means necessary. The male does not want that to happen. There are obvious reason why the elements are called "Mother Nature" in short the woman is Mother

*Nature she is a natural, she can at will arouse the elements against you. It is irrelevant rather you or anyone except the fact that your wife is the epitome of the female power and what a woman truly stands for, it is not because her skin is white but because of her female instinct to rule and control. Imagine if all the women came together with one thought in a moment of unison we would see the environmental elements bow to her command and we will witness the true power of **thought**.*

*I look at my wife every day and I'm sure you do the same, at lease when she is there. But do we really see the woman for who they really are? How can man invent a law on earth and yet not uphold the very natural laws in creation? "Impossible" This invented law [the Mosaic] can never give proper justice to those who violate the natural law in creation. Polygamy is the exception and not the rule of law in this country. The first Amendment Right give an individual the right to practice their own religion, if monogamy is the rule, then why does the invented constitutional law bar a person from marring more than one wife? On the one hand the constitution is saying a man religious right is protected on the other hand the man is not protected. **Please, give me a break**. We should be taking lesson from the black widow spider, the female need the male for one purpose and one purpose only, that is to procreate her. Many times the very nature of the black widow is to destroy and terminate the male after she has acquired her copulation. Mr. President there must be a stronger enforcement of [EPA] laws (Environmental Protection Agency) in this country, without the rigorous enforcement we will become known as the generation that was **consumed** by their own environment. This is the true power of the Creator. Hell is when the environment began to consumed it's creatures through toxin from the very things we manufacture from the earth. In closing Mr. President please take note of all the so-call powerful people in your midst, most of them are endowed with Doctorate Degrees [PHD] and Master Degrees, nevertheless these are the same individuals that have this world in turmoil. These are the same people that don't want African-Americans to have reparations. Common Sense has been missing from your Administration Mr. President and it does not take a college degree to learn this.*

Note:

<u>About the woman</u>, on January 19, 2002 the television program 60 Minutes depict the life of three women, one a woman was in the armed forces of the United States. A female Air Force Lt. Colonel name Martha McSally,

she had flown over 100 combat flights over Afghanistan an (Islamic Country) and other war zone areas. This woman was stationed in Saudi Arabia where Islamic dress is worn by the people of that Country. Lt. Colonel McSally was forced by her superiors at the Pentagon mainly the Secretary of Defense [Donald Rumsfeld] to wear the woman's Muslim dress when leaving the base going to officers security meetings for the United States. The Arabs had never required that American women should wear Islamic dress, they only ask that American women dress modest No heads of states were required to wear Islamic dress not even the previous Secretary of State who was a woman or other male soldiers and officers to wear the Islamic dress. Lt. Colonel McSally was sworn to uphold the American U.S. Constitution by which the First Amendment give Colonel McSally the right to practice the religion of her choice which is Catholic. This demonstrate how men of power in the year 2002 are still practicing women hatred. Then there was Lt. Governor Jane Swift who obtain this position through the voters in Massachusetts when she was pregnant with twins. Mrs. Swift was ridiculed because she had to be a mother to her newly born children and work on her job at the same time. There were other women who had been coerced by men of power to continue the ridicule because she had to attend to her womanly duties as a mother. The last woman was the person who blow the whistle on the Enron debacle.

The Environment & The Big Bang Theory

Mr. President, the big bang theory is just a theory not reality, there is no beginning to this vast creation, {even if there was a beginning it would be buried so deep into history it could never be resurrected or found in the history of the earth or universe} it has been made to appear that there is a beginning and an end. Death is not an end. Death is an experience that appears to be very complex and we have limited our understanding concerning death through fear and a lack of knowledge. This creation was here when we arrived just as it was here when others arrived and it will be here when we depart. At time intervals there always come along a philosopher or group of people who decide what is the right knowledge for the masses. The elite power structure understands with clarity that the masses don't have a clue in terms of why the creation is set up the way it is, they are made to believe what they have been taught and to except it as it is. They have no other choice. It is truly amazing that the Bible claims that the Earth was created 6,000 years ago yet the dinosaur was here millions of years before the earth was created.

Taking Responsibility for Our Environmental Thinking

As a conscience human being, we need to take some responsibility for our own thinking and what we think about. Many of us can't ever conceive of an original thought within our own mind. Many will think that there is no original thought, because just as you are thinking one thing someone else is thinking the same thing. This is not true. We use to think the same way until one day we thought. "If the lottery can choose a number out of billions of numbers and your chance of winning the lottery is one and ten million an original thought can be one in five billion". When you've been disconnected from the thought wave of power *(the Cosmos)* much of your energy has been drained, or zapped, from your brain. We have just enough energy in our brain to keep us in the obedient state of mind. This is why it is very difficult for many to think, it becomes hard and painful to think about things we had no knowledge of and it requires constant practice. We have been placed in a mode to where we want others to think for us, there is the religious concept, we want Jesus to think for us, he died for our sins. This is so elementary and brain washing until this very day many actually believe that another man can die for something another has done. Utterly impossible but we have a great majority of people believe this. Once this type of knowledge has influenced the thought process, it is very difficult to unlock the human psychic. ***Indeed this is a form of hypnosis.***

Here is where the curricula has meaning, it fits in with the overall scheme of deception, the many schools of thought knew that the people had to be guided in a way that the powers to be could maintain explicit control. This was done by design and can give meaning as to why many of the brain cells are not functioning as they should, since it has been said that we don't use a tenth of what we have. One side of the brain is larger than the other, we believe that over time the smaller side decrease because of the lack of energy which affected many of the brain cells on both sides.

After President Clinton was found guilty of adultery the very next year Rev. Jesse L. Jackson, Sr. was also found guilty of the same practice. This wasn't anything new, Rev. Jimmy Schwagger, Elijah Muhammad, committed adultery, Catholic Priest committing sexual acts with children, and it goes on and on under the auspices that God will forgive a hopeless sinner. The fact of the matter is the human being has many sexual urges but the objectivity is to control that urge. There is nothing religious about a man having sex with a willing participant. However, we do believe that there is a line between sexual intercourse with children and those who are forced into the sex act. Religion has some value, and we applaud those who have embarrassed their faith, as we too have been there as one who have practiced many forms of religion. I practice the Islamic Religion for over (35) years. We did it because we did not know what we know now. As my wife often reiterates that we had to go through these many fazes in order to understand what we know today.

Religion in many ways help tone down the urges for promiscuity or sexual gratification to a lesser degree. Unfortunately for the Rev. Jackson many of his following began to abandon him. Many lost respect for the Rev. Jackson and the ministers that once held him in high esteem was now backing away. This is what religion teaches, either you are sinless or your godly. *In reality you are neither.* You are a human being with faults like every creature in the universe. When we understand the environment we live in, we will understand that it is the environment that help influence the sexual urges. When we are close to someone we are attracted to and they are attracted to you, the urge seems to escalate and our sexual energies seem to rise. *What is that chemistry in the environment that cause this to happen to us?*

Environmental Ozone Health Effects

We would like to switch gears for a moment to address the finer details of the environmental question. Alpine Industries was looking to hire people to sell home air cleaners in 1998, it was an electric device that once it was on, it helps clean the air in the home from many of the environmental elements such as dust mites and other hazardous materials. They let you use one for thirty days to see how it performed and after the demonstration if you liked it, it would cost from $600.00 to $1500.00 depending on the size and model. We tried the *Living Air XL-15* for 30 days but could not afford it at the time. But the literature and brochures that came with it was valuable and we decided to share this information with the Victory Heights Community. This article was printed in The Victory Heights West Pullman Hard-Times Newsletter in 1998.

Many are not aware just how deadly the air quality is inside our homes, and it is much greater in-doors than out. We as a people must become more environmental conscience of the air and things we ingest into our lungs, otherwise death is always just around the corner. Here is what some researchers found in that literature.

"Ozone or trivalent oxygen is perhaps the most misunderstood, hated and loved element in the air we breathe. On one hand we are told that it is a harmful, poisonous gas capable of doing great harm to our lungs". On the other hand we are told that it has the potential of being the greatest natural purification element we have available to deal with man-made pollutants. The truth lies in the understanding of the nature of ozone itself, the mechanisms of ozone formation, the nature of the pollution problems that requires a solution and finally any adverse health effects involved with ozone as compared with others.

In November 2008 Barack Hussain Obama was the First African American elected as President of the United States of America. The Country indeed had turned its attention to Black America. I had corresponded with Obama when he was a United States Senator and Hazel Johnson had worked with him as a State Senator, her daughter

Cheryl had always kept me informed as to what Obama was doing for Altgeld Gardens. Obama's Champaign cry was **"Yes We Can"** and many Americans loved it. But after he was elected President, much of his promises fail by the wayside and he began to take up some of the same antics that President George W. Bush was known for. It was if someone was telling President Obama not to address the war crimes that the Former President and Vice President had openly admitted. We sent the President the following letter.

President of The United States Barack H. Obama

Dear Mr. President

Why are you continuing to entertain Mr. Cheney's recidivist behavior knowing that he and Former President George Bush has conspired to commit treason against the American People in the confessions and confines of the United States?

Your Administration appears to be afraid to charge Mr. Cheney of any War crimes, we would hope that you would cease to reiterate that you want to move forward and not address the crimes of their past.

If you do not charge Mr. Cheney and Bush with the heinous crimes of water boarding, lying about 9/11, not explaining the implosions of building 7, starting the Iraq war without justification in which he has admitted publicly and confirmed that he is guilty of this conspiracy.

Not only will your poll ratings go down but you would have turned your back on the American People. This suggests that you have abandoned your principles of Justice. For example, you indicated that you would allow certain detainees to remain in prolonged custody without a trial after Guantanamo has been closed.

You were the President of Harvard Law Review and a constitutional scholar, yet you would make statements inconsistent of the U.S. Constitution, especially with prisoners in the custody of the Attorney General of the United States. *How could you be so naive to allow a Former Vice President dictate to you (a sitting President) that he committed a crime in direct violation of the American constitution and you have not taken any action for on behalf of the American People? Why are you doing this Mr. President?*

How can you talk about change and in the same breath choose Bush Administration tactics to promote criminal activity? Mr. President, if you do not take aggressive action against Mr. Cheney immediately, you are doomed for failure and will sign your own impeachment proceedings. Mr. President, please don't allow this to continue.

Mr. President, we have awaited the confirmation of the Secretary of Health & Human Services Katheline Sebelius along with Dr. Steven Chu, Secretary of Energy & Environment and Lisa Jackson of the U.S. EPA. We would like a meeting with these three agencies or their representatives to discuss the feasibility and development of a monitoring system. This system should monitor, track and identify the elements in the environment that are associated with the ***root causes** of_illness, disease, behavior, death and the effects of magnetic energy fields*. We have identified several community-based organizations that are standing by to join us in establishing this needed system. We contacted President Obama during the primary election, and he concurred that such a system is needed. We have written letters to Katheline Sebelius, Dr. Steven Chu and Mrs. Lisa Jackson and their agencies requesting participation but have not had a reply, We would like to bringing these agencies or representatives together as soon as possible at place of equal convenience such as Chicago State University or University of Illinois. There are several community based organizations that would like to participate in the discussion for a monitoring system that could be duplicated in all communities where environmental hazards are the focal points for illness. Disease, behavior, death and the effects of magnetic energy fields.

The Three Agencies

Reasons for these three agencies are as follows: **Health and Human Services** … has the daunting task of addressing all forms of illness, disease, behavior, death and magnetic energy fields, each of these entities are associated with environmental factors. **U.S. Environmental Protection Agency** and subsidiaries [EPA] **Center for Disease Control** [CDC], **The Agency for Toxic Substance Disease Registry** [ATSDR] has the daunting task of addressing all diseases associated with environmental factors. **Department of Energy** [DOE] has the daunting task of tracking the energy grid that flows from things that are hot, cold or in between, snow, ice, wind, rain, oceanography, outer space, sun, moon, stars, planets and the darkness that hovers above all life in creation.

These agencies has to work in consortium with each other in developing the monitoring system, the system *must* be able to monitor each element in a geographical location within a one mile radius of any targeted community. To identify an element ATSDR must work with scientist, chemist to determine which elements *single or collectively* causes the onset of illness, such as the common cold, that can enter the disease faze, root cause of recidivist behavior, the impact of magnetic energy fields and ultimately causes death to the human body.CDC has recognize low levels of Lead in young children can cause learning disabilities, dysfunctional behaviors, violence and other forms of brain damage. Mercury is another element that also has some of these same effects. Lead when broken down has traces of sulfur and oxides, one can keep breaking these elements down and find other elements that cannot be broken down. When body inhales and exhales, the oxygen we take into our lungs are generally accompanied with air born particulates in the body and travel to the morrow of the bone and will lay dormant until the immune system breaks down which can cause illness, disease even death.

Monitoring System

During the mid-nineties at the Old Dutch Boy, International Harvester Brownfield site on the far south side of Chicago, the Advisory Counsel for the West Pullman Community requested that a monitoring system be establish in and around the contaminated Brownfield site. This system was effective when identifying lead dust and the direction of the lead dust when the wind was blowing. This monitoring system helps identify and track the elements that moved into other communities. It is with this type of technology that could be used in hospitals, schools, penal institutions, businesses, corporations etc. This system will help identify, track by name each element ingested when moving in a collaborative formation or within a geographical location. Emissions are not the only form of toxicity that haunts those who are ill from the effects of environmental hazards, there are many elements that are not named yet scientist must take a closer look at those elements ATSDR have on file.

Altgeld Gardens

President Barack Obama has indicated on many occasions that he worked as an organizer in the Alrgeld Gardens Community, we believe that this community along with Hazel Johnson [CEO] and Daughter Cheryl Jackson of Community for Recovery should continue to be the driving force for this community that is haunted by environmental hazards for decades should be the *first targeted community* to establish this monitoring system. Alrgeld Gardens is situated in a toxic donut Land fields to the east, Calumet Sage to the West, Sherman Williams to the North and Water Reclamation just in front of this community. Although some of the toxic waste has been removed, except that which was buried in the land fields, it is the residual effects that the community has to continuously deal with because of the community's location. U.S. EPA has confirmed that the residual effects may lay dormant in the community for years to come. Therefore, Alrgeld Gardens should and must become the Pilot for the Monitoring System.

On the question of health care reform or the Health Care Bill, I have yet to see or hear the talk about illness, disease, behavior, death and the effects of magnetic energy fields associated with environmental factors. Rather there is a public option or not this issue has to stand out clearly for public review. The public has the right to know and understand the root cause of illness, disease, behavior death and magnetic energy fields as a precursor associated with environmental factors. Without the explicit language written into the Health Care Bill where as the public can clearly understand what is happening to them, this health care Bill is DOA. It is imperative that the Public understands the ROOT cause of all illness, disease, behavior, magnetic energy fields and death as an environmental factor that cannot be ignored. In my review of the Health Care Bill I have not found this language, why?

Presidents statements on
Health Prevention

Knows the cause or root cause of illness, disease, behavior etc. For the past two months we have seen numerous attacks against President Obama either because of his policies or his character. Did Former President Carter get it right by saying that these attacks are a result of President Obama being an African American and Black people are incapable of ruling this country even when an incompetent White President put the whole of the country in an unparallel recession? **Here is the Question:** "What has caused this ref in continued negative **behavior**? Even after the majority vote has elected President Obama with a land slide election. **Behavior is a serious health care issue.** We cannot proceed with Health Care Reform until we reform the mind set and thinking of those who perpetrate negative behavior in social and economic paradigm.

2.) Micro elements or particulate matter is the true beginning of human life

Identifying those elements that create life, the sperm and its nutritional value, food.

3.) What should we look for in the Environment to ward off illness and disease?

We monitor, identify and track the elements that cause the illness, disease and behavior etc. To truly address health care reform, we need to look at the whole of society and the human body which is a walking, talking chemistry, or (laboratory) what we do not understand today is the complexity of the *formula* that creates this mass technological structure. Here is what we do know, we know that the sperm and ovum must be join together to create the fetus, but what is the chemical composition of the sperm or the ovum, Such as; atoms, neutrons, protons, electrons maybe all of the above. These elements feed into our daily nutritional intake? Having said that we must always and forever look at the elements in the environment that created the human being. We must go back to the beginning of the sperm and look at how it is created in the brain for the male, hear is a question to Ponder: "What are the elements and nutritional components for both sperm and ovum"?

4.) What can the Church do to help educate communities on environmental hazards?

First, the church must understand what the environment consists of, then began to teach the church group what to look for in the environment, that is the cells, bacteria that acts as a magnet toward human flesh, what we inhale into our lungs, why we bath and wash our hands.

5.) Working with the conference of ministers on a national scale to get the word out.

Collaboration with other churches and scientist to better understand the working environment.

For the past two months we have seen numerous attacks against President Obama either because of his policies or his character. Did Former President Carter get it right by saying that these attacks are a result of President Obama being an African American and Black people are incapable of ruling this country even when an incompetent White President put the whole of the country in an unparalleled recession? *Here is the Question:* "What has caused this ref in continued negative **behavior**? Even after the majority vote has elected President Obama with a land slide election. *Behavior is a serious health care issue.* We cannot proceed with Health Care Reform until we reform the mind set and thinking of those who perpetrate negative behavior in a social and economic paradigm.

To truly address health care reform, we need to look at the whole of society and the human body which is a walking, talking chemistry, or (laboratory) it is a magnet for bacteria and germ warfare, what we do not understand today is the complexity of the *formula* that creates this mass technological structure. Here is what we do know, we know that the sperm and ovum must be join together to create the fetus, but what is the chemical composition of the sperm or the ovum, Such as; atoms, neutrons, protons, electrons maybe all of the above. These elements feed into our daily nutritional intake? Having said that we must always and forever look at the elements in the environment that created the human being. We must go back to the beginning of the sperm and look at how it is created in the brain for the male, hear is a question to Ponder: "What are the elements and nutritional components for both sperm and ovum"? As an environmentalist, I have focused much of my life work looking at the cause and effects of environmental hazards associated with illness, disease, behavior, death and the effects of magnetic energy fields. President Obama, in his speech last week said: *"If we could prevent illness and disease before if happens then we would be well on our way in addressing real health care reform"*. Georgia Doty HIV/ Hepatitis Community Outreach is doing just what the President has suggested, focusing on preventive care, and if GDHHCO Outreach was State funded this work could continue on a national scale.

Illinois could lead the nation in health care reform with the ideas of the Georgia Doty HIV/Hepatitis Community Outreach Program. GDHHCO has a track record of making a difference in the community by teaching health education to prison inmates on real health care reform and economic security upon release from prisons and county jails. We have not seen or heard of any other organization nationally that have taken the same initiative as the GDHHCO. Today we are now confronted with many viruses, disease, sickness etc. The Department of Health and Human Services has issued a mandate for all individuals and families to wash their hands vigorously and often, but why? Because it is an environmental hazard and if we as a people do not take the advantage of health care reform, it will be the environment that will ultimately destroy us and literally wipe us from the face of the earth. The environment will kill us as it is so obvious with the illness, diseases and behaviors we are faced with today.

Don and I both have communicated with the President of the United States on health care reform and the President has responded very favorably with many personal letters supporting Georgia Doty Health Education Fund and HIV/Hepatitis Community Outreach Program.

HIV/AIDs, Hepatitis and other communicable diseases are all associated with environmental factors. It is the environment that we are living in today that ushers in these strict precautions in our time. Don and I have worked Inside the Illinois Department of Corrections talking with inmates on what they thought were the main issues effecting their incarceration. They told us that living in a small cell where the toilet was next to the sink and when you flush the toilet fecal matter and other bacteria would splash on their toothbrushes and clothing, hair brushes etc. Where is the preventive health care for the inmates in prison? This was only one fraction of the hazard's inmates were faced with while incarcerated. The prisons themselves are an environmental hazard because of the behaviors within the prison walls. "We cannot reform the greater percentage of inmates until we first address the psychological health needs that exist within the penal system. Real Health care reform is impossible without a stable economy; we must begin to look at employment preparedness for the next generation.

As Vice President of the Georgia Doty HIV/Hepatitis Outreach (GDHHO) this is my personal goal is to seek new ways to advance and develop new industries for today's economy and the next generation. I was informed that in the next 15 to 20 years there will be vast amounts of *technological unemployment*, this is because the jobs we have today will no longer satisfy the needs of tomorrow, computerized machines will take over manufacturing, retail even road construction, and we will need a better way to build our houses. Brick, mortar and wood will become obsolete we will need a better stronger foundation for a more lasting shelter for living, we will need to look at rebuilding a whole new city as a mean to keep up with the ever-changing technology of today and tomorrow. I raise these concerns to stress the urgent need for the "Baby Bombers" and our senior citizen to begin learning how to use the Internet to better educate themselves and the next generation. With your help and the George Doty HIV/Hepatitis Community Outreach, I will continue to work as an environmentalist and advocate for true health car referral.

We later turn our attention toward developing a needed

Environmental Curriculum at Chicago State University

I was quite shocked to hear this morning that Chicago State University might lose their accreditation and federal funding as a result of students not graduating from that university. We have known for many years that the university stood to lose many students that would drop out of college because of the lack of economic resource, learning disabilities, recidivist behavior, poor health care, and the list goes on and on. I was watching President Barack Obama who spoke at *Former Bill Clinton's Global Initiative.* The question was: ***"What kind of future do we want to build for the next generation"?*** I paused to think about my own grandchildren and what they could do to make a difference in their communities. Dr. Watson; "Public Service" is something each and every one of us can do and should do for the greater good in our society.

Students at our universities and colleges spend 80% of their time in schools reading and testing, the other 20 percent is use for leisure role play and games. Real progress does not start from the top down but from the bottom up. The bottom Dr. Watson as you well know, is in the community where the student grows up and learns what the community need and what it lacks as a community. We need to reverse the traditional education curriculum to and *on hands student development curricula* that will enhances what the student is familiar with in his/her surroundings. Students become more creative when they are working in their own communities. I share this in hopes that you would consider developing a new approach for higher learning at Chicago State University by establishing more of community service skills for the student and less time spent in the classroom reading and testing.

Secondly, we need to give the students more incentive than just a degree that may or may not develop into a career of choice, today we see literally thousands of students with PhD degrees, master's degrees working at McDonald's and Burger King, flipping burgers. Point is this, it does not matter what the subject matter is at these prestigious institutions **"Public**

Service" is available in each and every curriculum of learning. When the student volunteers, this help develop his resume and it gives him hands on experience in the area of his choice providing that the student is ready for real work. Yes, *Reading is fundamental, and testing is a necessity for learning* but what good is the book when the professor or teacher is pulling out all the stops with words and phrases that the student may never use in the real world?

We are presently working with Mark Bauman, U.S. EPA, Department of Health and Human Services, Department of Energy and other community-based organizations to develop a monitoring system that would track, identify particulate in hazardous communities like Altgeld Garden. Mr. Bauman whom I have had the pleasure of knowing for many years, is one of the most outstanding human being on the question of environmental contaminates. We have stumbled upon something very enormous for Chicago State University and we believe with the corporation of the university and its faculty we can develop a whole new curriculum of study for students and the university. There is more I would like to share with you on this subject at a later date and time, unfortunately, I just lost one of my siblings yesterday and I'm in route to Little Rock, Arkansas and will return a week from today. Thank you Dr. Watson for taking the time to read these few words.

Trinity Church was brought to the Group. Thank you for the immediate response, I am the Founder of the Organization below and I am also Vice President of the Don Doty Hepatitis/ HIV-AIDs Foundation. RRID was founded in 1982 to address criminal behavior associated with environmental factors. We worked with EPA and Chicago Department of Public Health in the mid-90 in the West Pullman Community along Hazel Johnson in the Altgeld Gardens Community. Below is our proposal to three government agencies, we have received replies from them in the last week. We believe that Rev. Moss could be an asset to this growing problem in communities of color not only in Chicago but communities nationwide. We would like a scheduled meeting with Rev. Moss or his appointee as soon as possible so that we could have a representative from Trinity at our table for the discussion to develop a monitoring system.

We are approaching November and we have not heard from U.S. EPA on *People for Community Recovery Planning Grant* that we spoke about at our last meeting. PCR is in dare straights as you can see below. Alan we are requesting that you ascertain the status of the planning grant as soon as possible, the work at Altgeld must continue in a more organized environment than what it is today. The educational system along with the environmental conditions of that community begs the question as to:_ *"Where is U.S. EPA, Illinois EPA, City of Chicago Department of Environment on the financial needs of this deprived community"? Mr. Walts, we are extremely existed about our meeting in September, however, we cannot sit ideally by and watch the violence, destruction behavior associated with environmental factors become the stone that sunk the ship, along with our children and the educational system to become the OUT-OF- SIGHT,OUT-OF-MIND neglect, in this targeted community. Where the President of the United States did his community organizing, allow this community to determinate because of the lack of funding to keep this Community Based Organization vibrant in a time when we need it the most. We are requesting that Mrs. Jackson enter vine and provide the necessary financial assistance needed to keep PCR open.*

Thank you for responding to PCR, Listen to this Alan, **seeing that the President did his organizing in Altgeld Gardens, what about making Altgeld Gardens a center piece for an environmental summit to erect a statue of the President on this land? Maybe at the top of the land field where it could be seen when driving on the Bishop Ford freeway?** This would generate funding from all over the world because our President began his organizing in the most poverty-stricken community in the state of Illinois and the most hazardous environment surrounded in a toxic donut where dysfunctional behaviors, learning disabilities, educational deprivation, lack of resources, most of all health care disparate. *The backdrop for this statue would speak volumes for the state of Illinois.* **This would place Mrs. Lisa Jackson in the forefront on Environmental Education for depressed communities.** My suggestion at this point to help PCR is to look at a *fund raiser* for the efforts of PCR maybe at Chicago State University with all educational institutions in and around the Chicago areas along with other communities are invited. Let us do a conference call as suggested at out last meeting to discuss the details of this proposal and talk about the small grants program that Margret Mallard has suggested. Why don't you set a date and coordinate it with Mark Bauman, then send it to us all. After this we should be able to set a meeting date for the beginning of next year.

We can now develop **CONFLICT RESOLUTIONS** as it relates to all educational institutions, penal, hospitals, schools, health care providers with the backdrop for an *"Environmental Health Impact Study"* on behavior as a health epidemic. How do you want to proceed with this? Would you like for the group to weigh in on this? Get back with me ASAP and please do not PROCRASTINATE with this.

This document was sent to me by Mr. Alan Walts at U.S. EPA for the group to review, I agree with EPA approach addressing a growing problem in communities in Chicago, the State of Illinois and across the nation. We will set up a conference call in early January to discuss the particulars of the Partnership. We could also re-visit People for Recovery's Planning Grant. We believe that such unprecedented agreement with HUD, DOT, and EPA would require more funding For planning than PCR originally requested for our targeted area.

We will also look at HHS to ascertain what they could bring to the table as a health component in the Partnership for Sustainable Communities: This would be a necessity as announced by Mrs. Lisa Jackson in her address to the United States Senate on environmental health. (Please see the full announcement). *Our group must be able to view this partnership as a City, state, nationwide objective, with a view of bringing other community organizations with health care disparities, affordable housing, transportation choices in a safe environment, with these issues together. That will address this partnership agreement from a depressed community like Altgeld Gardens.* However, Altgeld Gardens cannot be the only community to reap the benefits of this vast Partnership, EPA is looking for a collective Partnership with other communities in similar situations. We would like to cover the whole of Chicago with the help of our educational institution's city wide with a focus on Altgeld as a pilot for development.

This group will work as the liaison for other community-based organizations. It is my objective to keep our group small as a control group for our conveyance. We could look at our group as the Advisory Council to oversee the progression of the Partnership or we could utilize key organizations as committees and Sub-committees that would have certain responsibilities. These are just a few thoughts we should consider before the telephone conference. Please e-mail or call me on your thoughts so that we can move our agenda forward.

We have sent out a copy of Partnership Agreement document to all group members, however EPA, HUD and DOT did not include Health & Human Services which would be an ***imperative*** for community

Development. Department of Energy would also become a key player for the *"Partnership of Sustainable Communities"*. See can you reach out to EPA Administrator Mrs. Jackson on this question **"Healthy Sustainable Communities"?** We already have HHS at our table and will need HHS for this project. See what kind of response she will give you.

In light of the Partnership document, we will need the participation of the students at Chicago State University, mainly researchers, grant writers from all disciplines at the University. It would be helpful if you could consult with President Watson concerning this massive venture. The grant writers should not exclude the Universities own personal grant writers nor those students who aspire to become grant writers or researchers. This Partnership will include other community-based organizations that may have similar situated issues, we would not exclude other Universities around the city or State of Illinois. However, we could identify Chicago State as the educational Lead University for the Redevelopment of the Southeast Calumet Region should President Watson agree to such a partnership.

Mark, all the cards are not on the table yet, this is just the starting point of a huge undertaking and <u>PROCRASTINATION</u> is not an option, we want to move *our agenda* with *aggressive and progressive speed.* This is a good opportunity for Chicago State to recapture the legacy as a prestigious institution. Should Chicago State Decline to take the *"Lead Role"* as the primary educational facility for this project we could bring in several Universities collectively that could take the lead role as a matter of choice. If you would like to meet or discuss the particulars before we have the upcoming telephone conference, you can set the date and time at your convenience. Know that we want to move forward ASAP.

Greetings, Mr. Fletcher,

Thank you for following up. I have been receiving the emails from your colleagues as well about other Environmental Initiatives. Let's try to connect tomorrow afternoon by phone. I am thinking that another member of the Green Committee should meet with us, so that you have a contact in addition to me. We also have an Associate Pastor for Justice Ministries, Rev. Rochelle Michael. It would be wise to also seek a representative from the Justice Ministries who is experienced with activism and organizing, for us to be clear on how the church might participate with you. When we talk tomorrow, let's look at times for in the next week or two when we might convene with those additional two parties.We met with Rev. Trent last week and it was indeed a very good meeting, She referred me to Veronica Kyle's of Faith-In-Place whom I met with yesterday at her office. We sent her a copy of our proposal and the EPA Announcement. Because Mrs. Kyle organization reaches out to all religious denominations this will help us reach many churches city, statewide. We informed Mrs. Kyle's that since Barbra Boganey has represented Trinity Church from the beginning, we would like to keep Barb as the liaison for Trinity and the representative for the church in *our focus group,* unless Mrs. Boganey chooses otherwise. However, Mrs. Kyle's Organization has to appoint someone to represent Faith-In-Place who has a vast undertaking in galvanizing other churches to participate in our Partnership. Because the church has a great influence on communities, we need to enhance our focus to include all religious groups who would like to participate in our movement.

Our immediate task is to develop a planning grant which is now in operation with Cheryl Johnson at People for Recovery in Altgeld Gardens. We would hope that Trinity and Faith-In-Place will contact Cheryl with their grant writers and researchers and work with Cheryl to develop an *air tight* planning grant for the four Agencies HUD,DOT,EPA,HHS. Please be advised that *PROCRASTINATION* is not an option in our group, we stay focus on the issues in the communities and we aggressively move our agenda forward with stern progression. We will send copies of this memo to the main group for any comments. (See e-mail below), we think the church would be a vital organization to help galvanize community-based organizations for the Partnership. Faith-In-Place will choose a representative to work with us, we have sent them a copy of the announcement for their review, Barbra Boganey is a setting member of the focus group and would hold a vital interest for the church. Cheryl is working to develop a planning grant but she needs help, we would like to acquire writers and researchers from each of the participating Agency Partners to help with grant writing to add to the success of the grant. If you could identify writers and researchers from EPA and someone from HUD, DOT and HHS to meet at Chicago State University along with Cheryl and Faith-In-Place before the conference call, I'm find with that, we would like to get the financing we need to move this agenda forward. After reading much of the Announcement, there is no doubt that each agency has to contribute to the planning and development of our agenda, *Alan, we need seed money for operations.* Have you identified a representative from each of the agencies? We need to bring each agency representative to the table to look at the available financing for the partnership ASAP.

For the past ten to fifteen years this area was the focus for redevelopment, grants were written by many community-based organizations, what we confirmed was that many of the proposals that were written for our area was used in other areas of the **country**. Once we seen the grants that were awarded, the language in the grants from our area were used word for word. During that time much of the funding ear marked for brown fields were spreader across all projects working with Brownfield's. The Federal government sends the money to the State and the State shares it with City, the city shared it with politicians and the politicians shared it with the mob. The communities that really needed the money never got the share that was needed for redevelopment, consequently this area is still in the same predicament it was in 15 years ago.

This is why we need to meet with the representatives of HHS, HUD and DOT. Many community-based organizations see this as being the same ploy used to deceive the community's years ago. We have already spoken to quite a few organizations about this Agreement. *There has to be a direct line of communication for funding for this area so that the communities can have a sense of promise.* We do not have a problem writing grants, the problem is getting the funding allocated for job creation. Unemployment is increasing by the hour we do not need a bandage for an open wound, we need sutures to close the wound.

We need a financial reassurance for the development of this area. The way to achieve this is to bring the representatives to the table to ascertain how their finical structure will be used to address community concerns. For years we have talked about job creation and its longevity, *people in the community want to see action.* Mrs. Jackson has already talked with HUD and DOT, now it's time for HHS, HUD and DOT to sit down with us and unleash their strategy. Once we are clear on their direction, we can start job creation. The Announcement does not provide a strategy for job creation because it is unaware of the specific needs in the community. If you through raw meat out to a pack of hungry dogs, they will all attack it trying to get a bite, that the way EPA and other agencies has provided grant funding in the past. There is an old 'cliché.' *"Can you teach old dog new tricks"?* Answer is *"Only if the dog is willing to listen"*.

As you well know the Georgia Doty Hep/HIV Community Outreach mission is to address the healthcare needs in depressed communities Hep-C/HIV are healthcare issues and in the announcement, Don sent to you there are three possible grants that you could focus on. When you click on the announcement the second site and the two at the bottom of the page are RFPs that takes you to a health care site. Although you might be looking for a Hep-C or HIV specific grant, that not the case. Healthcare encompass Hep-C/HIV, Health care expands to all illness, diseases, behavior, death and the effects of magnetic energy fields. Hep-C and HIV is a disease component of the health care treatment. This suggests that your grant could include *prevention, recidivism, housing, transportation, any and all diseases associated environmental factors*.

Don has all the right components for any RFP the above agencies have to offer, GDHCO has laid the foundation and groundwork for this entire announcement. This includes the Re-Entry program that would require "Job Creation" upon release, "Housing", food, clothing and shelter, Transportation, medical care for treatment etc. EPA has already indicated that we could bring in other agencies such as Department of Education, Department of Energy and any other agency that is needed for this Partnership. This suggests that each agency has a budget, each agency has discretionary funding, and each agency is required to produce financial resources for the Partnership. Have I missed anything? If I'm missing something, please tell me so I can bring it to the attention of our Group. EPA choose us for this project and we are bringing to the table any community based organization that wants to participate, City, State, Nationwide.

You indicated that our group focus must expand to include City, State, Nationwide to address employment creation, Valerie Jarrett has sent out e-mails requesting community assistance and input for job creation as a community outreach movement. Alan we are all proud to have an energetic person like you to be able to articulate the group's mission. I believe the entire group is grateful. However, here is a little food for thought. We all try to follow the rules for engagement to acquire financial resources needed for community development. But many times, the process is neglected by those at the top, for example, Treasury Secretary Palson submitted to the United States Congress a three page document and requested over $800, Billion dollars of the tax payer money and the United States Congress approved the request. This money or our money was used to bail out Wall Street and to give Bonuses to executives who did nothing but help our economy collapse. Then there is the Iraq and Afghanistan wars in which we provide both countries with Billions of our dollars for financial assistance to redevelop there infrastructure. But when it comes to financing community based organization and groups like ours, it always appear that bureaucracy is implemented to deny our groups success as you have clearly sent us the EPA process for acquiring financial assistance (GRANTS). Alan, we all know that Mrs. Lisa Jackson has access to the President as well as Kathleen Sebelius, HUD, DOT etc. We are not fooled by the message you sent us. What we want is ACTION not rhetoric. Alan, we need no less than $5, million dollars *from each agency* to provide financial assistance for a planning grant that could address the issues below and attached to this e-mail. We are still looking forward to the conference call the part of the New Year. We have contacted several other organizations that would have great input to our movement. Please contact Mrs. Jackson and let her know that we stand by her but we want action not rhetoric.

The Development of the Delta

The Delta is a stretch of land from Arkansas, Louisiana, Mississippi and Tennessee. Routes 65 and 69 are highways that go's though these States, the indigenous people in this area have been exploited for the past 200 or more years. The conditions are virtually unchanged by time. When you drive this area let's say from Little Rock to Pine Bluff, there is marginal change, but from Pine Bluff to Dermott you fine decade property, old factories closed and decade, no jobs, no big factories, no fast food restaurants, not even a bus station for those people to travel from Dermott to Pine Bluff or Little Rock, no taxi cabs to transport people from one small town to the next. Halley, Arkansas is another small town and the home of Congressman Danny K. Davis whom I've had the pleasure of talking with him concerning the Development of this area.

Congressman Davis has supported the development of this area once a proposal is put in place. State of Arkansas has been instrumental in building highways to travel through these rural areas.

However, what is needed now when traveling through the Delta are jobs to help these oppressed communities, there has to be more housing developed in this long stretch of land, HUD-Housing of Urban Development, DOT-Department of Transportation, U.S. EPA-United States Environmental Protection Agency and HHS-Health and Human Services has an obligation to address these serious needs in this depressed area of the Country.

What we suggest at this point is to look at a planning grant that would bring all the above agencies together under the existing Partnership Agreement to help resolve some of these poverty-stricken areas. The Department of Education has an obligation to sit at this table to develop a curriculum that would help educate this indigenous community. Recidivist behavior has been the turning point for most of these areas, drugs and gang violence has taken over this area because of the lack of developing programs.

We will bring this suggestion to the group at Chicago State University and will request that U.S. Congressman Danny Davis be informed to ascertain rather or not he has put into place additional plans for this development. We will also request that the Congressman assign a representative to sit with the group to explore as planning grant proposal.

For the past ten to fifteen years this area was the focus for redevelopment, grants were written by many community-based organizations, what we confirmed was that many of the proposals that were written for our area was used in other areas of the **country**. Once we seen the grants that were awarded, the language in the grants from our area were used word for word. During that time much of the funding ear marked for brown fields were spreader across all projects working with Brownfield's. The Federal government sends the money to the State and the State shares it with City, the city shared it with politicians and the politicians shared it with the mob. The communities that really needed the money never got the share that was needed for redevelopment, consequently this area is still in the same predicament it was in 15 years ago.

This is why we need to meet with the representatives of HHS, HUD and DOT. Many community-based organizations see this as being the same ploy used to deceive the community's years ago. We have already spoken to quite a few organizations about this Agreement. *There has to be a direct line of communication for funding for this area so that the communities can have a sense of promise.* We do not have a problem writing grants, the problem is getting the funding allocated for job creation. Unemployment is increasing by the hour we do not need a bandage for an open wound, we need sutures to close the wound.

We need a financial reassurance for the development of this area. The way to achieve this is to bring the representatives to the table to ascertain how their finical structure will be used to address community concerns. For years we have talked about job creation and its longevity, *people in the community want to see action.* Mrs. Jackson has already talked with HUD and DOT, now it's time for HHS, HUD and DOT to sit down with us and unleash their strategy. Once we are clear on their direction, we can start job creation. The Announcement does not provide a strategy for job creation because it is unaware of the specific needs in the community. If you through raw meat out to a pack of hungry dogs, they will all attack it trying to get a bite, that the way EPA and other agencies has provided grant funding in the past. There is an old 'cliché.' *"Can you teach old dog new tricks"?* Answer is *"Only if the dog is willing to listen".*

Thank you for signing up to hold a community jobs forum in your area. Just like the Jobs and Economic Growth Forum hosted by the President at the White House, these events are opportunities to gather ideas for continuing to grow the economy and putting Americans back to work. Hearing from working Americans and communities across the country means understanding what's really happening on the ground, what's working, and what's not.

At the link below you will find all the materials you should need to host your own jobs forum with your family, friends, and co-workers, including a suggested guide for hosts and a list of suggested questions that we hope you will touch on. Use the same link to share the feedback from your community jobs forum once you have finished. We will be reviewing submissions and compiling your feedback into a report that will be sent to the Oval Office and will be responding to what we hear on WhiteHouse.gov afterwards.

Download the materials or provide feedback from your forum at http://whitehouse.gov/CommunityJobFeedback Professor Danny Block, We met with the above organizations last week because we are certain that each organization has input into this Partnership undertaking. Mattie Butler has worked with CHA and CTA over the years to help depressed communities in housing and transportation. We have given seminars at the Roseland Community Hospital with Dr.Cave' and Dr. Peter Orris of the University of Illinois and we have also given a seminar at Chicago State University along with Dr. Balogun, Dean of the Health Science Department, We will at some point bring the Dean to this table for a Health analyses for HHS. We believe that financial assistance from the four agencies HUD,DOT,HHS, and U.S.EPA could be obtained to help develop our job creation plan.

We need Stats for the Delta project and the Southeast Calumet initiative. The University of Wisconsin has a professor that familiar with the Delta Project also Loyola University. **Unless,** Mark Bouman has some stats from years gone by, hopefully so, we will be talking to Mark in early January. We also think that the American Innovative Healthcare Solutions could have a role working with us at Chicago State. There are also other organizations on the Westside of Chicago that wants to participate, and there is still "Faith in Place" and Trinity Church that will also be on this list. We will look at February for a meeting date to bring these organizations together and decide how we will work with each organization, but we strongly suggest that they bring to the table their expertise in their line of work and their organization can work with the core group. Our mission is to coordinate and fine tune our proposals so that it will address the financial needs for the job creation initiative. *Dr. Block please keep in mind, we do not want a government takeover of our project, We do the work, we get the financial resources needed for our project, we don't want anything less than that.*

Robert=HHS;

That whole idea, we are looking at the first week in February for the entire group. Alan Waltz will do a conference call with the *main* participants in January. The conference call should point out what *each organization within its own capacity* could or should do. *Unless*, HHS would like to have a *separate meeting on Healthcare issues?* If this is the case let me know ASAP and we can ask Dr. Block to set up a meeting room at Chicago State. Not only does HHS have funding, the President has already assured that much of the stimulus money will be divided among those agencies that will help develop and create jobs. Either you are in the know or you are not. *You have access to Kathline Sebelius*, if you do not have access we will get access, we want to make sure she is abreast to what we are doing. We know that each agency in Partnership with the HUD Agreement has access to additional funds. The mere fact that we brought HHS to our table and the Presidents Healthcare initiative is on the table is an indication that Funding is already present for job creation. The Question now is what would *you like to do?*

    I have already replied to The White House Request, their formality has been complete, they asked about six questions concerning community needs, we sent them what we proposed, and our immediate task is still focused on working with the Partnership Agreement, and announcement by HUD, DOT, EPA, and HHS. I just sent you an e- mail requesting a room to meet with Robert Herskovits from HHS. We would like to have Dr. Joseph Balogun, Dean of Health Science at Chicago State University to attend this meeting on the 17th around 10:00AM if you could accommodate and confirm this meeting.

Benzene / Air Born Quality

It is good that EPA has air monitoring systems in the Gulf, however, the air quality in Chicago and around the country also has bad air quality. You already know that this is what our meetings have been about for the last year. ***To develop a monitoring system that will track, identify all elements in the environment so that the people will know what is causing*** *illness,*

Disease, behavior, death and the effects of magnetic energy fields.

What do we have to do to get a monitoring system set up in the Chicago area? Do we have to have another bigger catastrophe before EPA realize that a monitoring system is a necessity for the entire country? Or must we reliy upon another big corporation that does not have a clue as to what to do should another catastrophe bigger than the Gulf Oil spill

Elements In The Environment

We are now at a cross road in understanding the true meaning as what the elements in the environment are, what they truly mean to our everyday life, how they affect our each and every thought, action and movement.

This oil spill gives us the best scenario as to what can happen when the elements are put to the test. The microorganisms work together as the most powerful elements in creation. BP has worked long and hard with the OUT-OF-SIGHT,OUT-OF-MIND,SYNDROM mentality. In BPs mind they never cared about if there should be an oil spill of this magnitude, so they never could conceive a clean up as the one in the Gulf. Once you ascertain what the microorganisms do with all of creation, then we can truly understand who, what, where the real GOD controls. You cannot name one thing in creation that the elements do not control, NOT ONE.

The elements have always had control of each and everything in creation. It is the elements that gives us life and death, they cause us to become ill with disease, they cause negative and positive behaviors, it is the elements that provide us with intelligence, gives us the food we eat, the speech to communicate, the technology to advance our thinking. You can't see these elements with naked eye, they are invisible but you can feel these elements just as the wind blows you feel a cool breeze. No one can deny the power of the unseen elements in creation.

Part 2—Elements In The Environment

Did you know in religion most denominations believe in the one God principle and have never equated the God concept with the elements in the environment. Traditional teachings in religion has placed many believers in the OUT-OF-SIGHT,OUT-OF-MIND SYNDROME mentality. It does not matter what religion one believes, the process in creation has always been the same. The difference between the God in a religion and the Elements in the Environment is that *all religions are manmade* and the ***Elements are the natural creation***. There is no equal between the two, one is far greater than the other. The word God is a noun but so are the elements in the environment. In religion they are taught that God created the havens and earth, but so did the elements in creation.

Here is a dilemma, when a suppliant prays what is it that they are praying to? In religion they say God and God is within you. In reality you are praying to the self which are the elements that live within you. Follow this scenario, prior to your birth the sperm has to be created and what is the sperm created from? The sperm mixed with ovum are created in the brain from the nutrients in the foods we eat. Our food grows from the earth, the energy along with the vegetation feeds the animals. plant life insects etc. The food chain is the vehicle that transports the nutrients which gives us the energy to live. Energy is created from the Sun, the Sun is created from ***Helium and Atoms***, these elements moves throughout the universe causing wave of energy, It is the energy that causes the earth to spin, our blood to flow from our heart which causes the human body to function.

When we pass away what happens? The body is returned to the earth and after time the body disintegrates and each element returns from which they came, the energy or (breath of life) that caused you to live is returned to that vast ocean of energy in the universe. Here is food for thought, *nothing in creation is ever lost,* the problem is you just can't find it. Fire consumes an object, and we say it is gone and disintegrated. What happen to the object that was disintegrated? Like Sybor space. Where did it go,. did the contents move to another dimension? Many have never even given this a thought. This is called the *OUT-OF-SIGHT,OUT-OF-MIND, SYNDRME. e*pa-ej] $75 Million in Funding Available—HUD-DOT Announce Community Challenge Grants and TIGER II Planning Grants

Energizing Creation Produce Constant Change

From time to time I find it important to share certain information with you as an environmentalist. Education is a key component for learning, the human psyche is something many have capitalized on for many years until till this very day! The whole of Creation is energized by the billions of stars and suns within our universe, this energy not only energize the the earth and its habitation, but it causes all the planets to spin in their own orbit. *Each and every single thing in creation began from a small microorganism.* **We see this within our own individual (birth) creation.** There is a constant change in creation, we need look no further than the age of the Dinosaur, the Neanderthal, Roman Empire, British Monarch, America's Discovery etc. There has always been changes in creation each and every fraction of a second and thereafter. Former Vice President Al Gore began to publicize *"Climate Change,"* Then President Obama came on the seen as the President to bring about **"CHANGE"** with the slogan *"Yes We Can".* In the mind of the human Being, this change must first begin with a thought in the brain. It has to first resonate deep into the sub consciousness of the mind.

Many times, this is very difficult especially when there have been many years of deceptiveness either in chattel slavery, religion, and politics and in many case a deprived educational system. Many do not like change and become rebellious when change is presented as a fact of life, we can see this with the Obama Administration. Let's take Religion for example, religion is like any other made device, it was never intended to remain on the earth forever. It too must come to its final conclusion. Tradition prevents many from accepting change, whereas tradition is like of a *"Pandora's Lock Box".* No matter what you put before them they are lock into their beliefs. Change is very difficult even in politics. It is the element, the **ATOM** of life that began Creation, not the Adam that is mentioned in the Bible in Genesis. We spoke about the *OUT-OF-SIGHT, OUT-OF-MIND, SYNDROME,* when we neglect to see the intricate details as to how the elements work within us, we become disconnected from the **COSMOS.** Our focus become blind we allow any and all kinds of bamboozle, trickery to influence our thinking and behavior.

Manipulative Knowledge in Religion

From an Environmental stand point and as human beings, *one can believe what ever they want to believe,* however, we must take a very serious look at religion and what it has produced for us world wide. We must do all that we can in **our life time** to educate and address the concerns of the people in matters of religion. We have found that the majority of the world population has embraced some sort of religious beliefs and it is this reason that so much war and deception exist in the world. Many theologians believes that most religions began some five or six thousand years ago, even if it was ten thousand years within the time warp, this would only be seconds on a scale of life of existence or a fraction of a second to say the lease.

Creation has always trumped religion, you can never equate religion with creation, and religion is an unnatural practice in human behavior. Religion is an addictive knowledge like any other addictive behavior; it can consume an individual's every thought. So much so that the human mind takes on a superstitious belief. The theologians added another factor in religion, for the Christians it was the belief in Jesus Christ, for Muslims it the Prophet Muhammad, Buddhism, Buddha etc. Each religion has a prophet or son of a God.

As a creative fact of life, one can believe in anything they choose to believe, the problem with this is that in choosing to practice a religion it does not raise to the level of creativity. Religion is repetitive and has no foundation as a creative source. All religions rely upon a book written by men thousands of years ago and in many cases these writings are unfounded by research. It has been said "that a mind is a terrible thing to waste", however, from a religious point of view it is the financial resources that keeps religion powerful.

Traditional religious beliefs have produced an addictive behavior that becomes a very hard habit to break. This process is like the Pandora's Box, many are locked into this belief for life and they believe that death will ultimately transport them to heaven or hell which ever their deeds produce. It will take someone with a key to unlock the mysteries in religion to free the mind from religion. *The truth of the matter is that death is an extension of life in creation. Death transports energy from one dimension to the next. **Energy is the source by which all things exist.*** There is nothing in creation that compare to the works of energy, <u>NOTHING!</u>

It is the microorganisms, elements, particulates, and nutrients in creation that gives us life and all things on earth life, how is it that we equate the natural creation with the development of religion? **Religion has no place in the study of creation.** Religion is an unnatural practice; you cannot equate one thing in religion with the elements in creation. **NOT ONE.** The word God has been used as an idol of worship for all believers and like all theologians in religion, no one will ever question the word of God.

Allen:

I am the Chairman of this Group, most of these members have been meeting for a year and they have brought something to the table in the past, our agenda dates back a few years, however *we are not trying to publicize our meeting agenda at this time.* We are not trying to bring a lot of people to this group meeting, only those we send this agenda to. Should you attend, this would be your first meeting with us, it would be good to come and listen to the Group then offer your assistance.

Mark Allen:

I truly appreciate what you are saying we both can see what the "Black Political Leaders" are doing(dog and pony show) to President Obama and we both need to work with those Congressional ties that might have a reach into The White House that could ultimately get his attention. Mark, if we could get him to come to Chicago State University to do a speach on "Health Disparity" or "Educational Reform" or" Race Relations" that could well be a great accomplishment. The objective would be to reach out to all those who want to see "Change" in our communities. This suggests that we reach out to Reverend Jackson and anyone that has a direct connection with the President or Michelle Obama. Do you know his Barbara in Hype Park? I'll talk with Dr. Britt at Chicago State and get his spin on how we could bring him to the University, meanwhile see what you can do from your end then let us meet up and compare notes for the next step.

Request for a Presidential Town Hall Meeting At Chicago State University

Dear Mrs. Jarrett:

I am the Chairperson for an *"Environmental Health Group"* at **Chicago State University,** our focus has been on public policy relative to health care disparities, racial insensitivity, educational disparities, food deserts, and economic disparities in Altgeld Garden, Roseland and West Pullman Communities respectively. We are presently working with U.S. EPA, HUD, DOT and HHS in the <u>Sustainable Community Program</u>. What we have found is that Altgeld Gardens as you well know set within a toxic donut on the far Southside of Chicago, to the East was a land field, to the West a steel mill along the Cal Sag River, to the South CSX railroad, to the North was Sherman Williams Paint Company and to make matter worst just in front of Altgeld Gardens entrance is a waste purification plant.

Surely you are aware that even after EPA removes contaminated matter from a Brownfield site, *it is the residues that are still prevalent in and around these communities.* Illness, disease, behavior, death and the impact of magnetic energy fields are still live and well in these communities, gang violence is the norm and order of the day, education and the lack there of seems to be the normal way of life in these areas. President Barack Obama has told the world how he did his organizing in Alrgeld Garden and you would think that the President would have made Altgeld Garden his first priority once he was in Office. Obviously, this was not the case. Many who are living in these communities cannot understand how or why the President has neglected to come back to these **grass root communities** with discretionary funding to help in re development of this area. After all it was these community residents that help the President when he needed them most and it was these communities that helped him get elected.

We are requesting that your Office as Senior Advisor please assist us in getting the President to come to Chicago State University and do a Town Hall Meeting on Race Relations, Environmental Health, Economic Development and Educational Reform. We think that the President could reach out to these poverty communities with words of encouragement as he has done for other communities all over the Country *who did not help him as the community of Altgeld Garden*. Surely you are aware that our President is for all of America and we understand that, but you should never slap the hand that fed you nor burn the bridge that took you across.

Mrs. Jarrett, we are asking you and your Office to please help us accomplish this itinerary, your thoughtfulness in this matter would be greatly, appreciated.

Why We Desperately Need
a Monitoring System

We have discussed in the past the need for a monitoring system that would monitor, track and identify the movements of the elements in the environment. We have also discussed how energy in the environment gives life to our brain that causes us to think, we discuss how the prefrontal cortex on the left side of the brain controls human behavior. A chemical function in the brain. Today we are looking at the up rise of human deceptiveness in behavior, in politics, a dysfunctional educational system, gang violence, children killing children, religious bigotry, joblessness, homelessness, material greed etc. Many of people are wondering how or when this will ever end.

The masses of the people do not understand why these things are happening and no one is trying to educate the masses of people as to the outcome of this up evil diabolical behaviors. The difference between an earthquake and a tsunami is that the earthquake swallows massive amounts of earth and the tsunami floods the earth with water and both are controlled by energy waves. When we speak of negative and positive energies, we should not take this lightly. It is the negative energies that is causing much of the up rise in human behavior in all our communities. The financial greed has prioritized the thinking of the people and has become the rule of the day.

The People can easily predict what is about to happen just by watching the daily news. Change has come and destruction is alive and well not only in America but global and the continued uproar of violence, lies and deception will one day real soon will reach a fever pitch and race riots will accrue on a scale never before in the history of the world. The issue is, **how can we stop this before it reaches the fever pitch?** If we do not understand the *root cause* of what is happening to the *mindset* of the people, we have no concept as to its conclusion. We talk politics all day long and care less about the destruction of the brain. Nevertheless, if we do not change our way of thinking we as humans will experience an earthquake right in our own back yard and a tsunami of epidemic proportions this is called a brain drain of positive energy.

Creation is Constant Energy Creation is Constant Energy

Every single thing in creation is energy driven and balanced. If we neglect to study Creation we neglect to study our own human intelligence and anatomy, books are great to read and we learn many things from them. However, if we turn our attention to the internal workings within us there is much more to learn than you could ever dream possible. When you study the organs, the blood, the cells, the microorganisms, those tiny animals in the one blood cell, there is enough education within one blood cell to last a full lifetime. The most exciting thing about the *study of yourself* you don't need a college degree; you merely turn your thinking internal and began your journey. The bigger question is how did we get so turned around that we were never taught to study ourselves in pre-school, elementary, high school or college?

Environmental education is an extreme necessity

The words bamboozle, hoodwink, trick neology comes to mind, financial greed, politics, religion are all ***mind control devices.*** Creation is factual, religion and politics are fictional, they are nothing more than a mirage that is here today but gone tomorrow. Like Houdini They both are entertainment and theatrical at their best. In religion we see the Pope of Roman wearing a custom, in America it is our so call Ministers or Preachers wearing the same custom or robe as a symbol of the robe of Christ. In Churches there is song and dance, in politics there are lies and deception, these symbols and images are divisive tools that have kept us blind for centuries on end. We should have been taught about creation and the human anatomy from birth. Just take a brief look at our situation today, should we become sick, the system tells us to go to a hospital or doctor and the reason is what? We have no idea as to what is wrong with us other than the pain or imbalance that we are feeling.

It is good to have teachers and professors to teach us the basic fundamentals of the human body, *but, it becomes our own responsibility as we grow and develop to go internal to learn about our individual selves.* We should learn about **every single working organ** within our bodies. If a physician can learn it, why can't we? Many libraries have the same books the colleges and universities have for their students. Why are we paying for something we can do ourselves? The internal organs are locked in total triple darkness, a direct contrast with the darkness in the universe, isn't it true that you can feel energy but you can't see energy? When you don't know yourself, you are compelled to take advice from someone else like a physician, psychologist, teachers, professors etc. It is this reason why health care has become a commodity, a multi-billion-dollar industry, and it has become necessary to get the help we need to better understand the many illnesses, disease, behavior, death, magnetic energy fields and to better understand our selves. In our world today, at every turn we find ourselves paying for help to save ourselves and for someone to tell us about ourselves because we don't know ourselves.

Religion Is A Unnatural Practice

If a person truly understands the workings of the elements in the environment, they will clearly conclude that *"all religions are unnatural practices"*. Today we hear about the burning of Qurans and a few years ago we heard about the burning of Bibles. The Afghans are the second poorest country in the world with 90% of the total population living in ignorance but are true to their religious beliefs. Religion has always been a tool for enslavement. No matter how many times a person believes that God exist, and Jesus rose up from the dead. The belief system has worked for those who believe in this type of enslavement. The conscience and the sub-conscience have **locked** this belief into the brain and mind of the believer. That's how slaves are indoctrinated. They have been locked into a system of belief that there is a heaven and hell. Heaven is for the good and hell is for the disbelievers. We can truly understand why Science and religion could never mix. If you have ever visited Chicago State University, they have a Department call Health Sciences. It is called Health Science because _*Heath* is a *Science* and not a religion. This is because it can never become a religion.

Religion is taught in Schools of Theology, this word *theology* is short for **theory** and a theory is nothing more than a made up _*fairy tale*. It is like the Santa Claus theory at Christmas time, The rabbit and the chicken egg at Easter time with the idea that Jesus rose from the dead after three days. Alice and Wonderland, the Wizard of Oz etc._*This type of teachings is embedded in the mind of our children from birth to adulthood*. Today these theoretical practices still exist in our society. *There has never been a God in the Creation of the Universe*. Within one atom of life there are numerous organisms that are design to create all that we see present. Because you happen to prosper in this life, it is because you *embrace positive energies* with a *minor in negative energies* .At the time of your death, the energies that have kept you alive will depart from you, the body you once occupied will be place in the earth for decomposition or you can be cremated into dust which ever you prefer, nevertheless, that energy that kept you alive will return to the vast ocean of energy that abides all around us consistently and will join the massive creation of energy in the universe.

Environmental Education

As the Chairperson for our Group, I have thought long and heard about doing *"Fund Raising"* for **"Environmental Education".** There are literally thousands of *'Environmentalists'* that shares our views on this topic. We hear all the time about fund raising for different diseases, *[although all diseases originate from environmental factors],* we do fund raising for our schools, churches, community organizations etc. This is something we could bring up at our next meeting for those who are interested, however, it would be great if I could get some feedback on developing this idea. We could try to make contact with Environmental Activist and Actor Robert Redford who has a long reach into environmental activism around the world.

Environmental Education As A Curriculum at Chicago State University

Dr. Britt.

I really don't think the people is all that concern about the environment because of ignorance to what the environment does.

The immediate concern is finding a job to take care of their families. En Ed is the *OUT-OF-SIGHT, OUT-OF-MIND SYNDROME* and not visible to the conscientiousness of the people. Religious enslavement is the worst kind of slavery, **it takes control of the conscience and the sub-conscience.**

The majority of the people are locked into some kind of religious belief and it is very difficult to pierce the armour of religion, especially after years of traditional religious enslavement.

Because Environmental Education is a <u>necessity</u> and <u>Juxtapose</u> to Health as a Science, what is the feasibility of developing a *"environmental curriculum"* within the Department of Health Science? Because environmental education is not taught as a curriculum, this would be an *addition to the present curricula and a necessity before student graduation* within the preview of the "Health Science Department". Environmental Education has never been a prerequisite for a license to practice under Illinois State Office of Professional Regulations. Chicago State University could become the first University in history to develop environmental health curricula as a Health Science. Could you speak to Dean Balogun and the Pro Vost to ascertain this feasibility?

The Micro-Organism Factor

Many times we get so caught up in our daily activities until we neglect to turn our attention to the life forces that keeps us alive. The "Micro-Organism" is the *OUT-OF-SIGHT,OUT-OF-MIND* function that is never given a second thought as to how it operates in the brain. As you read the words in this email something is happening, it is the "micro-organism" at work creating each letter to produce the silent word. If you have ever witness a typist that type over a hundred words a minute without watching the movement of his fingers, that is the organisms that's causing it to happen, they move at such an incredible rate of speed until you would not even give them a second thought. *We humans never really give credit to the little small increment details as to how, why and what gives us the air we inhale and exhale.* We only concern ourselves with the oxygen we need to stay alive and not the process by which we maintain our daily life. We speak of "Dreams" but pay less attention as to how the images are formed in our dream's, again these are the works of the "Micro-Organisms" in the brain. **It is this neglect that have cause many to embrace religion.** Religion does not teach you to learn the increment details of life, you must attend a school of science to understand the teachings of the anatomy and you will pay dearly to understand this knowledge. We should be teaching our children from birth these increment detail workings of the "Micro-organisms" so that *"the child can reach the higher goals of creation"*. Our children are stuck in a Pandora's box of ignorance and religious bigotry. We are not raised to challenge the workings of the "Micro-Organisms" because of their tiny life existence.

To truly understand the windows of the eye is to understand what it is that gives the individual the vision to see. This process is often neglected because the Organisms are moving at such a high rate of speed to give the individual the images of light to maintain sight and focus, so that the person can comprehend what it is they see. We might call this *"INTELLIGENCE"*.

The Micro-Organism Factor Part I

There are 5 or more parts to this segment on "Micro-Organisms". Here are just a few that we will explore in the weeks ahead. "Addiction", "Choices, "Death", "Viruses", "Bacteria". _**Did you know that our entire life is an addictive process?**_ Food, sex, drugs, alcohol, religion, politics, money, and ignorance. Ignorance is a serious addition, with ignorance, there is the don't care attitude, lethargy, weak morals, wanting for someone to die for us, someone that can forgive us for our sins etc. _The whole world pays a price for ignorance, we see it in our homes, our parents, our children, our schools, churches, political leaders etc._ Why is it that the mother who is pregnant with a child talks to the father with such intellectual agility before the child is born? But when the child is born, she talks to the child with Koo's, boos and ooh's? The mother, baby talks the child until the child is about 7 or 8 years old and sometimes the mother is still baby talking the child even at that age. The point is this, if the child sees, hear, breathes all that the mother see, hear, breath why are we still baby taking our children? The child understands everything you say if only you would talk to the child with sense of purpose. The mother Koo, boo and ooh the child until that's the language the child began to understand.

Then the parent is left with the task of teaching the child twice and with some three time before the child can truly understand what it is you trying to teach it. Our teachers are having a hard time teaching the child and students because we fail to teach the new born from birth. The reason why the "Micro-Organism is so crucial to learn is that _the child was created from the "Micro-Organism"_ and has a birth right to know why he was created in the form as a human.

However, if the parents are ignorant of the workings of the "Micro-Organisms" and rear the child with no understanding of what, how or why he was created, then ignorance continue to follow ignorance it becomes an addictive process that keeps our children in a perpetual state of dysfunctional behavior.

The Micro-Organism Factor Part I

About 95 % of the total population of the earth do not believe that the little, tiny "Micro-Organisms" created all that we see today, this **include all that is in the universe, the darkness in space, the stars** *and planetary systems etc*. You would be hard pressed to hear a Scientist talk about the **"Blackness"** in space and not *associate the **"blackness"** with the production of the organisms*. When we look at the "Organisms" under a microscope *we witness energy and nutrients in motion*. The scientist in a laboratory looks for mutation and the spread of viruses and bacteria, but there is *something much greater within each organism*. Plum Island off the coast of New York City warehouses viruses, bacteria and can release these viruses at any time, any place, anywhere they please. If you have ever read the book "Laboratory 257", your amazement would be how scientist developed the "West Nile", "Swine Flu", "AID"s and other diseases in a laboratory to increase the pharmaceuticals bottom line. We will talk more on this subject later. There is something much greater with a higher intelligence when looking at the organisms, it is how they have created **"Balance" or "Equilibrium"**. We have been taught how the earth is balanced on it axes, the earth along with the *entire universe is balanced,* we see this with all the planets, the stars, galaxy's etc.

This balance is seen with the development of the human, example, some children will learn to balance themselves and start walking immediately, and there are others that must crawl before they learn balance. they fall down and get up until they learn how to balance themselves. *This balance is an intricate part of the human behavior.* Not only must the child learn to balance him/herself physically, but they must learn to balance themselves psychologically, Socialy, economically etc. Without a proper balance we become unbalanced in our thinking, our actions and how we communicate with others. ***You must not by any means take these organisms lightly, they are the real powers in creation***. They create the winds, the rain, snow, ice, earthquake, hurricanes, tornadoes and each and every single living thing we see on the planet earth all ***forced by energy.*** These organisms give life and causes death. The organisms along with energy also transport human thoughts from one dimension to the next dimension. Because we neglect to understand the working process of the micro-organisms this leave a lot to the imagination.

The Organism Factor-Part II

Did you know that ***one word in a dictionary is connected to all the words in the dictionary?*** We call this the *oneness* of the word, this same principle is within the creation. *Your individual creation is connected to* *the whole of creation.* All words have meaning, many *sound* alike but have different meaning, let us look at the following words, and how they are connected: Orgen, Organ, organism, organizing, organization just to name a few. The first word <u>O</u>*rgen* like the State of Orgen or a *state* of mind both could have dual meanings, then the word *Organ;* what comes to mind is the key board *organ that gives us sound or music.* But so does the *heart organ* also a instrument that beats in the human anatomy by which music was created; then there is the *organism;* to carry on a vital function; this alludes to the practice of *organizing;* to give organic structure; and gives us a disposition; then there is organization that produce structure and this structure is produce in the whole of creation.

Let us now discuss the word **choices** which means to choose; Many of us think that we have many choices to choose from but in reality, there are only *two* choices. You either choose *"negative"* or *"positive"* at any given thought. You can **never** choose both at the same time because *two things* can never **occupy the same space at the same time**. If you went into a supermarket, you see many objects and these object gives you the appearance of many choices. But you can only choose one item at a time. Example, if you choose a *"negative"*, you must accept all that comes with that negative choice, until you change that choice to a *"positive"* and when you choose *"positive"* the same acceptance applies. This is happening at such a high rate of speed until it gives the **appearance** that you are making multiple choices at one time, but in reality you are only making *one choice at a time.* That is the beauty of understanding the workings of the organisms.

Every Country on earth at one time had absolute power and dominance worldwide, Take the country of Greece, at one time the Greeks had the most greatest scientist in the world. Surely, we all have heard of *"Greek Mythology"*. The Scientist that began to research the universe seen something that had to be taught to the masses of that time. They had to develop something that could be understood as a means of power and control. They seen Astronomy as something greater than their own life force. They studied the universe and for many years the scientist discovered Astrology and from Astrology religion was given birth. The God Zeus was prominent in the universe and had power over heaven, earth and hell. these scenarios still stand today in all religions. Nevertheless, the Greeks were more concern about the power to control the masses, they knew about the power of persuasion and the addictive nature of the human mind. Astrology as we know it today is not the Astrology we see in newspapers and magazines. Real Astrology however does have a great impact on a person's time of birth and a chart that guides his destiny. A man once said; *"that every human being born is dealt a hand of cards and every hand is different"*, and each person must play the hand that was dealt to them.

Every one can't be the President, nor can everyone be a scientist, however, **"everyone can play a part in the advancement of creation"**. We know that energy is created from helium and atoms, but when we look at the sun we see a massive amount of fire and we know that the sun provides energy for the earth and all planetary systems. When we look at a massive planet like Jupiter our mind just can't conceive of something that is so massive was created by something so small as a Micro-Organism.

The Micro-Organism Factor-Part III

We as human beings are vessels controlled by organisms, these organisms are influenced by energy, the energy gives the organisms power that allow you and I to think and choose. If you choose negativity, you must endure all that comes with that negative choice. Should you choose Positive energy the same principle applies unless you change your mind in midstream.

Technology and the computer as we know it today operates on the **"organism principle"**. In fact, the operation of a computer and the *mother board* is a direct reflection of the functioning of the brain, except the *organisms have explicit power and control* over the human brain and the computer. The *"Space Station"* and the *"Hubble Telescope"* has been searching for years to ascertain the secrets of the space odyssey and for years has failed in their attempt to ascertain its secrets. For centuries on end the *"Galaxies"* and *"Cosmos"* has held the secrets of the universe, it is one the center pieces of high knowledge, but the great scientist of yesteryear was *disconnected from the Cosmos.* and when the disconnect happens, **you are truly disconnected in the worse way.** It is like unplugging the circuitry to the mother board in a computer. We will talk more about the Cosmos later, but the broader question is how do we **re- connect** with the "Cosmos"? We said in previous writings that *"nothing is ever lost in creation"*, the problem is that we can't find it unless the organisms lead us to find a particular thing. Like *cyber space* when knowledge is sometimes misplaced or moved into cybor space many times the information cannot be retrieved unless you are a **Experienced** *"HACKER"*, the intelligent Hacker can retrieve certain information from cyber space because the *organisms has lead them to it.* The issues are, "what will the Hackers utilize the information for? Would it be used for positive or negative means?. Because of the *"OUT-OF-SIGHT, OUT-OF-MIND"* phenomenon, ignorance, blindness and short sightedness and religious beliefs,_*many will always dismiss the notion that the organisms have explicit power over the human brain.* Nevertheless, *"they can not name one thing that the organisms did not create"*. **NOT ONE.**

The Micro-Organism Factor-Part IV

Fear is a chemical reaction in the brain and when we speak of death, for many, fear becomes the operative as a means of control. Traditionally, fear has been used as a deceptive tool to control e- motions. Long ago ancient scientist seen that fear and death could become a lucrative commodity that would control 99% of all the world's economy. The very threat of death puts the mind in a fearful state. *In reality death is an extension of life as we know it.* However, if death is never taught as a curriculum therefore the students will never truly understand the true meaning of death. Today when a person dies, the following process takes place, the body cease to breath, the heart stops, the **energy and oxygen** that kept the brain alive escapes the body and it immediately *returns to the ocean of energy that abides all around us at ever fraction of a second.* When death comes almost always the *Clergy is called*, the *Funeral Home* is call, depending on the type of death, **the Corner is call**, the *pathologist is call*, the *cememtary is call,z* then the *insurance company* is called. and that list goes on and on a very, very lucrative commodity. "Death is only a **horizon** that *appears* to be to complex for human limited understanding". However, death is not complex at all, if a person lived to be a thousand years old, death would find them as this is the law of nature. *["If the person wishes to live that long"].* Ignorance cause death to become complex. When we look at the seasons of the year, one season dies for the next one to take its place. We know that energy is the source of all life as we know it. a common battery has energy, but when all the energy is used, what do we do with batter? **Some batteries can be recharged with a battery charger and reused. the same principle**

is done with energy we inhale and exhale, exercise does this for the human anatomy. At the time of death, the energy escapes the body and returns to the energizing life force that disperse energy *wherever it is needed in the Universe*. Today we use energy in many forms, solar panels, petroleum, gas for heating, batteries, water, agriculture to grow our food and list is endless.

Traditional education has locked us in a box, a Pandora's box of ignorance, if someone would come along with something new to unlock the box, most would reject it because they were taught a certain knowledge a certain way at a certain time and they do not want to depart from those ways. *The old cliché "can you teach a old dog new tricks"? Only if the dog will listen and act upon what he is taught.* President Obama stated that "Now is the time, and *this is our time"*, meaning that this *generation of people will change the dynamics of the way we think and perceive life as we know it today.* There are millions of people who will never change the way they think about life, like our political leaders, they remain sleep at the switch. The most common thing the Democratic Party have with the Republican Party is their logo, the *Elephant and the Donkey are both vegetarians*, but when you look at the Wolf and the Fox, one is conniving, the other is slick. One will stalk his prey and the other will out right attack. Nevertheless, their commonality is the same, as they both are members of the dog family and they both love lamb meat. We must turn our attention inward and look at our own life force, everything we live for is *within* us individually. We all think differently, and we must learn to except other people's understandings and opinions even if they are not your own.

The Micro-Organism Factor Part V

Many of us will never want to understand true reality, We have shared with you what the environment is and what the environment is not. *The environment is not a religion and could never be a religion.* The *environment is a natural phenomenon created by the natural environment.* Atoms, protons neutrons electrons etc. *All religious books were written by men.* It is utterly impossible to take something that was developed by man and try to say that it is natural. *Natural means that it was created by nature.* Religion was never created by nature it has no environmental beginnings associated with the natural elements in creation, this means that *it is unnatural. {*95% of the world population believe in some kind of religion} there are over 250 different religions worldwide. But hold on, we cannot throw the baby out with the bath water, **there can be and will continue to be an imperative use for religion and the church.**

When you get ready to look at creation in action, close your eyes and look at the sun spots, when you try to focus on one image of a sun spot, the image change right before your eyes, and they move in such a rapid pace your sight can't keep up with just one, because the images of the sun spot change, your consciousness begs to see the external images when the eyes are open. It is also like watching a television without a picture image, you see the small snowy like images, millions of little snow dots. The practice of "Yoga" teaches you about the *"Kundalini" ["the flickering light within"].* We said in earlier articles that everything that you *see externally is also everything internally.* When we are conditioned to except external life and neglect the internal working of the "Micro-Organisms".

When you attempt to watch the sunspots in their movements you are *watching reality,* you are watching *CREATION* at work, you are actually traveling at a tremendous speed as you attempt to follow a sunspots they will generally take your vision into another image of your choosing or you will drift into a sleep state and the images of dream might come into your sub-conscious focus. This suggest that within darkness all light is created, but why are so many of us afraid of the darkness even though you were created in total triple darkness? A blind man can form images just as the person with 20/20 external vision, in many cases the blind man's vision is more acute than the person with 20/20 external vision. **In future communications we would like to discuss what happens with the intelligence you accumulated during your lifetime after you have passed away. We need to begin looking real deep into our own intellect as energy extract the oxygen of life from the human brain.**

The Harmonious Whole

We as a people has almost always focus our attention on the external thing in life and very seldom look at the internal workings of the human body until we become ill and sick with disease. The external things has put us in the *OUT-OF-SIGHT, OUT-OF-MIND, SYNDROME.*

Everything we do is primarily focused on the external things in our life and we very rear pay attention to the workings of our internal organs within us. When we look at the universe, many are thinking that all of this massive creation is just for show. When slave masters long ago looked at the benefits of the external world, they seen explicit control over the people. If you understood the association of the human body with the operative work in the universe you would be stunned to know that we as people have been totally deceived about creation and how creation is linked to our own behavior and intelligence. *Our educational system is turned upside down and this keeps the mind of the people on external things like money and trinkets.* The mind has to look within and search for the secrets of life. We have been conditioned to focus on things that take us away from the real person within. Consequently, we have lost our way and we became disconnected from the Cosmos which provides harmony within the anatomy and keeps harmony with the entire universe.

How do we change the dynamics of life?

How do we change the dynamics of life? When we hear the voice within us, we are listening to the Micro-Organisms that created us. In religion they say this is God talking. The word God is a modifier or a term that religious believers can relate to. As we have said in many of our articles, if you never understood the root cause of a thing, you will be forever lost in a maze of ignorance and disbelief. Traditional teaching locks the mind of the believer. You have a right to your own beliefs, however, here is what is happening all around you as we speak. Today the power of money has taken center stage and the addition to obtain it has put many in a shell game of greed because with money you can buy more stuff and it would help feed your family. There are people that will do anything for the sake of money. It is difficult to change the world if the people are stuck in an addictive trans to acquire financial necessities. We spoke about the Cosmos, the universe is regarded as an orderly function and a harmonious whole, if we have been disconnected from this harmonious whole, how do we reconnect our thinking to become harmonious with the whole? Our children are dropping out of school at an enormous rate, because they see and feel that the educational system is not offering them anything of substance to sink their teeth into. Our students are constantly fed the same knowledge over and over and over again. It does not matter if the student is grade school or college. Gang violence has taken precedents in most metropolitan cities and communities.

If all *churches in every community* in Metropolitan City this could help change the dynamics of life as we know it. But change has to begain within yourself first. This remind me of a Movie, I think it was "Notorious B.I.G." P Diddy told Biggy Small "We could change the world". Biggy Said: "We can't change the world until we change ourselves". These are true words. We have so many churches in our cities, but they are not used to truly help the people, there need to be organization in the churches to work in shifts, wlking the street of the community in great mass to stop gang violence and paddering to the politicians if the churches would come together for the purpose of changing the community. Now that is real change.

For The Record

For the record, our Group at Chicago State University is a "*NON-TRADITIONAL ENVIRONMENTAL FOCUS GROUP*", this implies that we are *above the traditional thinking* as to how and what the environment is. The substance of our discussions as the chairperson, we have researched many issues that most would never think about, nor *challenge the traditional teachings of the environment*. As Chairperson we knew all along that most members would disagree with the focus as to **what the environment really is** and most would agree that our focus is far from what is being taught in our educational system.We brought Chicago State University, Trinity Church, Park National Bank now US Bank, Roseland Hospital, Illinois Consortium, University of Chicago and Community based organizations because we felt that these entities were necessary to bring about a good cross section of businesses in these communities. For more than a year we have met at different locations to bring attention to the needs of the total community with a focus on Roseland, Altgeld Gardens, Pullman and West Pullman communities. After speaking with Alan Waltz, begining next year 2011, we both agreed that our group at Chicago State University is strong enough to hold the attention of The United States Environmental Protection Agency and *it would not be necessary for our group to meet monthly or by-monthly, but we could meet once or twice a year to review what is needed in communities local and nationally*. If there are any questions concerning issues that need assistance on environmental questions or if the group wish to call a meeting on issues, please contact myself, Dr. Britt or Mark Bouman.

Understanding the focus of *Non-Traditional environmental education* is like sitting on the highest peak of the earth on a clear day when your sight or vision can see for miles and miles on end, this is tantamount to the existence of creation, it is endless. It has to be on a clear day because a cloudy day you can't see nothing but clouds and fog. *When you look at death you can see that the brain and body surrender to death in a state of unconsciousness*. Rightly so,I really don't think an individual would want to experience a conscious death transformation.

A person that dies with his eyes wide open does not physically see the transformation of death because there is no oxygen or energy to render the individual conscious. When examining the process, we see that **Oxygen** and **Energy** are the key elements that makes the exist from the body. The blood and organs function are controlled by energy and oxygen. There is something else that exist the body from the brain, knowledge and intelligence. *When we break our knowledge down we can see that our so call knowledge and intelligence is nothing more than sounds*, we utilize our vocal cords to produce certain sounds from our throat as a form of communication we call language. To produce these sounds we must have oxygen and energy. For a deaf mute, they utilize their hands, a blind man use Byrle to express their *thoughts*.

Speaking of thoughts, what happens with our thoughts? *"Thought moves faster than light"*. What happens to a thought after death? Oxygen and energy produce sound, so after death comes, all sound has to return from which it came. Most people have the idea that when they die and their spirit (oxygen & energy) moves from their human body and that **same silhouette image of the human body** will enter the next dimension, or as religion puts it, it's in heaven. *["Anything above the head could be considered as heaven"].* Sense the **whole human body is a chemistry**, it would be fair to say that all chemicals will return from which they came in due time after death. This is why we have suggested to U.S. EPA to develop a tracking system to track, and identify elements in the environment so that we can have a better understanding as to which elements will cause illness, disease, behaviors, death and the impact of magnetic energy fields.

President Of The United States

Dear Mr. President:

I have followed you from the Office of State Senators to the Office of President of the United States and your statements of the Republican Party working backwards has more of a *self-indoctrination*. As a environmentalist we always look at the *root cause* of a situation so that we truly understand the problem and address the issues at hand. Mr. President, *it is utterly impossible to place a square box in a round hole of the same dimension,* meaning this: The Constitution of 1776 is inapplicable to the year 2010 and beyond. *In logic you can not add to a document that is complete at its original conception.* Amendment implies to *"add too."*

Amend implies to_*"re-write".* At your inauguration you sworn your duty to uphold the United States Constitution, nevertheless *your oath is to keep the people of the United States in a retrograded monopoly.* Your words just a few weeks ago, was; 'your car has a reveres and drive gear shift", when you want to go forward you put the gear in **"D" [Democrats]** and when you want to go backward you put the gear in **"R" [Republicans].** There are nine justices with life tentures at the U.S. Supreme Court who interprets the Constitution any way they choose and surely you learned this in Law School. This document was always written for the rich to maintain power and influence over the masses, it was never intended for the poor, this is why the 3/5 of a human is still written in the document today.

The founding fathers wanted to keep slavery alive and well on into the future, so today slavery still exsist, in reailty greed is a form of slavery, "a slave with money is no different than a slave without money". Most people choose to be a slave with money. There are 435 U.S. House of Representatives and 100 U.S. Senators and they all want to keep the Constitution as it is. You spoke about change, *"where are the Founding Fathers of our own generation that want to change this Constitution to a document more applicable to our time"?*

Members:

Over the weekend I was contacted by the ***Chicago Department of Public Health***, Dr. Arnold's Assistant, Chad Brose who had indicated that Dr. Arnold wanted to invite our group to attend his ***"Environment Coalition Committee"*** sometime in mid-November. From my understanding there will be three meetings, one in Chicago, another in Springfield, another somewhere on the East Coast and a panel from different agencies. The date for the Chicago meeting has not been set, for all who are interested please call Chad Brose.

Good Afternoon Mr. Fletcher:

As previously discussed, please find below a link that will provide information regarding the upcoming Chronic Disease and Health Promotion Task Force public hearings. These meetings are open to the public and testimony will be sought from participants to be incorporated into a report to be delivered to the Governor's Office and

General Assembly.

http://www.idph.state.il.us/cdpahptf/hearings.htm

November 4, 2010

Dear Mr. President:

Thank goodness the election is over, we hope that the lesson learned was that the "American People" ***Congressman Boehner was referring to was not the same American People that you are referring to.*** House Majority Leader Boehner was referring to the *Rich Corporate Businesses*. Look at how much money they spent on this election. You did indicate that change was coming. *This is also part of that change you so vehemently talk about.* You are experiencing the best of both parties. ***This is a good thing for you;*** this will either confirm what you have been saying all along about the Republican, Democrats and Tea Party. Or they all will come together and start doing the businesses for ***all*** the people of the United States. ***If they go backwards, you win and if they go forward you still win again.***

Mr. President:

The Movie **"Fair Game"** is a very thought provoking and entertaining movie, the critics has indicated that there was nothing added to the plot to enhance the drama supposing all factual. There are several things we would like to bring to your attention, it appears that you have lost your luster with people that wanted to change the way our government does business. In reality you are doing the exact same thing the prior Administration was doing. *In fact, you are aiding and abetting the same philosophy as George W. Bush.* When you look up the word *"TREASON"* it means: "Betrayal of Loyalty, Trust, violation of allegiance owed to a Country, the people or government. *"CONSPIRACY"* is to break the law *deliberately, the agreement or oath between persons to mislead, deceive or defraud the people or persons of their legal rights.* You were the President of the Law Review at Harvard University, how could you be so careless as to get caught up in the same game? You know for a fact that Mr. Bush, Carl Rove, Mr. Cheney, Scooter Libby and All those involved who conspired to commit Treason against the United States are guilty. **It is best to die with dignity than to live a life in "tierney" knowing that you have the power as the President to bring these men to Justice for the American People.** *It is less important to be a one time President knowing that these men have conspired to violate the peoples trust. You should not want to seek a second term knowing these men have committed treason against the American People without first bring them to justice.* **As an Environmentalist this negative criminal behavior constitutes "High Treason".**

Mr. President, at some point you have to stop allowing the negative behavior of those around you, both political parties and utilize the Power of the Presidents Office to *rectify true change in government.* You appointed Eirc Holder as the Head of the Justice Department and he moves around these same issues as he too is afraid to speak or tell the truth. You have allowed politics to control your Office, You are the President and you have the power to change the course of history. *Mr. President you can't be afraid to utilize your power as President to prosecute those who are guilty of conspiracy to commit treason against the United States. How can you honestly look into the face of our troops knowing that thousand were killed in a war that was not authorized by the Congress? You know that George W. Bush and all those who participated in the conspiracy cover-up is guilty of Treason just as you know the mold on your face.* Don't be surprised if someone later on want accuse you of conspiring with the Bush Administration for the same conspiracy, simply because **"you fell to act and bring them to justice" for the crimes committed against the people of United States.**

Mr. President, you taken the Oath of Office, sworn to uphold the United States Constitution, now your actions indicate that the Oath of Office is inconsequential to the Office of President. We voted for you because you said you would bring change to our government; *how can you bring change to the American People and allow acts of treason to go unpunished?* This furthers the conspiracy to deny Justice to the American People at the highest level of government. *We would hope by the end of your Presidency, Justice will be fully served.*

Human Behavior

Each and every one of us has a duty to perform in our life time, many will not help you even if it was only for the time of day, It always come back to, *(what makes a person like this?)* *Again the natural environment plays a part in human behavior.* The President has urged every one to get involved. My issues may not be the same as your issue but I choose to get involved by writing those who are responsible for the issues I'm concerned about. I have worked with President Obama long before he was a State Congressman, U.S.Senator and now President. I fill strongly about change and what the President is doing and will continue to support his efforts as long as he is in Office. There are many things the President is involved with and he needs our help to guide him. I am only one person but I communicate to thousands. So in my own way I have to reach out to the President the best way I can in hope that my words will reach him. Each person should try to reach out to the President with whatever issue that you fell should be addressed. My issue may not be your issue. Nevertheless, the late **Teddy Pendergrass** said it best in his recording: ***"Wake Up Everybody"* no more sleeping in bed"**. Now Balladeer **John Legend** has reproduced the same song, is it because Mr. Legend also see that the people are still asleep? We can get on the phone or face book and talk about senseless nothings, but want pick up a pen and write the President and tell him the real issues that are plaguing our communities.

From the White House...
Tell Us What You Think

This is my response to *"The White House"* on *"what I think"*. Every human was created to do a specific task in this world wild on the earth. Creation was designed to teach the human advancement for creation, this is true intelligence. There are five things that have held us back as a people from true progress in the world and in our generational lifetime. Money, Food, Sex, Religion and Politics. These five things have cause the human being to loose his focus as to why he/she were created in the first place. Our educational system is proof as to how far away we are from true reality. *All that we can see in the Universe was not created just for show.* We are so far behind in technology and science it will take approximately 15,000 years to to update our *thinking* and put us back on the trial of real true intelligent thinking. *We are so bogged down in these addictive behaviors, we don't want to think of anything else other than these five things.* These five things are a hum drum of our daily thinking such as war, sports, education, employment, the economy etc.

As a people we have been conditioned to think and believe in those things that are *UNNATURAL* in the **environment** of human creation and to except those unnatural things as a natural part of the creation. *We call this bamboozled, hoodwinked, tricknology etc.* As a people we need to better understand our past in order to focus our attention on the future. Meaning this: "Since religion has only been on the earth for about 6 or seven thousand years which is fairly new in the scheme of time on the earth". *"What was the people like before religion can on the seen"?* Religion has produced more wars, poverty, deception, fraud, fabrication, mayhem, rape, robbery, politics etc. than any other theology in history. Religion has shown three faces of the same thought. **EVERY ONE MUST CLEARLY UNDERSTAND THAT RELIGION IS NOT CREATED FROM OR BY THE ELEMENTS OF THE LIVING ENVIRONMENT**. Today, politics and religion dominate the news on a daily bases, the media is guilty of this charade and the owners of these media out lets are the culprits of this frenzy. Example, *Sarah Palin is in the news on a daily basis, you can't be angry with her because she seen an opportunity to launch her notoriety on a worldwide stage and capitalize on it!* This is done because of the powerful and *"Super Rich Slave Masters"* of today. They will use by any means the opportunity to use the *slick of hand* in politics and religion to make their point clear. The Republican Party call this the American People.

Our children are not taught about the real environment, their teachings only consist of reading and testing, they are hardly ever out in their own community learning about the real elements in their own environment and what these elements are doing to their brain. They are on a continued marry-go-round with the same learning disabilities that are taught to them over and over and over again, and then they are given a degree for learning totally nothing about the living environment… Our children need a new curriculum of environmental education that focus on the *natural elements in the environment and what these elements are doing to our brain, our thinking at every second on a daily bases.* This is the true nature of learning the ideas of human development and the advancement in creation.

Environmental Curriculum

Dr. Britt:

Hope you and your family are bathing in the Thanksgiving festivities. Additionally, I just wanted to reiterate the necessity of developing an ***"Environmental Curriculum"*** at Chicago State University. You did indicate that CSU had an environmental program but not as a curriculum. Here is what I see in the politics of our educational system. With all the negative focus on President Obama, with the Democrats, the Republicans, the Tea Party participants etc. We as a people can't seem to rise up from the grips of the powerful rich slave masters of today, Michele Bechman had the courage to organize the Tea Party with some success, we the African Americans can't seem to organize any kind of political party other than the "Black Caucus", NAACP and they appear to have no political influence to enhance the the African American Political Agenda.

    Our Environmental Group at CSU has the potential to set the political agenda for the entire educational system nationwide, ***"I can not see any one talking about what we are talking about when it come down to addressing the environment."*** If you know of any Group let us bring them to our table to help enhance our focus. DR. Britt, if we could pull the key people together, like Dr. Joseph Balogun, Dr. Sandra Westbrook's, Dr. Rong Lucy He, Austin Harton Chris Botanga, Jane Crossley, Mark Bauman all staff at CSU. Additionally, after speaking with Alan Waltz at U.S. EPA who has already indicated that EPA could provide the necessary people to help structure the curriculum once the idea has taken forum. Then there are the community businesses and organizations that are setting with our group. Why are we procrastinating on this issue Dr. Britt? We should be writing our own environmental textbook. Get back to me on this ASAP.

Forces of Nature

When society becomes unbalanced *"The Forces of Nature" comes alive*, nature has its own way of reckoning the balance, Look at the four seasons of the year and how they impact the tsunami, earth quakes, volcano' swith hot lava, tornado, hurricanes, freezing cold, wind, rain, snow, heat, insects, animals, bacteria, disease etc. just to name a few. All controlled by the forces of nature. Our President has step into the hot lava of politics, he was never really aware of all the problems he would be faced with. Americas debt is in the Trillions of dollars and our government is constantly borrowing additional money to offset the debt that has spiraled out of control. The reason why companies are moving to other countries for cheaper wages is because America owe so much money to these countries and the manufacturing businesses are there to help work off Americas debt at cheaper labor. Our government is borrowing money that it does not have. *The Rich and Wealthy are the root cause of our government being in debt.* We can understand the President's rational for supporting the Republican tax cuts, however, the two million unemployed that does not have compensation does nothing for the 300 hundred million Americans that might suffer from the on slaught of nature. Meaning this:

Chapter Fifteen

Any one can predict the future outcome of society, *but it does not mean that the prediction will come true,* for example; Nostradamus predict that there will be a catastrophe of monumental proportion in the year 2012. I believe that Nostradamus was trying to educate the people of his time about the *"Forces of Nature"* when things go awry. Because America has allowed every race of people to enter her land, these people have brought much of their own culture with them and America is trying to turn this nation into a culture that is unnatural to its original intent. It was the behavior of the Founding Fathers that brought this upon the American people. Look at what was done to the Indians, slavery etc.

Nature has a way of teaching the whole of society, everything we see upon the earth was not always here and at certain times and intervals nature will cause people to make an abrupt change, additionally, when we contemplate on times gone by, we can better understand why the earth wipes away whole nations and start the whole process over again, *I just hope the people are not so naive to think that because we are living in the twenty century that our living conditions and technology was the first upon the earth.* The earth has destroyed millions of nations with higher intelligent than America. This is the whole purpose of nature is to bring about change. As we move forward things are changing before our eyes every fraction of a second and sooner, so why are we procrastinating? We must change the way we think about life here on earth. The Rich and Wealthy Americans live way beyond their means and this has cause us to rob Peter to pay Paul, **this is the root cause of the American debt.**

We should not continue to look at the environment as just seasonal but look at it as a tool of retribution should the society continue with negative thinking and actions.

Dr. Watson:

The whole idea of teaching our children was to educate the students in our community. During chattel slavery, the slave masters thought that if they educated the slaves and taught them what the masters needed them to know, the slave masters would not have to stand over the slave and watch them. The slave would then teach the other slaves and would report to the slave master if there were any disturbances among the slaves. The slave driver would report back to the master whereas the master had complete control of that educational system as is today. *A structured curriculum should be based upon the needs of the community, education should not be hinged on reading a book and taking a test. The student has to have hands on experience as to what is needed in his own community,* the teachers and professors at our schools and colleges has to make a concerted effort to take tours on a daily/weekly bases to guide our children in the community *as to what is truly needed,* instead of setting at a desk dictating to the students about reading a book for the next test, this supports the needs of the rich and wealthy slave masters to continue the increase in colleges tuition. It is all about the increase in funding for education.

This is not education but economic robbery, It is so plan to see what is really happening with our educational system. Our students are not being truly educated but truly manipulated in thinking that education is costly. "***This is call the Houdini effect***". The masters have hoodwinked, bamboozled, and tricked the leaders of the community, schools, universities, colleges in thinking that the cost of an education is sky high. *There is really no cost at all, but it has been made to appear that the cost of an education is sky high,* all of this is for the rich and wealthy to continue to feed off the poor an uneducated slave. The student has to visit the many manufacturing companies, to ascertain the intricate details as to how these companies operate, they need to visit these construction companies to see how they build, they need to see what goes on with the police department, hospitals, small businesses, all of these untapped resources in our communities, then devise a test on what the students have learn about the needs of that community, yet, the only thing most universities are interested in is funding to build more dormitories and to keep the doors open. They have totally neglected to utilize the resources in the community to educate our children. They are charging astronomical fees for tuition and hundreds of dollars just for books, this is totally ridiculous. At what point will our educators awaken to this fraudulent and deceptive practice? We have asked Dr. Britt to work with us to structure a environmental curriculum of which Chicago State University does not have. We have not heard from Dr. Britt in this matter, it would be greatly appreciated if your office would consider developing such a curriculum.

Absolute Power

December 27, 2010

Dear Mr. President:

As we look at the years end of 2010, We must say to you *"Heal To The Chief"* for the many accomplishments you were able to achieve this year and last year as well. However, there has always been a consistent drum beat from the previous Presidents like George Washington all the way up to you. All of the Presidents were forced to dance by the same tune of the Rich and Wealthy Masters of the world power. Mr. President," *we know that you will never ever get it twisted"*. Thinking that you hold the absolute power of the world. The Rich and Wealthy Slave Masters are also Puppet Masters and have had this power for *Centuries on end.* They not only have power over you, but power over China, Saudi Arabia, Russia, Europe, Asia, Australia and every President, Monarch, King or Queen worldwide. Mr. President: *"ALL MEN ARE NOT CREATED EQUAL".* If this was so, the Rich and Wealthy Slave Masters would return all of their wealth back to the poor people of the world. This will never happen, Equlity also suggest balance, since the world economy is held hostage by the Rich and Wealthy, they could pay off the American debt by the stroke of a pen and still have Quad trillions of dollars left over to pay off the entire world debt. Nevertheless, this would defeat their purpose of having **"Absolute Power."** All wars in every country world world are illusions and manipulation to keep control of the worlds economy of course you already know this.

   Mr. President, surely you are aware that the United States Constitution was never written for the Slaves and it is written into the United States Constitution itself, this document was written exclusively to protect the Rich and Wealthy Slave Owners from the tyranny of the poor. Case in point; *"when Former President George W. Bush needed the decision of the United States Supreme Court, to gain the office of President, what happen"?* The Rich and Wealthy Slave Masters decided they wanted Mr. Bush to be President and he was. The same principle happen with 9/11. **This** *is why you will never ever bring charges on the Former President George W. Bush and his Vice President Dick Cheney.* To be honest Mr. President, there is a consistant need for this kind of power as a means to keep the world in a check and balance. It is unique in many ways and it is not unique in others. The power has to balance in order to produce *"CHANGE"* in the worlds economy. We all have been used and manipulated by the Rich and Wealthy Slave Masters, no one can take this power because they rise their children to take control of this power from from birth and time on end. Even if it should ever happen, one Monarch would still Lord this power over the other. *This is the life we live in this demision of time*, it has always been and it will always be the **"Absolute Power"** of the Rich and Wealthy Slave Masters of the world.

The Portal

My Family to Your Family wish you and yours a very Happy New Year! We hope that this year will bring to you and your family all your positive hopes and dreams. We will look forward to seeing you again at our next environmental meeting. It is truly our work that will help change the world as we know it,we must continue to lay the foundation for positive change in our scientific, social and economic life.

To began our year on a positive note, it is hopeful that we understand the real meaning as to why we are here on this earth and in this dimension of time. As we have said, each and every one of us was brought here through a birth canal for a set purpose. We individually need to ascertain what our true specific mission is. Our Birth and form of delivery is also called a **"portal"**. <u>A</u> *portal is a gateway or entrance to another dimension. Death is also the* **PORTAL** *by which all life on earth transmits to the next dimension. Death must render all human life and primates to an unconscious state.* **I read somewhere that the human consciousness would not want to remember all the past events and lives it has traveled through in the archers of time.**

We were not sent here to learn politics and religion, we were sent here to learn **SCIENCE,** *the whole of creation is a Science Project.* We utilize the sciences each and every day of our lives, for those who do not believe in science, stop using the telephones, quit driving the automobiles, don't use microwaves, stop building and manufacturing etc. We have continued to requested that EPA develop a monitoring system to track and identify all elements is creation. It is because of the elements that creates each and every single thing you see in the universe and creation, if we could identify these elements we could stop disease in its tracks, we would understand what elements are responsible for recidivist behavior and we could better control the magnetic energy fields that magnetize additive behavior. The rich and wealthy slave masters probably would not want this because then we would understand.

WORTHY OF YOUR IMMEDIATE ATTENTION/ CONSIDERATION

Alan:

Many conspiracy theories have merit, my concerns are focused on the human brain development and its entire function within the universe since the whole of the brain was design to encompass the workings of the entire universe. However, we have only been taught to use one tenth of the brain matter we have. Most people have become satisfied with their one tenth use of their brain matter. I am not satisfied by this marginal use. *The whole of the environment merits my attention* seeing that the entire creation is a "*TOTAL SCIENCE PROJECT*" and it should merit your own attention since you work for the United States Environmental Protection Agency.

    Alan, you must never ever limit your own ability to expand your horizon and brain potential nor encourage others to stifle their legitimate concerns about the workings of the environment. There are many "*SPARES*" within the earth's gravitational pull, there is the: *Ionosphere, Stratosphere, Atmosphere, Troposphere, Mesosphere, Thermosphere, Hydrosphere, Exosphere, Hemisphere etc.* These spares are generated by the earth spinning at 1,000 miles per hour. *We need to know and understand what causes magnetic energy fields to impact human behavior.* Alan, don't fall for the politics that continue to bamboozle your thinking that tricks your mind. Remember, *we are all slaves to the Rich and Wealthy Slave Masters of the world.*

Dr. Watson:

Happy New Year to you and your family, I never received a reply from you requesting your thoughts on developing an "*Environmental Curriculum*" at Chicago State University. Many times, patience is indeed a virtue, you must be very proud of the work Mark Bouman and Danny Block is doing to help develop an *Environmental Curriculum.* I am very excited to know that Chicago State University has taken the initiative to develop this type of Curriculum. Having said that, you must also consider making this curriculum an imperative meaning that: "*this curriculum should be a prerequisite prior to admission to the University*".

Chicago State University has to develop a higher standard than any university worldwide. The reason is that *all subjects and departments at the University feeds into the **Environmental Curriculum.***

Thereby, a prerequisite would be necessary seeing that *all the elements of knowledge would require that the students be refreshed on how the environment impacts all of the knowledge on every level at every University and school of higher education.* What Chicago State University is doing must be ***duplicated*** to all universities, high schools, city colleges nationwide.

"MATHEMATICAL SYSTEM,"

The defibrillator is a tool or instrument that is used to shock the heart back into its life rhythm, the electrons in the defibrillator shocks so many voltages into the heart to jump start the rhythm, It is like jumper cables to a car battery to get it running, same flavor. We said in past articles that we must continue to *"Shock the Consciousness"* of the people in hope that they awaken to the true realities of life as it was intended to be. ***Politics and religion are not a science and they could never be a science, neither is created by the elements in the environment, atoms, electrons, nuetron, protons etc***. These two entities are unnatural to the environment, nevertheless, the Rich and Wealthy Slave Masters want you to believe that politics and religion are natural produces of the environment. However, they both were developed by a man's imagination as to what he thought to be the ultimate controlling system of governance. These two systems of corruption has blinded the senses of true reality and it will continue to lock the minds of the people as long as it keep producing vast amounts of wealth for the Rich and Wealthy Masters of the world.

The people are constantly bombarded with entertainment such as theater, song and dance, football, baseball, basketball, golf etc. and the list goes on, these games are ok in moderation, then there are games we by our children to keep them in a mind-controlled system. The child attends school and the teachers constantly teaches the child to read many books and take many test, if they are successful acquiring a good GPA they can attend college, while in college they are bombarded with the same books and test syndrome, [garbage in, garbage out]. You have to wonder why they are constantly teaching our children the same thing over and over, day end day out? Then there is the tuition to be paid by the student and what for? The teachers are paid by the state, the schools are paid by the state, who are the beneficiaries of the tuition the students are paying? Then the students have to pay for books, caps and gowns for graduation and this list gos on and on. ***Pretty soon in the near future high school students will be paying tuition to attend public schools.*** Where does it stop? It stops at the Rich and Wealthy Slave Masters bank account.

Our children should be able to understand what cause the forces of nature to respond as it does. They should know what cause the weather to react in the manner it does? The forces of nature react and respond by a *"MATHEMATICAL SYSTEM,"* these systems react to a calculated time response. Look at the four seasons of the year, spring happens on "Q", summer solstice comes on "Q", the fall on "Q" the winter solstice on "Q". These same Mathematical Systems control Hurricanes, Tornadoes, Earthquakes, Volcanoes, Tsunami, Rain, Snow, Ice etc. If we never understand the magmatic equation for these systems, we will always live in darkness and be dependent on someone else like the Rich and Wealthy Masters of the World to continue controlling these forces of nature. *If the Indians could do a rain dance and bring rain, what do you think the Rich and Wealthy can do?* The question is do they have this power? Of course they do, **You rarely if not ever here tell of a prison being destroyed by any of the forces of nature.**

Winning with Hazel Johnson

January 16, 2011

Dear Mr. President::

Winning is believing in yourself as did Hazel Johnson and yourself, everything we have shared over the years is because of my own belief in myself to advance the **"Environmental Justice Movement."** Going forward is proof and answer to the call of *"Yes We Can".* We have won the fight but not the battle. *Hazel Johnson was a winner for awaking our senses to environmental hazards and the consciousness of the Environmental Justice Movement.* Hazel Johnson, was the key focus for the cleanup in the Victory Heights West Pullman Community where the Old Dutch Boy Paint Company and the International Harvester Plant was located. Navastar International Trucking sold this Property to Reverend Johnny Colman for $1.00. Today on this same property the State of Illinois has allowed solar panels to be built as a conservation for solar energy. I last seen Hazel in September 2009 at a meeting with United States Environmental Protection Agency Administrator Mrs. Lisa Jackson and I kissed her before I left. At that meeting Mrs. Jackson appointed Alan Waltz EPA Enforcement Officer to work with us.

We wrote to you Mr. President concerning your role as community organizer while working with Hazel Johnson in the Altgeld Gardens Community, we never got a direct response from you since you became the President of The United States, but you have communicated with me ever since you were State Senator, we thank you.

Cheryl Johnson, you already know that we will always be there for you and will always help you in any way we can to uphold your **"Mothers Dreams"** of a clean, sound environment for each of us and the world.

My role as the Chairperson of the Environmental Group at Chicago State University is to share all that I know of the environment with our group and others**,** *I personally must do all that I can freely without compensation*. Many would want to be paid for the information we share, but *why should a person be paid to educate the the general public* *when it is the environment that has created us freely?* Each and every one of us have the ability to win, ***this power is within us all***. We only have to go within our individual selves and ***avert our attention to the power within***. Once we awaken to this enter power we become free from the illusions of the world. **"For our Mother of the Environmental Justice Movement"** *and I speak for many "Rest in Peace Hazel Johnson, your Daughter has taken the baton".*

The Incest Bloodline

The Bible has suggested that Adam and Eve was the first Man and Woman and most religious believers have never even questioned the idea as to how the population of the earth grew so fast in 6,000 years{**of course this is not true**} {*today the earth population is over 8 billion*} and seeing that this was the beginning of creation for the first man and woman. This analogy of which the woman being created from the bone of Adams rib. How could the people be so blind as to believe that the woman was created from a bone or rib of the man when each and every human being was created by the sperm and ovum through sexual intercourse? *Additionally, we must acknowledge that even if the Adam and Eve fabrication had any truth, this would undoubtedly suggest that the children of Adam and Eve practice incest between themselves.* **Early in the 13th century Incest or Incestum meaning; "intercourse between near kindred to the degree of consanguinity or affinity where marriage was legally forbidden by custom".** Each and every society has always practiced incest as taboo.

Then there was the slave trade where the Slave Masters would force the slave to mate with each other, mother and son, father and daughter, sister and brother as a means to increase the slave population. **The more slaves, the bigger the profit.** This practice has continued today and now our youth still practice this same old slave mentality without a second thought as to what this is doing to the minds of our children. **Sex is the sharing of energy and not necessarily intercourse nor is it what we think it is or should be.** Animals in the wild have more control of their sexual behavior than humans. Some animals have sexual intercourse once a year. Sex is an emotion of shared energy between individuals, regardless of who and how many. Nature teaches us that after so many years of sexual intercourse, this practice comes to an end, women have menopause and so does men, However, commercial advertisement has promoted Viagra, Cealis, and many other sexual Enhancement drugs to keep you sexually active as the slave masters intended knowing that it is natural that your sexual activity must come to a close at a certain age. Menopause can come early for many. *This sharing of energy has to stop at some point in human life* *and we should except this as a natural development in our life, many do not want sexual intercourse to ever end because of the **additive behavior of sex,** just as all life must end at some point.*

The Slave Masters did not care what slave he matched up or who he sold a slave to, **because the slave was like cattle and the slave had no rights, as indicated in the United States Constitution**. Today the slave trade is still alive and well. There is an underground network of the slave trade. Those who participate in this massive slave trade is" Asia, Russia, Saudi Arabia, the whole continent of Africa, China, Korea, United Kingdom, Australia, United States of America, Haiti etc. Today it is very difficult to trace your family roots without mixing of the races because the slave masters also had sexual intercourse with the slaves.

Then there is the Rich and Wealth Families like the Rockefeller's, and the Rothschild's *who forbid marriage outside of their own families* to maintain the wealth within the family. Take a look at the Video_*"The Zeitgeist"*, or read *David Icky's Book, "And The Truth Shall Set You Free."* Religion has turn the society upside down, many parts of the Bible has justified incest and other homosexual behaviors, Abraham slept with his daughter, Lot spoke of men and the same sex relations and this goes on and on throughout the Biblical mysteries , yet many religious believers continue to justify these acts as unlawful and devised laws to forbid these acts. Today Gay marriage has become a legal and bidding for same sex marriage.

The creation of the human has always been through sexual intercourse until the most recent development of the test tube baby and in fertilization, we need to better understand why certain laws were designed for the public interest but does not apply to the Rich and Wealth Slave Masters of today?

The Brain Addiction

In his State of the Union Address last night, President Obama confirm what we have been saying, we heard about the *"Chinese Tiger Moms"* and the culture they produce for their children; accordingly, these mothers have raised the consciousness to a NONE TRADITIONAL educational practice, it is self-evident that they are higher in all academic studies than American children. If we would just look at what is going on around us, we should know that there is something terribly wrong with the American educational system, our system focuses on traditional teachings of the United States Constitution, a document written over 300 years ago. Our culture wants to utilize this document as a bases for our democracy. This document is not applicable to our time of 2011. This document was written for the people of their own time, this is totally backward, and we have retrograded three hundred years. Here is what is happening in our brain, the *neurons* in the brain is like little wires, then there are the *axon* which sends out electrical charges in the brain, these *neurons* release chemicals and these chemicals work like computers. Surely we have heard that the brain is like a computer, you must know that *the brain operates like a hundred million computers at one time,* each computer has billions of memories. *This is why our brain was created to encompass the entire universe, but many of us cannot even comprehend utilizing the entire brain matter or cells.* These neurons are electrical charges, scientist call these EEG or *{electroencephalograph}.* Unless the brain has been manipulated to the point that someone else has control over the way you think and what you think about. *Again, this is an illusion of the mind and this becomes an unconscious addition.* Sex, food and drugs is the order of the day.

When we take a closer look; THERE IS THE RIGHT HEMISPHERE *OF THE BRAIN THAT CONTROLS THE LEFT HEMISPHERE OF BRAIN, THE LEFT SIDE CONTROLS THE RIGHT SIDE, one side control vision and the other controls language or sound.* The brain can be manipulated to the point that whatever pleasures or rewards given to an individual can be altered severely. We discuss slavery as an induced state of mind through years of servitude, sex was practice among the slave masters as a means to produce more slaves, this pleasure was also painful for many slaves because many were raped and didn't know what sex truly meant. *The slave masters raped the children as young as nine years old and had other slaves to rap young children as a means to produce more slaves.* This state of mind put the slaves in a state of docility, today things are still the same and nothing has changed in the matter of slave production. Today we see gang violence, rap videos where the young women dance provocatively as a means to insight sexual urges. This same practice has produced more slaves for the Rich and Wealth Slave Masters of the world.

How and when does this practice end in American culture? President Obama was correct saying that; *"people from other countries want to come to America because of our freedom of expression"*, but this freedom of expression comes with a terrible price. Just look at our economy and the recidivist behavior in our political and religious systems. If we do not change our system very soon, then Nostradamus predictions might come to a grim conclusion in 2012. *The Republican Party want the American people to believe that President Obama was the one that put the country in this economic parody, KNOWING very well that he did not create this problem, he inherited when he taken office. It does not matter how good you are in rectifying a bad situation as our President has done on many occasions, most republicans want to continue having a free ride at the American people's expense.*

Environmental Components in Religion

Your individual brain was given to you for you to think for yourself, to believe in yourself, not anything other than yourself, *When you came into this world or dimension, you came by yourself even if there were sextuplets in the same womb, the doctor delivered you one at a time, No one can die for you, but you, you will die by yourself even if one hundred died at the same time with you. No one can save you but you.* There is no such thing as sin, however, there is negative energy which is produced by your own individual thinking and actions just as you have positive thinking and positive actions. Here are some environmental components in religion, *the pinnacle of human existence is to;* **"know thy self"** *know, who you are, what you are, where you are and when you arrive.* In religious theology it is taught that you should believe in *something other than yourself,* preferably you must believe in God and his Son Jesus Christ. When you believe in something other than yourself, *you have denied your own existence as a human being,* this suggest that *you have lost all self-respect for your individual self and you believed in something other than your true self.*

Your true self is the belief in your own ability to excel with your own independent thoughts guided by your own intellect, by utilizing your full brain power that was given to you by the elements in the environment. Religion has done a fantastic job on the human Psyche, religion teaches you to believe in something other than yourself, when this happens the individual **becomes a slave to the belief that there is something greater than himself.** This mentality of thinking does not allow the individual to rise above their religious beliefs. This keeps the individual locked in the Pandora box of religion. The believer is easily influenced and guided by the language of the scriptures and religious teachings. Once the individual awakens to the hoodwink illusions of religion they are called *'Hippocrates'* and a nonbeliever, they cast that person out from cult and condemns that person to damnation.

This suggest if the person is cast out because they awaken to the true light of their individual selves, religion in itself is hypocritical in its own logical beliefs and conclusions. *Religion should want the* *individual to awaken themselves to the true light as to who they are and not to become a slave to the belief in God and Jesus as most religions ascend to.*

This would suggest that the individual believer is a true slave to a belief in something other than his true self *and* by a God of which they have no knowledge except for what they have been taught by religious clergy and what they have read in scriptures of inconstant and false analogy. The true focus of religion is about money, wealth and power. *If the parishioners are not close to the ministers that control the finances of the church, synagogue, mosques etc. or those who handle the treasury the rest of those parishioners will never know where their money has gone.* Most believers will never think to to follow the finances of these places of worship. **Make no mistake, we are all slaves to the Rich and Wealthy Slave Masters of the world, it is the daily appearance of the crumbs from the Rich man's tables that gives us the feeling of freedom.**

Albert Einstein was a Physicist known for his ability to use mathematical equations, high calculations and theories, his most noted accomplishments was the special theory of *"relativity"* meaning the the law of mechanics and the law of the electromagnetic fields. Einstein loved intellectual solitude and the theory of knowledge; he was also known as the founder of (E=MC2). *E=Energy=Mass Times the speed of light (C) squared at 186,000 miles per second (2). Human thought moving faster than light.* A theory has always been questionable as this alludes to questioning what a problem is opposed to the factual evidence. *Today Einstein theories are a permanent part of our universal thinking of physical matter as a result of particles vibrating at certain frequencies. A frequency meaning: "that if you alter, change or amplify your thinking in any way, you change your physical and current reality.* Remember, our thoughts are energy, and if we put more effort into what we think about we can Quantum Jump or Leap into other parts of this vast universe we have never known before. *Our world as it is taught today does not focus on the numerous universes within ourselves and the solar system. Each and every human being has a universe that is untouched by human thought.*

Quantum Jumping is the process of jumping into parallel dimensions and alternate verions of yourself. Alternate universes were proposed by Hugh Everett's in 1954, so this is nothing new except for those who have never heard of this nor experienced it before. We spoke of how data and information linger and hovers around in space and it has always been there for the wide awake, because when we think of something like a new idea, our thoughts reach and retrieve it out of thin air, this is how energy works within our own thoughts. As we think, energy is moving inland out of our brain and in our thought process. We have learned that quantum matter behaves erratically which require constant focus and attention, this is the voice that you hear within, that directs you to the higher self you have never known.

Chapter Sixteen

The Woman

As ***Chairperson of the Environmental Group at Chicago State University.*** Last semester I worked with 5 interns from different universities and colleges. What I generally tell these interns is this: "To better understand the cause of a thing you must ***ascertain the root cause***". *"A history of all subjects are best qualified to reward research"*. This means that the individual must do a vast search on all subject matter, you can't just take a few thousand years as the gospel when history dates back hundreds of thousands of years. Religion as we know it today only exceeds seven thousand years give or take a few years. You mention the history of the so-call Devil or Satan. ***This concept stems from religious scriptures and beliefs, these beliefs began with "WITCH CRAFT" and the demonizing of women as we have indicated below.*** However, these are human behaviors that have been orchestrated by the Rich and Wealthy Slave Masters of the world. *To be truthful we need to understand that in reality there was never such thing as a Devil, Satan or Sin.* These are just religious concepts to instill fear into the hearts and minds of those who are ignorant of their true self. Check this out for size, each and every single thing you can see or imagine was created by the elements in the environment, there is not one thing you can name, see, feel touch or imagine, that was not created by the elements in the environment. ***NOT ONE!.*** With that being said; we must conclude that the air we breath contain oxygen and energy. As human beings we need energy to perform all task, Our brain needs energy and our thoughts also needs energy to contemplate ideas, there is negative energy and positive energy. Negative energy is generally identified as satanic energy, however, the human body operates like a car battery, which has a negative post and a positive post, but it takes both to jump start the automobile and keep it running. So, like the automobile the human being operates on both positive and negative energies. When you know the history of religion then you can pinpoint the inconsistencies in all scriptures regardless of the denomination, Christianity, Islam, Buddhism, Judaism, Hindu etc.

During the 15th through the 18th century the *{"Woman"}* was demonized as a *witch* and was prosecuted by religious and political laws during that time. If we observe the history of women we can see substantial change in women behavior, this is because the **"Woman" is female of the first power in creation of the human being,** the system and the process of human and animal birth has never changed in the history of the world, the very notion to think that the woman was created from the rib of Adam violates every conceivable rule of common sense. King James wanted the people of his time to believe that the woman was subservient to the man. To take this a step further they condemn the woman as a witch that practice magic and curses. She was the first to become enslaved long before chattel slavery and considered personal property. The man has always knew that the woman was the first power, the man deliberately instituted false information as a control system to keep male dominance in the world. Lies and deceptions are *"Environmental Hazards",* and unadulterated fabrications can not only manipulate the senses in the brain but can turn the intelligence of common sense upside down and keep the individual in a docile state locked in a box of ignorance. The *"woman"* has always had the dominant power in the world, she gives birth to male and female, she bleeds but never die, she generally lives longer than the male, she carries "Y" & "X" cromazones and she is the Childs first teacher.

Today, she is not only the dominant force in the world, she controls the psychological, social, economic and corporate status worldwide, she has awaken to her true status in the world, she has always been stronger than man, *Men only **think** they are the stronger sex because she allowed it to be* . Today the man wants to continue this old ancient practice by trying to control the women right to abortion, they used fear in the past and continue to use this tactic today by advocating that abortion is unconstitutional even in cases of rape, incest, or obtaining communicable disease. But should you ask the male to have a vasectomy or become celibate he would say that is preposterous.

What is Success?

Do you find it ironic that material wealth is the ultimate means for success? Let us examine this for true understanding. We teach our children to go to school and get a good education in hope that they will acquire lucrative employment, today employment has developed a serious problem among the unemployed. Let's look at this objectively, if you do not own your business, it is imperative that you work for some else that will provide you with a salary or pay check to support your family. Much of this is hampered by politics, religion and a lack of employment skills that will give you the necessary income to support you and your family. Unless your salary is substantial and your living is among the middle class and above, your life can be an extreme struggle just to live day by day. **Education was never design to produce employment.** Education was design for the *human to acknowledge the activity of creation.* Have you notice how the political system continue to focus on the American debt? America could settle its debt in one day if it really wanted to, America has troops in just about every nation around the globe and for what? If America would with draw all of its troops around the world, there would be enough money to pay off its debt. America gives Israel over $2, Billion dollars Annually, Egypt another $1.2 Billion and the list go on and on with its allies. Americas armed forces all over the world is given unprecedented amounts of money just to keep wars and espionage.

Then there are the Rich and Wealthy that continue to dangle materialism in the face of the poor, they have used ever conceivable means to keep the minds of the people in continued state of docility. They allow a few to become rich and those few believe that if they can do it you can do it, then they provide programs that reflect the same ability to acquire materialism and wealth, they feed this belief into the minds of our children in the public schools, university and colleges so much so that when you ask the child what they want to be when they grow up, the child may respond, **"I want to be a doctor, lawyer, teacher, scientist astronaut etc".** with the thought that this is the ultimate success in life. This becomes a merry-go-round for every generation. *The politics is never far away and is never* *discussed at the breakfast table. To be a doctor, you must be in bed with the pharmaceutical companies that keep the masses on prescription drugs, to be a lawyer they must learn how to deceive the public utilizing a constitutional document that's over 400 years old and inapplicable to the people of today. To be a teacher is to keep the student in a docile mentality teaching them the same thing day end day out so that the student will never awaken to the real realities of life. To become a scientist is to continue to develop illnesses and disease in a laboratory and impose these upon the masses at will to keep the financial market at odds with the investors. This gos on and on and no one is keeping watch.*

When we look at the Universe it appears tranquil and allusive, we can see it as creation being expanded and formed at every fraction of a second and faster, we can only see what has been taught to us, like the big bang theory. The truth is **the big bang is only a theory and a theory is not factual evidence.** However, this form of teaching has inspired millions and is continued in our public school system today. They have sent untold rocket and spaceships into space and we still don't know what it is that they are building in the space station 200 miles above the earth. They claim that America went to the moon, but has never gone back in over 40 years or did they wag the dog? Our children are being rock to sleep at every turn by keeping entertainment in the fore front of their minds, sports, money, sex, food, drugs, politics and religion. Our children can never excel beyond these material beliefs. *We asked US EPA to develop a monitoring System that would monitor, track and identify the elements in the environment in every community and around the country so that the people would know from day to day what elements are causing illness, disease and violent behaviors.* This would be broad casted just as the weather is being broad casted. *Alan Waltz has indicated that this would be expensive, yes, but it is the best system anywhere in the world and it could cost us nothing if we would with draw all of our troops from around the world and cut our allies and military spending.* We have all of this monitoring systems and espionage around the world but America does not want to monitor the elements around its own people who are dying from illness, disease and violent behavior.

I truly love President Barack Obama but I also know that he is just a figure head with a title and has no power to change the status of American politics and religion. These are ancient practices that would take many years to change. However, we and the President began and will lay the foundation to change these insidious behaviors.

What is Success=II?

A question for the group: "Why do we continuously by stuff other than the food, clothing and shelter we need to survive? We are never satisfied with the few things we already have. We worship money, trinkets and more material wealth, one house is not good enough, many of us want a house with 100 rooms? Knowing we can't occupy but one room at a time. A chair by any other name is still a chair, you cannot set on multiple chairs at the same time even if they are stacked on top of one another, so you have 90 rooms filled with furnishings, 40 bathrooms knowing you can only use one at a time. People buy houses now as investments, same thing with cars, boats, planes, stock market etc. At what point do we say enough is enough? We love to impress our fellow man, but what does this do for the human psychic? After years of this hording wealth, money and power. It Findley dawns on you that what is all this wealth for other than constantly looking over one's shoulder to see who is trying to rob you? As you grow older with age, you finely downsize to just a couple of rooms, you conclude that you realy did not need all that space from the beginning even if you own ten mansions or a castle, what have you gained? Most people believe that if they have plenty of wealth and power history will always remember them. *There have been billions of wealthy people that have never ever been mentioned in the history of time and there are those who thought that they would not be remembered are the epitome of what history should be.* So, what is the true reason for wealth, fame and power, is this what you really want for your life? You want notoriety as being famous rich and wealthy? ***Or would you want to be known as an individual with high brilliant intelligence with a good understanding of the creation and its purpose?***

There is something much greater than material wealth and power, this is put before your eyes at every turn on a constant basis. Case in point, The Hip Hop guru Russell Simmons found it in his new book ***"Rich".*** I watched the Biography of Russell Simmons and how he establishes Hip Hop Rap and Def Comedy Jam, Phat Farm, Baby Phat clothing line with his former wife. It was very interesting to see how his wife glorified diamonds and all the wealth they had accumulated after their success in the industry. Russell on the other hand found peace, contentment and solitude in Yoga, he attuned his mind to see the real wealth in society. He began to see that the material wealth was useless without the understanding of himself and what life truly meant in the world of entertainment. If the human mind can only see material wealth as the epitome of success that person is already lost from the start. *How can a person look at material wealth and believe that this is the epitome of success when it is the elements in creation that created the wealth from the beginning?* **The creation is bigger than anything created**. It is constant, infinite, and the ultimate entity in existence. Success is when you have awaken to who you are, your purpose, mission and you are able to execute your mission with a true focus in this life. Wealth was design to share with the people, it was not design to deprive or enslave the masses. Much of what we have learned in our lifetime is all fun and games. We have not focused on the real life of creation, many would render that creation is to complex. But how complex can it be when each day you awaken to a new life? ***Now that is true success.***

Espionage The Art of Deception

When Valerie Wilson was placed on the worlds stage as a spy, all countries worldwide taken notice, we often wonder why world governments practice espionage?

The idea is to acquire advantage over other countries secrets, and to become more powerful as a means of clandestine deception. Many strategies are deceptive by nature, this practice is to trap the opposition and take advantage of all secret information. ***When we study Creation, we can see that creation is not deceptive, creation has brought you here, taught you to become human and through its mathematical systems, creation and its elements will cause you to die, then all the information you acquired in this life is taken from you and it becomes the soul property of energy created by atoms and helium that abides all around us continuously even as we make the transition of death to our next destination, where ever that may be.***Energy is what makes each and everything we can imagine come alive.

Energy is the only entity in creation that we must be very mindful of. However, as we look at positive and negative energy we can assume that deception is in negative behavior, we can see this in animals and human. ***Most deceptive practices originated centuries ago through witch craft, black magic,devil worship and religion, those who practice the art of deception hid themselves in places of worship like the church, mosque, synagogues etc. They practice this as an illusion to their craft. Today, witchcraft is alive and well, to prove the point is to look at the many people who still practice superstition beliefs. If that person does not pray daily, that person will not earn the favor of God as taught by the scriptures in religion.***

It is sad to see the millions of people that still believe that there is a God over the creation. I understand the body chemistry and how the element in creation controls all body functions, but for the life of me why can't people see the reality as to what has happen to them? It is as plane as the nose on ones face, however, I can agree with the writer who wrote: *"One cannot make the blind see or the deaf to hear, because the majority of the world population have been entrenched and indoctrinated with this belief for so long, that there is not much you can do to ward off this insidious behavior, someone once said: "At some point you have let sleeping dog lay", unless you can shock the consciousness of those who are willing to see and hear.* These individuals has to have a desire to want *a **higher truth*** than what they have been taught. **When President Obama was talking about change he was speaking of a total change in the way we think about life and the creation**. As President, there are certain things he cannot say because he realize that there are millions of people that are still hung up on their religious beliefs and they are afraid to venture away from these beliefs in fear of their friends, neighbors, family members, God and clergy.

Genetic Chemistry

My Daughter-in-law asked a question concerning genetics here is my reply. Below are just a couple of articles I wrote for the "Environmental Group at Chicago State University". As the Chairperson for this group it is my responsibility to insure that our group understands the real issues in the environment with accurate information through investigative research. This means: *"A history of all subjects are best qualified to reward research".* This also means that the individual has to go deep within their own subconsciousness and sort out the true chemistry of their existence and what that existence is made of. *The whole creation is a science project in* **Active Motion,** *having said that t*he human body is a chemistry created by energy and this energy is always in active motion. Energy is created by the sun, moon and stars because they all have atoms and helium which creates energy. It is energy that brought you here, and each and everything you do is done because of the workings of energy, when you have completed your work here on planet earth, it is energy that will cause you to depart from this dimension and it is energy that will transmit all of your acquired knowledge back to energy from which it was given to you in this body to study creation. We acquire knowledge through trial and era through the chemistry of the brain. Your brain was originally designed to encompass the entire universe, but something went wrong. When women controlled the earth things were in great harmony with creation, this is why the woman is; *"female of the first power in human creation".*

It was the woman that allowed the male species to become dominant on the world stage, it is her that bleeds but does not die, it is her that carries male and female in her womb, it is her that carries "X" & "Y" cromazones, it is her that carries the fetus for nine months, after the fetus is delivered, it is her that teaches both male and female and it is her that lives longer than the male counterpart. It was the woman that allowed herself to become a slave to the tyranny of the male species. Slavery itself gos back some hundreds of thousands of years. Slavery didn't just come here during the 14th,15th,16th, 17th,18th centuries of chattel slavery. Slavery Begin when *men were the slaves of women*, and women dominated men for centuries on end. It was the woman that gave up the ruler ship to men and it was done to prove her endurance of her own power and to resurrect herself at a certain period in time, *that time is now approaching.* When you study the process of human birth you must retrograde to the beginning of the fetus, because in reality it go further backwards than the fetus, this is when you began to look at the genome or the genetic of the birth. All of these factors are brought together long before to the forming of the fetus, this is why we must understand the chemistry of the human body. The genes can vary from human to human and it would be extremely hard to determine where these gene originated from.As you travel backward to your grandparents and great grandparents and you keep going backward, you go from 2 parents, to 4 parents because there are the mother and father on both sides of the human chain and from 4 to 8, then 16 on and on.

Prior to the forming of the fetus, the life that was formed from the sperm and ovum mix together is the product of energy, energy began the formulation long before the fetus is created in the womb, this is done through a mathematical system, this is why when you are born, it is at a certain time, and your death will also be at a certain time. ***Nature is always true to this mathematical system.***

My granddaughter Maddi is a true work of art. What you as parents don't know is how far Maddi had to travel to get here? When you hear people talk about time travel, you have to look at Maddi. I see 4 years old everyday and that generation of children is a special generation, they have something to offer, *they are the true time changers*, they see, speak of things many of us cannot comprehend. Meaning, they might say things out of the ordinary and we are concern as to where they picked it up at? Many children through genetic traits bring along with them something of their pass, certain information through energy is past on and it travels with them wherever they go with certain understandings that many cannot comprehend. This is how many children becomes geniuses and the word GENE comes from GENOME or GENETIC.

Genetic also can be associated with religious cults, *religion is a manmade discovery*, all religions are unnatural they are not created by the elements in creation such as the atoms, protons, electrons, neutrons, photons etc. Religion is the biggest control trap for human being to ever embark upon the earth. This is why it is so difficult to remove this brain washing practice from the mind set of religious worshipers. There is no such thing as a good religion, they all are illusions of the worse kind,

they are only made to appear to be good, but the bottom line is they all entraps the mind just as any drug or alcohol, it is an addition of the worse kind and because of the superstition beliefs there are no rehabilitation clinic to address this horrible behavior. Just look at how many Churches in the African American communities, drive down Halsted Street or Madison Street or any well know poverty stricken community in any city across our nation and count the churches, mosques, synagogues and places of worship, even on the west side of Chicago and count the churches, not to mention those that are not on a main street. What is this doing to the mindset of the people? What is so remarkable about this, is all of these religions are saying the same thing, it does not matter what the denomination is. President Obama is the real game changer, but the world will not change until the woman is fully awaken to her true power and to who she really is.

Media & Politics

Many do not understand the true meaning of "Media" nor "politics", media is any type of writings, books, literature that can be shared with public interest, ideological with diversity. When certain knowledge is taken out of circulation from the general public this leaves the public without clear vision as to history nor the future. When Michael Angelo destroyed the Library of Alexandria in Egypt, it is said that much of the history of science was destroyed along with the past history of the woman. This was done to shut down all communications and information concerning women for thousands and thousands of years of their reign. What was left is guarded by the Pope of Rome in the Vatican. There is certain information that the Rich and Wealthy Slave Masters do not want in circulation. This would spoil their plot to rule and control the world. For thousands of years man wanted to control the world, as the woman had explicit power over the male species for thousands of years. **How do we know this?** First things first, *"the mind indeed is a terrible thing to waste"* When you learn to tap into the workings of the subconscious mind which is controlled by energy, many things are made clear to you as to how and why certain things are the way they are. Have you taken notice how men want total control of the woman body? Man wants the right to say when a fetus should live or die, and the woman should not have any say as to what she wants. The argument is that a fetus is a human embryo, and its life should not be taken at any cost. What you don't hear is the male getting a vasectomy to stop women from getting pregnant.

Here is the big question, how was it that man taken ruler ship from the woman? We need to first understand how_ ***"ENERGY"*** works, as we have pointed out previously, you can't look at *traditional education* for answers because you will never ever find it. It was designed that way by men to maintain power. Energy is the storage entity component for all information throughout the entire universe, the universe and energy is expanding continuously. Why is it that your human ideas are formed in your mind at the flash of a second? They just pop up, it is because of energy that hovers all around each and every individual constantly and when it is time for you to depart, what is the first thing that leave the dying body? *"ENERGY"* along with *"oxygen"*. But what happen to all that knowledge and wisdom you accumulated? Energy taken that because it was energy that taught you all that you knew. **Energy has the history of all things in creation**, energy never ages. *The Creation is Quad trillions upon Quad trillions of years old and beyond that, Creation has always been here and there is no beginning of creation as man want to suggest by teaching the big bang theory, there was never a big bang, all of that was just a theory to make man appear to be intelligent.*

For centuries the Woman ruled the earth with compassion for life and all living things, the male was her slave and wanted her power, this same power could free him from bondage. Because of the political climate at time, the woman never believed that the man could turn the world against her since she lived in luxury. The man petitioned the rulers of that time and said: "if you allow me to rule, I will turn everything on earth against you", *does that sound familiar?* The Woman granted the man his request to allow him to rule for a time as the woman had ruled for centuries. So, man started to put things in motion, he condemned the woman as a witch long before religion was brought to lite and began to develop a religion that would prohibit women from voicing any opinion and that she would become a slaves and property for all men. Additionally, man did not think that anyone would ever know nor understand the history of the woman; he thought it would conceal forever. The man never anticipated that the knowledge of the woman would ever be told. ***Cleopatra, just to name a few was one of the last emperors of her time to rule over men and that was just in Egypt, There was a world power of women and we can see and understand now why this information was taken out of circulation and never made for public view.*** That's the media you will never see. There have been millions of women that ruled over men for long periods of time, but you would never know this by today's standards. It was man who came up with the many Gods theory, then later he developed the one God theory, it was always man who thought to confiscate any and all literature pertaining to women's rulership. So today you see the woman on the rise to power again because of man's inability to rule and govern effectively. Man has always had an aggressive thirst to start wars as a means to commit mayhem in order to maintain his power, he does not know anything else but war.

Hear is another tid-bit, many believe that "Technology" is something knew within our generation, but it is not knew even with today's standards. Technology has been among us for centuries, things passed away as all things do and at certain times it is brought back as a teaching tool. The workings of a computer is all energized by ENERGY. When you are blind to a knowledge and have no desire to rise up from a dead state, you will remain in a docile state. Dr. King said it best: *"If you don't Stand for something, you will fall for anything". The individual must stand up for what they believe is right, then after you have thoroughly researched your mind of this information **and not from the traditional literature that our educational system** is providing for our children today, but from in-depth search of the sub consciousness where all of this information is stored.* Each and every part of a computer is manufactured through the use of ENERGY. You will find energy in inanimate things, in fact you could not build a house without the use of energy which is in food, wood, metal, steel etc. utterly IMPOSSIBLE to look at life without ENERGY.

Environmental Hazards with HIV

Maria: I want to thank you for your response and please note that it was well taken, I am an *"Environmentalist and Chairperson of the Environmental Health Group at Chicago State University"*. My focus has always been on environmental hazards associated with *illness, disease, behavior, death and the impact of magnetic energy fields.* In the past we have look at *"Micro Organisms"* having an impact on human health and the environment. HIV is associated with these microorganisms, and I would like to help educate you to better understand how these organism work as a health hazard. I believe it is imperative that people and those who are affected by this disease have a clear understanding as to the root cause of this disease and not be fooled by not understanding how the *"elements in the environment"* has played a major role in executing the true cause of this illness, disease in human behavior. We can no longer look at this disease on the surface of blood transfusion, sexual acts etc. these acts are also a significant part of this disease, but we must look at the intricate details of this disease by understanding the root cause. There is a book that you must read, it is call *"Lab 257"* which tells you in detail how certain disease are developed. I am extremely busy these days as Chairperson and I have to communicate with my colleagues on environmental issues and concerns, I would like to add you to my list of members in our group. I would also like to share your story with Dr. Britt and Dean Balogun of Health Science Department at Chicago State University. Please send me your story and Bio.

President of The United States Barack H. Obama

Dear Mr. President:

As we approach the ***changing times,*** I felt that you have entered a cross road, first of all you should not be alarmed by the Republican Party or the Democrats ignorant behavior. The American people with intelligence can see the none patriotic behavior of both parties. The whole idea of the Presidency was to unite the parties and Congress to work for the benefit of the people. After looking at the Republican debate the other night, I am sure that the great majority of the American people are convinced that these people are totally absent of morals, self-respect, ethics and patriotism. ***They continue their racial motivation as a means to discredit you for the positive work that you have done.*** The American people want to see these parties and group work together to bring about the *need for change.* We understand that "Energy" is a motivational factor and controlling source in human behavior, but as we have said on many occasions there is energy in a car battery that works the same way in the human brain, ***there is a positive post in a car battery and a negative post, but they both work together to start the automobile and to keep it running.*** This same principle should be applied with our Congressional Representatives. If they had any ideas how to create jobs as patriotic Americans they would have done so long ago, *unfortunately they have no idea as to how jobs are developed.* President Obama, even if they could take your place they would do less that what you have already done for the American People, they have no understanding as to what to do when faced with a critical crisis's.

My feelings are tantamount to most Americans when talking about the deficit. ***Why are we as Americans borrowing money from other countries by increasing our debt? Then we turn around and give other countries like Israel, Egypt, Japan, Haiti, Iraq, Afghanistan and many more third world counties $20, Billion Dollars or more to*** *support their causes and leaving Americans with their debt?* Putting these things in perspective, I understand catastrophes, but America lost over $100, Billion dollars in the Iraq war and no one knows where it went. Why are we spending hundreds of Billions for defense with American troops stationed all over the world? **What is the purpose of this?** America cannot police the world. Mr. President, if you would pull our troops out of these third world countries, our debt will be reduced by three quarters of a per-cent of the total debt. Today unemployment has increased, millions of homes in forecloser, businesses are closing, our public schools are closing, our States are in a whirlwind of debt and can't balance the State budgets. We know that you take on this responsibility from President George Bush, but what is the end game?

Mr. President we would greatly appreciate your immediate response to this missive.

Thank You Sincerely,

We have not corresponded for several months due to my focus and attention in writing my book and hopefully it will be published before the end of the year. We would like to turn your attention to the many weather-related catastrophes in America and around the world that are associated with environmental factors._For every action there is always a correspondent reaction._ We know that when a cold wind is intercepted by massive heat waves this can cause lightening and can form hurricane winds and funnel clouds, we also know that many of the fault lines in the earth can shift and cause an earthquake which can trigger a tsunami. Each of these scenarios are environmentally related. We know that **energy** is the root cause of these catastrophes. However, **"we are not aware of the chemistry that forms and cause these events"**. We have requested that U.S. EPA develop a tracking system that would track and identify each element in community environment so that the people could learn, know and understand when these catastrophes are about to form and to protect them from the on slaught of community diseases. How can we get these politicians to see what is really happening around our country?

It appears that our United States Congress is so out of touch with reality, they can't differentiate truth from fiction and there is a continued drum beat of total ignorance and their only focus is the election and who can galvanize the most money,and how they can defeat Obama care. *They are not concern about coming together to address the serious environmental needs of the communities.* "*They have no interest in the vast devastation that is caused by environmental factors.*" It does not matter which Political Party is at fault, they both have one objective, that is "*to raise as much money as they can*". "**Money is always the operative word to get their attention**". It is never about the environment which is the true reality of our life. It appears that we have to pass on to our children our responsibility in addressing the impact of environmental factors associated with the many catastrophes we are experiencing today. This is truly a sad affair for America and its political ignorance. When will it stop, what can we do to overcome this consistent and continuous madness?

President of The United States

Dear Mr. President:

There are no words to express the continued barbaric behavior of your cabinet, the Republican Party, many Democrats and the many dissatisfied American People who have turn a deaf ear to positive thinking and right-minded consciousness. It is important that I share with you the terminology of the ("N" word) "Nigger"! It is a noun, and it is used in a pejorative context. It depicted a people of the Sahara

African descent. In America it spoke to the Negro Race and the Black people of today as you are well informed. In 1619 during the Colonial American slave trade, it was **John Rolfe** that used the term "Negar" when describing the African Slaves. It was the Dutch who coin the Fraze *"Begraafplaats van de Negar"* (meaning) (Cemetery of the Negro which also implies *dead*). The Slave or Negar had no life and it contributed to the rape of the women and men who were captured for the use of slavery and had no knowledge of where they were going. For centuries the White Race has perpetrated this same mentality, they are under the assumption that they are forever the ruling power of the world. But there is another scenario of the "Negar" terminology that most White People fear, and it contributes to why they fear the rise of the Negar to power, *you are very much aware that the real power is not in the Office of the President*. If this was true you would not have the Donald Trumps of today speaking in abstract terms the way they do. They feel contempt from your presents as the Leader of the Free World even though you were elected by the American People through their own political and electoral process that they empowered and enforced by Congressional Law.

Mr. President, the other "Negar" was the violent Mandingo warrior who was also captured as slaves, but many of the Slave Masters feared these warriors because of their rebellion to become a Slave. The Slave Master feared these Mandingo warrior slaves because they thought these particular slaves would attack them and rape their women as they had done earlier. This is what we are facing today, these people still think that you are still a Slave and they still have power over you and you must bow to what they think is right for America, the nation and the world. Mr. President, we both know that *racism is alive and well in America,* Many of these race haters, Birthers, Republicans, Tea Partiers, and many Democrats all have one thing in common, they cannot stand to see a "Negar" in the White House. This remind me of something Elijah Muhammad and Malcolm X said decades earlier. They said: **"You never bury the "Nigga that's in you because you might have to call on him again."**

President Of The United States Barack H. Obama

Dear Mr. President:

The media has portrayed you as an animal, a clown, a misfit, not to mention the birth er issue not born in the United States, and now the Donald Trump with his ignorance and challenging you as to your educational background. I am very appalled that your Attorney General has not step forward to challenge any of these issues. Surely you are very much aware of the case, **United States Supreme Court vs. Sullivan, Supra** on the First Amendment right to Free Speech. The Court has ruled unanimously that *"the First Amendment Right to free Speech **shell not** be infringed"*. It appears that your First Amendment Right is constantly being infringed upon and the United States Attorney General has been looking the other way while these attacks are being bombarding your infringement. We said to you in October, 2010 that ***Absolute Power*** is in the hands of the Rich and Powerful Slave Masters of the World. Your religious beliefs dictate that God has all power. These are only allusions in your mind and those who truly believe in religion. *Energy as you and* *everyone else knows is the only true source of Absolute Power.* **How is it that you can see the devastation that Nature produce and then you contribute this act to the power of God when you know for a fact that nature is the act of science in creation?**

Mr. President, at what point do you crawl out of your shell of fear by allowing punnets like Sarah Palin, Rush Limbaugh, Glenn Beck, Michele Bechmann, Donald Trump and thousands of mis-educated, mis-guided individuals that the Office of President is not a carnival, nor an institution where individuals can say derogatory statement, lies, fabrications about the President and his Office then call this FREE SPEECH and get away with it? **If you were white, and a African American made the same statements about the President, The Attorney General would have exercises his powers and convicted the individuals and placed them in prison.** But since you are African American, these white individuals believe that Free Speech gives them the Constitutional Right to treat you with derogatory disrespect as a setting President. Nevertheless, you do have the power to stop this charade and put an end to this craziness. *I am extremely appalled that the Secret Service, FBI, CIA and the entire Justice Department has not came to your aid to stop this madness.*

President Of The United States Barack H. Obama

Dear Mr. President:

As we approach the ***changing times*** I felt that you have entered a cross road, first of all you should not be alarmed by the Republican Party or the Democrats ignorant behavior. The American people with intelligence can see the none patriotic behavior of both parties.The whole idea of the Presidency was to unite the parties and Congress to work for the benefit of the people. After looking at the Republican debate the other night, I am sure that the great majority of the American people are convinced that these people are totally absent of morals,self respect, ethics and patriotism. ***They continue their racial motivation as a means to discredit you for the positive work that you have done***. The American people want to see these parties and group work together to bring about the *need for change*. We understand that "Energy" is a motivational factor and controlling source in human behavior, but as we have said on many occasions there is energy in a car battery that works the same way in the human brain, ***there is a positive post in a car battery and a negative post, but they both work together to start the automobile and to keep it running.*** This same principle should be applied with our Congressional Representatives. If they had any ideas how to create jobs as patriotic Americans they would have done so long ago,*unfortunately they have no idea as to how jobs are developed.* President Obama, even if they could take your place, they would do less that what you have already done for the American People, they have no understanding as to what to do when faced with a critical crisis's.

My feelings are tantamount to most Americans when talking about the deficit. ***Why are we as Americans borrowing money from other countries by increasing our debt? Then we turn around and give other countries like Israel, Egypt, Japan, Haiti, Iraq, Afghanistan and many more third world counties $20, Billion Dollars or more to support their causes and leaving Americans with their debt?*** Putting these things in perspective, I understand catastrophes, but America lost over $100, Billion dollars in the Iraq war and know one knows where it went. Why are we spending hundreds of Billions for defense with American troops stationed all over the world? **What is the purpose of this?** America cannot police the world. Mr. President, if you would pull our troops out of these third world countries, our debt will be reduced by three quarters of a per-cent of the total debt. Today unemployment has increased, millions of homes in fore closer, businesses are closing, our public schools are closing, our States are in a whirlwind of debt and can't balance the State budgets. We know that you take on this responsibility from President George Bush, but what is the end game?

Mr. President we would greatly appreciate your immediate response to this missive.

Thank You Sincerely,
Charles Fletcher

President Of The United States Barack H. Obama

Dear Mr. President:

You could consider the next faze for change is the belief system in all religions in the greater population of the world. Rachel Meadow of

MSNBC said it best in a recent commercial. She said: *"that we must look at "energy" in other ways and its usage, what and how it provides the usage for things other than petroleum and fossil fuel etc"*. You are aware that energy is everything and **"every single thing is energy driven."** You cannot name one single thing that was not created by energy. **Not One.** You will find energy in inanimate objects because these object were created by energy. The homo-sapiens, animals, insects, objects in outer space, other planetary systems and the like all created by Energy, All acts of nature is created by Energy. Earthquakes, Tornados, Hurricanes, Tsunami, Snow, Wind, Rain, Heat, Oxygen all created by Energy. You cannot name anything greater than Energy. **NOT ONE.**

If there was ever a God in creation it would be ENERGY. **"Energy is the God"** that all religions have worshiped and always will be the God in every religious belief". Energy is the unseen spirit, Energy is what brings life into our world, it is Energy that will remain in all creation forever and always. It takes Energy to teach us and to learn, to speak, to breath, it takes energy for your organs and blood to function, it is Energy that provides the intelligence we learn, it is Energy that will cause us to die and it is energy that all life death depends and all life will always return to ENERGY.

Thank You Sincerely,
Charles Fletcher

President Of The United States Barack H. Obama

Dear Mr. President:

I am very confused and concerned about the debt crisis's as you try to move forward, for eight years the George Bush Administration along with Dick Cheney, Halliburton and crew increases the debt by $13,Trillion dollars funding two wars, then providing Billions of dollars to third world countries like Israel, Egypt etc.They did not pay one dime toward the debt. This tells me that the Rich and Powerful Slave Masters knew that this extraordinary debt would have to be paid. **So what they did was choose a Black President that would take the blame for this massive debt.**

Why would you ask for a $4, Trillion Dollar debt increase with a ten year payment, knowing that the Rich was totally responsible for this massive increase? *Why did you not request for the full $14, Trillion Dollars that would cover the existing debt to be paid in full by the people who caused the increase in the debt in the first place? You have a Constitutional mandate to correct this debt without Congressional approval, why are you playing games with the Republican Party when you have the Power of Executive Order?*

Mr. President, the American People want you to LEAD this Congress not play games with these leaders, Dr. King said it best: *"If you don't stand for something, you will fall for anything"*. Mr. President, why do you continue to play games with these ignorant Republicans knowing you already have the upper hand? Are you afraid of these people? What are you trying to prove? They have already drawn a line in the sand as the Party of "NO", Where is your line? *Mr. President, you have to stop this craziness pretending that you are doing the right thing when all the while you are looking none Presidential*, **settle the debt issue and move on to producing jobs for the American People.**

Thank You Sincerely,
Charles Fletcher

THE ABYSS

Dear Colleagues:

The *"ABYSS"* is a very deep or unfathomable gorge chasm such as time, despair, shame or a bottomless pit. Everything in creation is an **"ABYSS"**, action, dreams, desire etc. There are many levels of the Abyss; the whole universe is an Abyss that is forever toiling toward change within the universal environment. The Atmosphere, Ionosphere, Stratosphere, Troposphere, Mesosphere, Thermosphere, Exosphere etc. are all different levels of the Abyss. *Each and every thing in creation begins from a microcosm and the end results can be as awesome as the planet Jupiter.* When we learn about the cosmos and how we have been disconnected from this magnetic energy field, we can take flight back into the Abyss and learn about these different levels of the brain that can reconnect us to the cosmos.

For many years we have looked and studied religion as a *"UTOPIA"* meaning an ideal community or society possessing a perfect Socio-Politico-Legal System. ***This word was imported from the Greek in 1516. The term has been used to describe both intentional communities that attempt to create an ideal society and fictional societies portrayed in literature such as religious scriptures.*** Utopia is also leaked to *"**Dystopia**"* a neurological movement disorder **repetitive** movement as in abnormal postures, Juxtapose to the Republican Party. *All religions are utopian and in many cases it has used the ideology of God to substantiate their inability to examine the true nature of the environmental elements that created the human being.* The word God and its terminology was design as an illusion so that the human brain would not absorb its full potential limiting the brain's function.

The terminology of God has always been a way to limit the individual from looking into him/herself for the answers to creation. They always tell you what God said by using the scriptures and can never tell you what their own individual thoughts are saying. Religion teaches you to believe in something other than your true self. An over whelming amount of individuals (*some three quarters of the total* *population*) have refused to look and examine the knowledge of those elements in the environment *(it was for this reason we requested EPA to develop a monitoring system that would track, identify each element in the environment)* that created the human being from the beginning.

They think it is too time consuming to look at how each individual was created and by what elements. They would rather take the word of the bible or scripture, or a minister than to look and examine their own self-knowledge. Those that practice religion is forever lock in a Pandora's box and refuse to exit, they are conditioned to live in this illusion of God, Church and Jesus. We have said many times that religion is a unnatural practice because it was developed by man and not by the natural elements in creation. We said in our last article that: "If there ever was a God in creation it would have to be ENERGY".

There is absolutely NOTHING in Creation greater than Energy. **"NOTHING"!.** Please remember: *"Religion is not a right but a privilege".* Today the power that be is trying hard to introduce religion as a Science (Just look at Scientology) and religion could never be a science because of it unnatural and inability to create.

"Deepak Chopra the Endocrinologist" quoted *"Stephen Hawking"* A **New Creation Story: Beyond Religion & Science.** He made worldwide news stating: "A Creator is not needed to explain how the universe was created," physics is separate from metaphysics". In fact, he points out "There is a way to abolish metaphysic altogether, why bothers with God when Science is on the verge of delivering a theory of everything?

Thank You Sincerely,
Charles Fletcher

Death & The Here After

Many fear death because of the unknown consequences, Religion has put death either in a heaven or hell consequence. Meaning that if you are saved and righteous, heaven is the alternative and destination for those that believe in God. Opposed to hell where the individual would be sent for violating Gods laws and Principle of the Bible, this would send the individual to a place in Hell where the individual will burn for damn nation if he/she were a lier, killer, cheater, hypocrite and have no faith nor a belief in God. **This kind of understanding in religion is an animated illusion.** Let us look at death from a practical stand point, when an individual die,the following takes place and it happens to each and every thing that dies regardless of how it dies. Energy is extracted from anything that has life, rather its the human body, animals, insects, agriculture even inanimate objects like mountains, rock all has the exclusive protection of ENERGY.

Energy always makes its present known through the many signs in nature, Earthquakes, Tornadoes, Hurricanes, Tsunami, Rain, Snow, Cold, Heat, Lightning, Wind etc. We experience all these actions in nature as a sign to make you aware of the true power of Energy. *"Death is only an horizon that appears to be to complex for human understanding".* Death is not complex at all it never has been, but if you believe in religion, it automatically becomes fearful and complex. Death is a natural phenomenon just as life, death is a necessity that other life might prosper. The whole of creation is energized by and through Energy, therefore when death comes to all things living the very first thing that happens at the time of death is that energy is removed from all objects of life. *All energy and knowledge is retrieved from all objects of life, this is the clear operation and destination of energy, then all life with energy returns to the energy grid and the energy grid exists throughout the entire universe. The Abyss cannot exist without energy.*

Most people within our lifetime wants to know what will happen after death and where do we go, many believe that heaven is a place of streets with golden pavements, angels with wings and you will see all your relatives. *Let us look at true reality, energy has the power to recreate, reincarnate and place that energy wherever it needed or where it pleases. But first let us truly understand how energy works within each individual. Energy is what created the sperm, then it causes the sperm to move into the ovum causing all organs to develop and function, such as the beating of the heart, causing the blood to flow, energy nourishes the brain developing the necessary wisdom and knowledge for the human being and other life to exists. Then energy created each and every thing in existence so that the brain can function as an independent organ. Each and everything with life has a brain.*

Thank You Sincerely,
Charles Fletcher

Dodecahedron & Consciousness

It is time for us to look at the universe on another level. When we look at the universe from a physicist stand point we see a blue sky with a sun on a clear summer days. At night we see stars galaxies and the blackness in space. It has been understood by many physicists that our universe is in the shape of a *"DODECAHEDRON"* Pronounce Do-dec-dron this emblem is found on the Chrysler automobile logo only the "Dodecahedron" has (12) faces evenly sided with the same shape as the Chrysler logo. For many years Scientist has thought of this as our universe locked in a "dodecahedron" box.

However, the human mind and thoughts want to venture out-side of this Dodecahedron; we would like to better understand what kind of creation is there outside of this "Dodecahedron"? Atomic Physics teaches us that the creation is boundless and endless. **Or Is It***? Or are we listening to unfound knowledge of the universe or are there other universes outside of this Dodecahedron?* ***If "ENERGY" is the controlling force of our universe would not it be equally understood that energy also operates OUT-SIDE of this "Dodecahedron"?***

There are many levels of consciousness and awareness, they both appear to be equal in analysis but they are quite different in meaning. "Awareness" is a cognitive perception, this lead us into the understanding of the different phases of consciousness, self consciousness, unconsciousness, sub consciousness and Double consciousness. This Double Consciousness was first originated by the late W.E.B. Du Bois in 1897. This two-ness was look upon as psycho- social tensions or split consciousness and disadvantageous of social positions.

Du Bois focus was on social values and daily struggles of the negro's and slaves who looked at themselves through the eyes of others.

Today many are still being looked at through the eyes of others as ¾ of a human as indicated in the writings of the United States Constitution; however, this same consciousness can be applied to all races meaning that we see each other differently from a totally different perspective. We can even apply this same behavior and analysis to the United States Congress and our President Barack Obama.

Thank You Sincerely,
Charles Fletcher

Disease & Addictive Behaviors

We define disease as an abnormal condition caused by internal dysfunctions, distress, social problems, deviant behaviors, atypical variations etc. Disease can ultimately alter the person's perspective of life and their personality. These diseases can be associated with addictive behaviors, what are these additions? Money, drugs, politics, religions, sex, alcoholism and the list can go on and on. Since our economy has shifted and unemployment appears to be extremely high, the real question is, how did we get in this economic downturn? We can see the political fallout between the Democrats and the Republican Parties, and this contributes to the Presidents inability to take control of both the House of Representative and the U.S. Senate. *"MONEY, POLITICS & RELIGION"* is the underline factor for both parties, The Republicans idea is to keep the rich RICHER and utilize funding from the existing Government programs like Medicare and Social Security.

It appears that many Republicans care less about the rest of the American people with no jobs, no health insurance etc. Money is the operative conclusion. How did we get like this? It will cost President Obama over a Billion dollars to run for President in 2012. This desire for more money has entered new heights in deviant behaviors and human internal dysfunctions. Acquiring money for food, clothing and shelter has placed many Americans and third world countries in a depressive state of mind bordering on insane behaviors that borders on a catastrophic disease of the mind and brain.

The more money we acquire the more money we want, and many cannot get enough of money. Money is an addictive disease, and it affects 75% or more of the world's population. The lack of financial resources has a tendency to control the individual's mental behavior as to how to acquire more money. *This causes the individual to want to do ANYTHING to acquire more money, this feeds into their psychic behavior even if it causes the person to kill another for a few pennies or less and many times they will commit mayhem for no reason.*

It is like the communities are feeding upon themselves to acquire more money. There was a time when the communities would share their resources with other communities until the invention of money. Money has taken the place of real bordering. We can look at this from another perspective. *Energy feeds upon itself, meaning this; when we see and hear thunder and lightning, volcanoes, earthquakes, tsunami's, rain, snow, ice, heat, and death etc. all of these functions are induced by energy and is necessary for the continuation of the use of energy. When these things are happening, this is ENERGY FEEDING UPON ITSELF.*

Thank You Sincerely,
Charles Fletcher

Nostradamus After Shock

Food for Thought:

Is America really ready for a national catastrophe? Nostradamus predictions for 2012 could have significant meaning based upon America's present state of affairs. Most Americans are not even concern about 2012 and most think is just a hoax. But when we look at the unemployed numbers. The Rich and Wealthy Slave Masters who refuse to pay their fair share, we can add this to our present state of politics. They want to cut all government programs that are on the backs of the poor. However, when Hurricanes or earthquake swallow up their property, they look to FEMA and the government for help. When the Dow hits below 5,000 the stock market will crash into a whirl wind of default.

The debt will skyrocket twice its size. Gas will climb to over 20 dollars a gallon and at this point the people will panic and chaos will become rampant. Our country will become suicidal, friends turning on friends, trying calm the beast. We can't seem to come together on anything, but we all need and want more MONEY to quit the beast within. Each and every day it gets worst for the poor. The Rich is just sitting on the MONEY until the catastrophe happens, then they will start using their slaves to finish off the starving masses. This is called the **"After Shock"**.

Thank You Sincerely,
Charles Fletcher

What is your true self

Your true self is the "Energy" within you. Those who believe in the God concept are in for a rude awakening. The God concept originated from the Zeus mythology until the one true God concept was introduced by writers of all religious scriptures. These Scriptures was written to show the power of politics in the church. Most people who are religious truly believe that there is a God and they pray to this God for guidance. Even though the entity they are praying to is the energy within. Let us look at this realistically.*"Energy" is created from Hydrogen, Helium and Atoms*, you can fine these same elements in each and every star in the universe, and you will also fine "Energy" in the clusters of our Galaxies, Planets, meteors and the blackness in space. *"Energy" is the Absolute Power in all of Creation there is nothing in all creation greater than "Energy".* This thing we call *"Mother Nature"* is nothing more than "ENERGY" Feeding upon itself. What happens when the storms,' earthquakes, volcanoes, Tsunami, rain, snow heat come? It will destroy any and all things in its path and many things it allows it to keep living or let it continue to exist for another time. "Energy allows things to exist for hundred even thousands of years. This same energy is within the human body, all of our organs are created by energy, our brain and all of its functions are all controlled by energy. It takes energy for us to awaken, it takes energy for us to sleep, energy is used to grow our food and it is energy that created our vision to see, to hear, to talk to walk and to die.

Many religious scholars will argue that this energy was created by God. There is no God and there was never a God that Created Energy. *The creation of energy was created long before the creation of the universe.* Study Creation! Energy controls all of the planets, stars, galaxies etc. *There is absolutely no knowledge available as to when the Universe was created.* To argue the big bang theory is totally, and utterly ridiculous, there is no knowledge of a big bang in the universe and there never will be a true understanding as to how the Universe began. The Universe is Quadrillions of years in age and time and no one knows how old creation is nor do we know how old the earth and other planets are.

Theory is not facts and has no bearing on true facts. What are the true facts? **We cannot keep pretending that these are facts when they have absolutely no bearings on the truth.** The Powers that be continue to utilize these theories as if they are true facts.

Thank You Sincerely,
Charles Fletcher

More Food for thought

History has always stated that we are all connected, **and we truly are**. "Energy" is what connects us to each other and every single thing in creation. Even after our death, it is Energy that provides an escort so that we will better understand what happens after our death, Energy has evolved for eternity. It is energy that teaches us about life on earth and it does not stop even after your death. Energy is a progressive element in creation; it provides all the necessities in creation. In our previous articles we spoke about the Universe in the shape of a *"Dodecahedron"* and my question was if the Universe was in a dodecahedron, (box like) then *what was there outside of the dodecahedron?* Was there other Dodecahedrons? And how many were there? Let us assume that there are numerous dodecahedrons beyond the one we are presently in, because as we study "Energy" we see that it multiplies, therefore would not create just one dodecahedron over the zillion ages of time. Additionally, would those dodecahedrons have the same type of universe as we have in our universe? I would wonder as to What kind of transition would there be from one dodecahedron to another?

As we make the transition from this life on earth, as a matter of natural law, energy will guide us as to what our mission was while on earth and what we have done during our stay. Do we progress to another planet, or do we reincarnate and return to earth based on what and how well we done on earth? It is Energy that makes these decisions for all creation. If we should travel with our soul, spirit, mind (all interchangeable and all energy) we must conclude that it is energy that created these senses of Consciousness and Super Consciousness or collective unconsciousness. The altering of the conscious mind is like Quantum Jumping which we have discussed in previous articles. This is the ability to step outside of the body throw chanting and talk to our twin selves. All is the workings of *"Energy"*.

Thank You Sincerely,
Charles Fletcher

Energy in Every Level of Consciousness

Many Physicists has said that the word *'TIME'* means: A **"Temporary Induced Mind Experience"**, this suggests that each human thought induced by brain matter is a temporary experience. The thought process causes the experience to look at other thought patterns that would better address the idea at the moment. The speed of our thoughts are produced by energy. *This is done before we choose the right idea and before the execution of a complete thought.* Energy is no doubt a true complex working of ideas and this complexity feeds into the many levels of consciousness, for starters we can look at the human body and see the many organisms created and controlled by energy. Each of our organs, blood cells, brain matter, internal, external body functions etc. are all energy driven.

We can never truly understand the real workings of our true self until we go within our self. The old cliche *"As Above So Below"* is juxtapose to_ *"That which is External is Internal"*. Religion has refuse to teach the people about "Energy", *The Clergy puts more emphasis on God and Jesus but never the true source by which they both must represent.* The same Energy that gave these two entities life in scripture language is the same energy that each of us share within. We are all connected to this same energy rather it is nuclear, atomic, rocket fuel, petroleum, natural gas, electrical all are products of the same energy.We look at the tall sky scarper buildings, statues and the many inanimate objects all has the natural force of energy. However, today we can see that the use of the negative and positive forces of these energies has become a hazard for many. Although we utilize energy to create new benefits for human consumption, the jury is still out on what scientist know about the next level of energy and human consciousness.

Thank You Sincerely,
Charles Fletcher

Complexity of Dreams

One day I was listening to the recording Artist R. Kelly's who recorded the song, *"I believe I can fly"*, as I thought how our energy leaves our bodies when we are asleep with our dreams. We all have the feeling in our dreams that we are flying, and we are truly flying because our energy is moving all around us at tremendous speeds rather we are awake or sleep. *As we are asleep, our energy exits our body, it actually moves out side of the human body during our sleep, your mind, spirit, soul takes a breather from the body and yet the heart continues to beat as our energy moves and hovers over our body while we are asleep.* Energy has the ratio of about 10 feet within the perimeter of the body as it is resting. Our breathing helps to stabilize the energy through as our nose, mouth, ears, anal cavity are all exits for energy that reside in us. Even our own skin is a breathing apparatus for energy. This reminded me of my Aunt one morning she went out in her back yard to kill a chicken for breakfast, she decapitated the chicken and the body of the chicken kept running around the yard without its head suggesting that the chicken still had a little energy within its body until the chicken died. *To better understand this phenomenon is to picture a person exiting his/her automobile and the car is still running until we get back into the car and start driving.* This is why death is so easy when we pass away. Energy will exit the body completely rather it is natural causes, accident, or mayhem. Energy has a way of solidifying our images as we develop in our body during our lifetime. When we die the image of our body is separated from our physical body that must remain on earth and our soul, spirit, mind intelligence will be raised up by energy. Once we understand how energy works there is no need to be fearful of death. Negative thinking and practices and the lack of true love always fall on the ignorant and those that hate change. Additionally, once we pass away there are others waiting to greet you upon death, they are able to identify you not only from this lifetime but from other past lives.

Thank You Sincerely,
Charles Fletcher

Holon's: Whole/Parts

There is a higher level of awareness and as we look at our true self (energy) we can see that there are many things we still do not understand, and our curiosity is always focused on the things that we cannot see. Atomic Physics teaches us that there is a system that exist between consciousness or **thoughts and the execution of our actions**, this system is called **"HOLON'S"** the governance or hierarchy of consciousness, this terminology means: *"Part of a whole or Whole/Parts"* this *system or process deals with cells, molecules, atoms and particulates*, these are functional elements and things we cannot see with the naked eye but we feel these parts through our conscious thought patterns in human behavior.

As we ponder these processes, we bring to light that there is indeed a process that takes place between our individual thoughts and the actions we take after the thought. It is call Holon or Whole/Parts. This Holon system moves so quickly during our thought process until we do not have time to even think about this necessary procedure that is happening at each and every level of consciousness. We never pay attention to this system as it falls into the *OUT-OF-SIGHT, OUT-OF- MIND, SYNDROME.* Whole/parts are constantly traveling vertically upward into other Whole/Parts into Whole/Parts into infinity, like into the point of a pyramid, it does not travel horizontally as our thought waves or vibrations travel, this is why we are able to feel each other's vibrations or frequency and thought waves.

Thank You Sincerely,
Charles Fletcher

Noosphere: Mind

If you have ever sat in your automobile looking out of the windshield or driving along a busy street observing all of life's creations, you are experiencing the replica of the human mind and its operational functions. There are many levels of this system that we have failed to recognize because of the many influences and illusions we adapt as our focus of entertainment. *Religion, politics, money are all entertainment for the human mind although we may not see these things in that order; they are entertaining our daily thought patterns consistently.* Today unemployment and the lack of resources is the focus of many worldwide, this causes the mind to wonder in the illusion as to how we must obtain financial freedom. Nevertheless, this is only a small fraction as to what the mind was originally created to do. There is a level of intelligence that never comes to the surface of the mind; ***"what is the true purpose and function of the human mind"?*** *Is the mind created for evolutionary changes?* When we come out of the womb we are indoctrinated with religion, politics and money which dominates and controls the individuals thinking from birth to death, we never really look at the true process as to how the mind truly works and for what purpose. The many levels and operational patterns of the mind almost never come into play because of these dominate factors. The human brain is the center of the mind, but the human heart controls the feelings of the individual. ***Absolutely no one can see the inside of an individual's mind, the mind is personal to every human being, Every individual is able to vision the mind from the INSIDE-OUT, BUT NOT OUT-SIDE-IN.***

Thank You Sincerely,
Charles Fletcher

Biosphere: Life

There is always something else that we should be thinking about and doing, other than worshiping religion, politics and money, (we shall call these three functions (RPM) these things has trap our thinking and most of us actually believe that this is all that is necessary to achieve success. The functions and operations of the noosphere are so massive until the RPM has dominated our thinking. We spoke of holons which travel upward into a narrow point of infinity, these are levels of intelligence we can't even phantom because we are trap in the RPM or a Pandora's Box of RPM.

We have talked about the Noosphere which is the workings of the human mind, and we will go back to the noosphere. However, the biosphere focuses on the surfaces and functions of organisms, when we say surfaces, we are speaking of the outside of all cells, atoms, organs, particulates etc. We should never ever lose focus on energy that gives the biosphere, noosphere and physiosphere the life to function. Within each of these cell's energy is the controlling source and power, the human cells within the body are also connected to the mind, soul and spirit of our consciousness which help keep us alive. Nevertheless, the mind or the noosphere is also operating within each cell of our body and there are over ten billion cells in one human body. The brain is the command center for our body, however, the command center or noosphere travels to the biosphere in every area of our body and as we mentioned earlier the mind controls each and every function from the INSIDE-OUT and never OUTSIDE-IN and our mind gives the order as all energy has commanded.

Thank You Sincerely,
Charles Fletcher

Physiosphere: Matter

We are always and forever practicing the **OUT-OF-SIGHT, OUT-OF-MIND, SYNDROME,** many are not even aware that there are layers and layers of intelligence that would impel us to greater heights than what our daily consciousness dictates as an everyday thought. Matter or physiosphere are the physical things we see and worship. *Religion gives us the physical ability to strive for an illusion that will never be reached in good consciousness.* *Politics are structured laws to keep the people subservient to the order of government.* *Money provides the necessary power to maintain servitude of the people.*

Thank You Sincerely,
Charles Fletcher

Magic & Mythology

Most religious believers would never want to hear the following information because it is contrary to what they truly believe, and it will cause them to become superstitious so much so that they would not receive the blessings of God. It does not matter what religion a person belong to rather it is Christianity, Islam, Jewish, Buddhism, Hinduism etc. *The principles are always the same.* In Religion the believers are always looking for a short cut in understanding their beliefs and differences in sciences and religion. For starters let us look at Christianity; it is the talking snake in the scripture of Geneses, or the creation of a woman from the rib bone of Adam or Jesus born from a virgin birth and not that of a man etc. Each religion has some of the same mythological creations as if they all magically appear by God and from the believer's point of view God can create anything. ***The thought never accrued to the believers that there was and always has been a unique process for the creation of all human beings, animals, insects and vegetation.*** One reason the United States Constitution prohibited the use of religion in politics was that the Church and State concept in religion was and is a myth and would violate the true principle in the Constitution. **"Mythology means:** *"it is not true."* *Today we still raise our children to believe in mythological concepts, however all religions will eventually fade into oblivion. **It is imperative that we believe in our self as each and everything in creation is within you.***

When talking about magic we can point to Houdini, David Copperfield, Harry Potter and the list go on and on. When great Mythological teachings became fashionable, it was the charlatan that brought the magic to the forefront in religious beliefs. The high-powered scientist seen how the mind could be hoodwinked, bamboozled, tricked and manipulated with certain ideologies and concepts. The high science teachers also knew that the ignorant masses would never understand the process of creation, so they put together information that would continue to trick the thinking of the human mind and they developed what we call today as the scriptures of truth, Bible, Quran, Torah etc.

Thank You Sincerely,
Charles Fletcher

The Creature

I was speaking of Energy operating in Total Triple Darkness and a friend asked me. ***"How did we form and how did it happen"?*** As we vision ourselves as human, we see an intelligent mind with high spiritual awareness. *We hardly ever think of ourselves as a product of reptilians, primates or Apes.* According to the Darwin theory this was a process of evolution. The larger question was, *how long was the interval of evolution from the birth of the reptilian to the birth and development of the Ape and what was the timeline between the development of the human and the Ape.* The presimian or primate was and always have ascended from a common ancestor. This evolutionary process take millions of years because of the brain functions in these individual primates. As we develop as human, we recognize that for many of us our thinking is very slow on issues we are not familiar with and it takes time for many to adjust and adapt to changes in the environment like climate change. There are three types of evolution the most common is Divergent, Convergent and Parallel. The human mind, soul, spirit is in all three and energy is the driving force for all three as the primary development for each species. As we advance forward we must ask another question: ***"What is the next presimian for development"?*** The Human Being, mind, soul, spirit in its present development is not the end of evolution, *the fact of the matter it is just the opposite it is the beginning of a new change in evolution.*

Also keep in mind this is just on Planet earth, Evolution on other planets are quite different because of their own environment.

Thank You Sincerely,
Charles Fletcher

Total Triple Darkness

If there was ever a God, it would require energy for it to exist. There is no magic or mythology with energy. The energy that was in Jesus is the same energy that is within you today if he ever existed. Jesus could not do anything during his lifetime that you can't do today. All religions have a beginning, and all religions will have an ending, it is because of the unnatural behaviors in religion that it most cease to exist. Remember, energy is what created the human being and the human being cannot create anything without the aid of energy. One would think that this would put an end to all religious beliefs; however, this will not happen within our lifetime, it will take a few thousand years but it will eventually fade into none existence. Religion has no natural origin. There is no beginning of energy and there is no ending with energy. Energy has always operated in total triple darkness, Light was manifested through energy, as you are reading the words on this page, each and every letter is generated by energy. We see the stars that set back in space trillions of miles away, but the sun within earth's atmosphere seems to be very near. This suggest that our mind, soul, spirit has the same existence. We close our eyes, and we see sun spots all around, when we open our eyes light pours out like a water fall. This is a process of energy.

Thank You Sincerely,
Charles Fletcher

There never was a God and the true concept of God dates back thousands of years, we will use the Jumping off point with Zeus and the Greek Mythology although the religious concept dates back to Africa some ten thousand or more years before religion was formed. The larger question is what was the people doing before religion? The Slave masters of old and those today, knew that if they could produce a religious belief in the people this would control 95% of the world population and so what do we have today? There over 200 religions worldwide. Please read below:

The Woman-II

Below are just a couple of articles I wrote for the "Environmental Group at Chicago State University". As the Chair Person for this group it is my responsibility to insure that our group understands the real issues in the environment with accurate information through investigative research. This means: ***A history of all subjects are best qualified to reward research".*** This also means that the individual has to go deep within their own subconsciousness and sort out the true chemistry of their existence and what that existence is made of. *The whole creation is a science project in* **Active Motion,** *having said that t*he human body is a chemistry created by energy and this energy is always in active motion. Energy is everything and it was energy that created the sun, moon and stars because they all have atoms, hydrogen and helium which creates another form of energy. It is energy that brought you here, and each and everything you do is done because of the workings of energy, when you have completed your work here on planet earth, it is energy that will cause you to depart from this dimension and it is energy that will transmit all of your acquired knowledge back to the energy grid. It was Energy which was given to you in this body for the purpose to study creation. We acquire knowledge through trial and era through the chemistry of the brain and heart. Your brain was originally designed to encompass the entire universe, but something went wrong. When women controlled the earth things were in great harmony with creation, this is why the woman is; "Konapha Kuun" *"female of the first power in human creation".*

It was the woman that allowed the male violent species to become dominant on the world stage, it is her that bleeds but does not die, it is her that carries male and female in her womb, it is her that carries "X" & "Y" cromazones, it is her that carries the fetus for nine months, after the fetus is delivered, it is her that teaches both male and female and it is her that lives longer than the male counterpart. It was the woman that allowed herself to become a slave to the tyranny of the male species. Slavery itself gos back some hundreds of thousands of years. Slavery didn't just come here during the 14th,15th,16th, 17th,18th centuries of chattel slavery. Slavery Begin when *men were the slaves of women*, and women dominated men for centuries on end. It was the woman that gave up the ruler ship to men and it was done to prove her endurance of her own power and to resurrect herself at a certain period in time, *that time is now approaching*. When you study the process of human birth you must retrograde to the beginning of the fetus, because in reality it goes further backwards than the fetus, this is when you began to look at the genome or the genetic of the birth. All of these factors are brought together long before to the forming of the fetus, this is why we must understand the chemistry of the human body. The genes can vary from human to human and it would be extremely hard to determine where these gene originated from. As you travel backward to your grandparents and great grandparents and you keep going backward, you go from 2 parents, to 4 parents because there are the mother and father on both sides of the human chain and from 4 to 8, then 16 on and on.

Prior to the forming of the fetus, the life that was formed from the sperm and ovum mix together is the product of energy, energy began the formulation long before the fetus is created in the womb, this is done through a mathematical system, this is why when you are born, it is at a certain time, and your death will also be at a certain time. ***Nature is always true to this mathematical system.***

Maddi

My granddaughter Maddi is a true work of art. What you as parents don't know is how far Maddi had to travel to get here? When you hear people talk about time travel, you have to look at Maddi. I see 4 years old everyday and that generation of children is a special generation, they have something to offer, *they are the true time changers*, they see, speak of things many of us cannot comprehend. Meaning, they might say things out of the ordinary and we are concern as to where they picked it up at? Many children through genetic trates bring along with them something of their pass, certain information through energy is past on and it travels with them wherever they go with certain understandings that many cannot comprehend. This is how many children becomes geniuses and the word GENE comes from GENOME or GENETIC.

Genetic also can be associated with religious cults, *religion is a manmade discovery*, all religions are unnatural they are not created by the elements in creation such as the atoms, protons, electrons, neutrons, photons etc. Religion is the biggest control trap for human being to ever embark upon the earth. This is why it is so difficult to remove this brain washing practice from the mind set of religious worshipers. There is no such thing as a good religion, they all are illusions of the worse kind, ***they are only made to appear to be good***, but the bottom line is they all entraps the mind just as any drug or alcohol, it is an addiction of the worse kind and because of the superstition beliefs there are no rehabilitation clinic to address this horrible behavior. Just look at how many Churches in the African American communities, drive down Halsted Street or Madison Street or any well know poverty stricken community in any city across our nation and count the churches, mosques, synagogues and places of worship, even on the west side of Chicago and count the churches, not to mention those that are not on a main street. What is this doing to the mindset of the people? What is so remarkable about this, is all of these religions are saying the same thing, it does not matter what the denomination is. President Obama is the real game changer, but the world will not change until the woman is fully awaken to her true power and to who she really is.

Thank You Sincerely,
Charles Fletcher

Past Lives & Creationism

When President Barrack Obama was championing for President, his mantra was "Yes We Can" and "Change We Can Believe In". As we look upon his accomplishments today, we can see small and big changes in his Administration. If you have ever walked in a wind or rainstrom and the wind or rain was so strong until you had to turn your face, then all of a Sutton it stop and your whole body, mind start to relax and at that very moment a change comes about from that horrible experience to that of calm. You have just experienced change. Change is the act of Energy and energy is the product of creation. As we drive our automobiles against the winds, we cannot visibly see the wind or see change but we can feel change on the surface of our mind. After things mature or grow and reach its full development then change becomes reality and then we see change in its full glory. Creation is always changing every fraction of a second and sooner. There are two types of changes going on simultaneously, there is negative change, and positive change, this gives each individual the opportunity to choose which direction they wish to go. When there is too much negative influence in the environment, much of the negativity will come to the surface and chaos accrues. When positive influences come to the surface of the environment it teaches the masses with inspiration and agility.

The Mind, Soul, Spirit (all interchangeable) will never, ever die, When a person dies, all energy leaves the body and return to the "Energy Grid" where all energy is dispersed. This energy exists all around us at all times. Most people think that past life is the life that we have already experienced in the present life. Past lives are the lives we have experienced prior to our present life. The energy in me is the same energy in you, it is the same energy in all those that passed away before us, nothing has changed with the production of energy, it continues to produce for quad zillion of years moving forward because it is constantly creating as we advance forward into infinity. To better understand this process, we must truly understand the purpose of death. Death transmits and is the transition of our life here on this planet we call earth. There are more individual dead than there are alive. Many of us have recognize others from past lives. It would not be unusual to know that Michelle Obama and Barrack Obama met each other thousands of years before with the same ideas they both have today.

Thank You Sincerely,
Charles Fletcher

Energy is in each and every single thing we can see and do

It was Energy that gave us the life within and life without

It was Energy that created the human, animals and insects It was Energy that cause your life to be created

It was Energy that created the organs in your body

It was Energy that created your blood and gave it life It was Energy that created the Mind, Soul, and Spirit It was Energy that taught you intelligence

It was Energy that provided you with psychology, Physics, and Science

It was Energy that educated you and created schools for your thoughts

It was Energy that created the Alphabet and Mathematics It was Energy that created sickness and good health

It was Energy that built shelter for your warmth It was Energy that created food for you to eat

It was Energy that created water for you to drink It was Energy that created the rain, snow, and ice It was Energy that created the Universe

It was Energy that created the Sun, Moon, and Stars & Planets It was Energy that created the darkness in space

It was Energy that created earthquakes, Hurricanes, Tornadoes, tsunami

If there was ever a God in Creation it must have Energy for it to exist

Thank You Sincerely,

The subject of Sex and money are the most sought after of all deities in our lifetime, they both are created from Energy. However, both seem to go together like hand in glove. First let us look at sex. Prior to the explosion of the sexual revolution and the baby boom era, most people had a great respect for sex because it was something that most people cherished. There are layers upon layers, upon layers to truly understand sex and the sex act. Slavery promoted the worse kind of prohibited sexual perversion in the history of human conception. Slavery not only turned from heterosexual to homosexual which is energy driven but in many cases, there was an act of **beastalism**. Sexual activity with animals, even today these practices still exist. The act of sexual intercourse was design for reproduction of the human being **after** the human had completed his task of study upon the earth utilizing high intelligence as the true focus of human thought. True sex is within the Mind, Soul and Spirit of the individual. As you well know, "Energy is within each and every part of the human body. With sex it is like connecting to an electrical outlet that energize a charge of direct current to the body, after the act itself, many feel energized after the sex act and for many it depletes the energy because of a sexual over load. Today, rape, mayhem, child abuse by priest, clergy and teachers has placed sex as a normal phenomenon practice of religion in the church and public schools. This idea of sex with children has promoted a new culture of sadistic behavior among the people.

Money has a way of promoting the most heinous of all acts in the sexual revolution. Meaning; that people with wealth and finance will pay any amount of money to "**see or experience unorthodox sexual acts or perversions**". This is no less than prostitution of the Soul, Mind and Spirit of the human. Because we have been disconnected from the true Cosmos of sanity and have embraced the illusions of ignorance, many have adopted sexual perversions as a mark of true sanity. Meaning that they think of sex as a normal activity and there is nothing wrong with a little sex every now and then. *The truth of the matter is that money gives the illusion and energy, that if you had enough money this would calm all the confusion and needs one has stored up in his/her mind. Money buys material things of the world.* **Intelligence acknowledge the whole of the universes and beyond.** If a person's mind is always on money and its illusions of the world, they will undoubtedly feed into the addiction process and forever trying to obtain more this energy we call money. Money is another form of energy, created by energy and distributed by energy, you must remember that Energy always has a Positive and negative effect that is produced by human choice.

Dear Mr. President:

The Supreme Court case of *"**Roe V. Wade**"* comes at a time when we should look at this case more closely. Additionally, this case has reviewed the woman as ***the fault keeper for abortion practices*** and haas allowed the male who is also a partner in the consent to copulate with the woman. Today more emphasis is place on the woman for getting pregnant and omitting the male from his part in the sexual act. The male is the chief culprit in a woman's pregnancy. A woman cannot become pregnant unless there is the male sperm ejaculated into the womb. *This is all the reasons why we reject the idea that the Virgin Mary (Mother of Jesus) conceived a child without the aid of a human male counterpart.* Today in the State of Mississippi the people of that State rejected the idea of Personhood and confirm that Roe V. Wade is the Constitutional Mandate. However, ***If life began at fertilization we have totally neglected the "Energy that produced life in one sperm cell, the Energy in one sperm cell is the same energy that fertilized the egg in the ovum that produced the ampulla of the uterine tube and the production of the zygote, initiating the prenatal development.*** The media and the powers to be has continue to violate *a woman's right to her own body* and allowing the man to be free of his responsibility as a father of the child, even when the outcome was the man participating in rape or incest in an act of copulation. If the woman decide that her pregnancy violated her principles of sanity, *she has that right to reject that pregnancy.* ***This is not a political issue rather it is human rights issue.*** *A woman cannot become pregnant by herself.* ***There*** *should be a law equally supporting vasectomy as a birth control. But there is no law written that the male should have a vasectomy. How can the law be so discriminatory against women who choose to abort? These laws are applicable to woman only and not to the male counterpart who help produced the pregnancy?* Prior to religion a woman's pregnancy had the agreement between both male and female, sex was a sacred participation and permission was required to perform this act. Today sex has taken on a whole new embrace, slave masters wanted more slaves for work and today the population has exploded to 7 billion and counting. Religion caused the acts of promiscuity as written in the scripture of most religious beliefs.

Thank You Sincerely,
Charles Fletcher

Does Life End at Death?

Life is "Energy" and *energy is life.* Neither life nor energy has ever, ever, never ever, never ever ended at the time of death. Energy exits the body and the body dies, the body is returned to the earth from which it came but the life or energy that the body had, returns to the energy that sent it to that body. The human body is always being consumed by energy and the nature of energy is to consume just as fire will consume a piece of paper or any object that connects to fire. It is Energy that allows the body to live for long periods of time, and it is energy that weakens the body, the body becomes old and frail, or if the person is killed or die from sickness, energy will exist the body. It is a sad day when people never go within themselves to truly understand the energy within. It is Energy that heats the blood and keeps it flowing rapidly in the body until the time of death. We witness our elders when they grow old and feeble; this is because the energy within them has almost consumed them through the exercise of their blood and organs. ***Today emphasis is on exercise because of many environmental factors, obesity, cancer and lung disease etc.*** But the critics will never tell us about the increase in energy within our bodies will also cause our body to weaken as energy is absorbing much of the body's functions during our life time. Energy controls much of our everyday life just as the use of Technology, like a computer or automobile must come to an end at a certain time. Can we trade this body after its death? Of course, you can, but once you have returned to the Energy Grid, you might decide to linger a few thousand years before you return to planet earth or you might go elsewhere within this vast universe.

Thank You Sincerely,
Charles Fletcher

The Elusive Life of Energy

On a clear sunny day standing on the top of Mount Everest, the highest peak on earth, a person could see for miles on end, and it will appear as if the world or so it seems is extremely massive at first look. However, it is barely a small dot on the rector scale in creation. The earth could set in the planet of Jupiter some two hundred times because of its massive size to earth. Because we view the external world greater than the internal mind, soul, spirit, within the life of one human, *we fail to see the real choices in our life*. Money, sex, drugs has conditioned the people to look for someone other than themselves and save them from the tyranny of the world and *there is no one that can save a person from tyranny but their own internal self,* (by you and for you). We are truly living in an illusion of the worse kind. When looking at the human mind we can vision our own mind as a replica of the entire universe, just close your eyes and you will see the universe, yet we cannot phantom the thought within our own mind that our internal thinking as a human being is far greater than our external vision. Chattel Slavery has done the greatest deception of hoodwinking the public's mind, soul, spirit and convincing the masses that there is a God that will same them from the tyranny of the wicked. ***This is the elusive life of energy which is nothing more than "Positive and Negative" choices.*** It is truly amazing how religion can purport the idea that Jesus died on a cross and suffered his death to save the life of others and couldn't save himself. 95% of the world population in Christianity still think that Jesus will save them from the tortures of a another. All religious denominations have bamboozled and trick the minds of the public to believe that one person can die to save the life of the many. ***We are living in a true sick society***. Just look at the Penn State debacle, we couldn't even save the life of a ten year old child from an act of sodomy,even after there was a witness. But yet the male does not want the woman to abort a child even when she has been raped and sodomized.

Thank You Sincerely,
Charles Fletcher

Seize the wealth of the One Percent

We are experiencing a time within our history that the Rich one percent has place a lock on the economic conditions in the United States. Today the real problem is that the Rich one percent has taken control of the financial resources in America. The United States Government must seize control of the financial resources of the Rich one percent. *President Obama has done everything possible to allow the Rich to do the right thing and SHARE their wealth, but the Republican Party and their Lobbyist do not want the Rich to share their wealth with people they tricked.* The Government of China has control of the wealth of their Country, The Government of Saudi Arabia, has control of that country's wealth and there are many other countries that have control of the wealth resources of their countries. *America allowed big corporations to take control of the wealth in the United States and the consequences are catastrophic.* Wall Street, big banks and corporations has bamboozled the country, and refuse to share their wealth with the nation. The *Wealthy one percent is rich on paper only and because they have tricked the public out of their wealth, it is now the responsibility of the U.S. Government to seize the wealth of the one percent and spread that wealth among the people that need it.* The biggest mistake America ever made was to allow the rich to take control of the big corporations and their resources. *There are no government regulations that would halt the one percent from hording the wealth from the 99%.* Like China and other powerful governments, the United States Government has no other option but to seize the wealth of the one percent by order of the Executive Branch if the U.S. Congress fail to act on behalf of the American people.

Thank You Sincerely,
Charles Fletcher

Treason

Today we are living in the initial change of our society worldwide; however, 90% of the world population is still living in the old traditional lifestyle. The Republican Party thinks the American people should have less government intervention and more corporate control. This is why they all vote no on all of the Presidents Bills, trying to make President Obama a one term President. If this is their view, then why don't they take a pay cut in their own government salaries first before they even think about cutting the programs of the poor and the middle class? They all taken an Oath to Uphold the United States Constitution but in the same breath they all have committed **"Treason"** against the Office of the President and the American people who by the way pays their salaries. *The definition of treason was once referred to a group or individuals that went against a King which was known as high treason and treason against a lesser superior was petty treason. In law a person who commits treason is known as a "TRAITOR" and a traitor is one who betrays their own political party, nation or President.* President Barack Obama is Not a King as you might find in England, Spain, or Saudi Arabia; however, his position as President of the United States holds the highest position in the Executive Office of Government in a Political Democracy within the culture of the American People.

They want to make President Obama a one term President because of his views on change which has already taken place. The Republican Party and many Democrats does not want change, they are members of the "Good Old Boy" network that never wanted change, they want to live by the old traditional standards of keeping the SLAVES in their place. Just take a real good look at what the Republican Party is doing with the 1% Rich population, the Republicans don't want them to contribute any money not one dime to help the middle class or the poor. They have not created one job since they have been in power. The Rich and Wealthy Slave Masters of today is pushing the American People backward into slavery. *We have said this a thousand times but it appears that it still falls on deaf ears; "When we referring to both some Democrats and Republicans*

"There is no difference between the Wolf and the Fox for one exception, the Wolf is an outright animal, he will aggressively pounce and attack his prey, whereas the Fox is keen and slick, he will stauk his prey before he attacks, nevertheless, these two animals have one thing in common, they both are members of the "DOG" family and they both like lamb meat.

Thank You Sincerely,
Charles Fletcher

The Sociology of Jay-Z By Professor Eric Dyson

Dr. Michael Eric Dyson of Georgetown University has begun a new curriculum that teaches the sociology of Hip-Hop and rap music. Professor Dyson is a true produce of the *"Hip-Hop Rap"* generation. This approach opens the door for a better understanding of our youth culture and elevates the sciences for the next generation of children that utilize Hip-Hop and Rap Music as another means to an end. Rap or Hip-Hop Music as it is call today dates back some four decades to individuals like Gill Scott Haran, James Brown, Author Prysoc and many more legendary entertainers. These individuals also saw the plight of the people in a regressive time. Many were jobless, living in poverty with nothing on their minds but drugs, violence, sex, mayhem etc. This lifestyle has plagued African Americans for centuries and much of this treatment was initiated by White Slave Masters. *Sociology is an education or endeavor characterized by aspirations for better progress.* This attempt by Professor Dyson opens up a whole new level for the music and entertainment industry, in reality this curriculum points to a higher level of consciousness within the Hip-Hop Rap generation. *"Intellectual Hip-Hop Rap"*? Within this level of Hip-Hop Rap it takes on a whole new meaning, it purge into the mindset of the community and allows high powered intelligence to intervene in a docile culture.

Today the rap music industry's whole focus is on sexual perversion and lyrics, this is because sex sales. Look at the music videos with young children dancing provocatively, rappers and singers using sexual lyrics with the beat of the drum has influence the next generation of children to a lower standard of consciousness and entertainment. For example; When a rap artist records an album and that album becomes a hit, the recording industry provide the artist with luxuries, money, a big houses, cars, a plane, a boat and all the perks money can buy. Most of our youth become so over whelmed with these luxuries they really don't know what or how to utilize these resources. They start buying the glitter, gold chains, rings, watches, clothing etc. The Record Industry fronts these lavish perks so that they will become the beneficiary of all the sales for the hit album. Jay-z, on the other hand seen the pattern of what the recording industry was doing at an early age. Jay-Z sole CD's out of the truck of his car and became successful long before he developed his own record label.

Thank You Sincerely,
Charles Fletcher

Theosphere: Religious Theology

The Theosphere gave birth to the religious dogma and its beginings and the theology of religion, men of history felt that this was all that man really needed, was having a true God and later Jesus the Christ would save them from the torments of hell fire. Unfortunately, many scientist went far beyond the theosphere.

We have discussed the Noosphere, Biosphere, Physiosphere, but not Theo-sphere nor **Whole Parts** in their perspective depths. The mind, soul, spirit has different levels of intelligence. The whole for a better understanding is the circumference of a circle or 360 degrees of a complete circle, this gives the definition of something complete but in reality, it is not complete. This is *only a part of something or an extension of something entering into another phase of something else*. We call these parts of the whole, (whole parts). It feeds into the circle of the true meaning of the Zodiac. *(The beginning and the formation of religion as a whole),* the Zodiac is broken up into 12 equal parts we call birth signs. These parts are equally distributed to form the zodiacal chart or birth signs or 360 degrees of a complete circle. Each sign depicts a certain characteristic of the individual at birth. The whole parts are layers and layers of a process that formulates the workings of the mind, soul, spirit of that individual, if you ever went up or down a flight of stairs, this is an indication as to how the mind, soul spirit really works. The point is that the process moves so quickly and fast until we can't even recognize the real process.This feeds into the *OUT-OF-SIGHT,OUT-OF-MIND SYNDROME.* Many can run up or down the staircase of the mind, soul, spirit, however many will take one step at a time and many times the individual will pause because of tiredness until he is satisfied then continues. This is tantamount of walking up or down any staircase, and each step is like being in a classroom in school filled with a multitude of different curriculum's until you reach a landing and on that landing, you discover that there are miles and miles of intelligence that must be processed to better understand the workings of the mind, soul, spirit of that individual. Religious theology tried to subvert this process of intelligent thinking by*rejecting the necessary environmental education and curriculum* which was never added to the public school curriculum or University. Religion is not a natural creation but a male dominance subversion, it is an illusion of unnatural behavior and not created by the natural elements in the environment.

Thank You Sincerely,
Charles Fletcher

Title 18 USCF Part 1 >Chapter 115: Acts of Treason

On December 1, 2011, we wrote an article entitled "Treason," speaking of our Congressional Leaders in the United States Congress, however, we did not refer to the criminal statutes that address the acts of Treason. We can now focus on how our Congressional leaders will violate these statutes and think that they have ***absolute immunity*** from prosecution. After reading these statutes (below) we would have to wonder where is the Attorney General of the United States Eric Holder? Why he has not charged these Congressional Leaders with Treason. If the statues apply to the American People, it should also apply to the United States Congress and any person that violates these statutes. ***Are they above the law and free to treat the President of the United States with Contempt and Treason and nothing is to be done about their acts?*** Title 18 USC is a Criminal Statute, Part 1>Chapter 115.

Title18 USC 2382 **Misprision of Treason.** *"Whoever, owing allegiance to the United States and having knowledge of the commission of any treason against, conceals and does not, as soon as may be, disclosed and make known the same to the President or to some judge of the United States or to the Governor or to some judge or justice of a particular state, is guilty of misprision of Treason and shall be fined and under this Title of imprisoned not more than seven years".*

Title 18 USC 2383: **Rebellion or Insurrection.** *"Whoever incites, sets a foot, assists or engages in any rebellion or insurrection against the authority of the United States or the laws thereof or gives aid or comfort thereto, shall be fined under this title or imprisoned not more than ten years or both, and shall be incapable of holding any office under the United States".*

Title 18 USC 2384. **Seditious Conspiracy.** *"If two or more person's in any State or Territory, or in any place subject to the jurisdiction of the United States, conspire to overthrow, put* down, or to destroy by force the government of the United States, or to levy war against them, or to oppose by force the authority thereof, by force to prevent, hinder or delay the execution of any law of the United States, or by force to seize, take or possess any property of the United States contrary to the authority thereof. They shall each be fined under this Title or imprisoned not more than twenty years, or both".

Title 18 USC 2382:

The Acts of Treason

Dear Colleagues:

Today we are living in the initial change of our society worldwide; however, 90% of the world population is still living in the old traditional lifestyle. The Republican Party thinks the American people should have less government intervention and more corporate control. This is why they all vote no on all of the Presidents Bills, trying to make President Obama a one term President. If this is their view, then why don't they take a pay cut in their own government salaries first before they even think about cutting the programs of the poor and the middle class? They all taken an Oath to Uphold the United States Constitution but in the same breath they all have committed "Treason" against the Office of the President and the American people who by the way pays their salaries. The definition of treason was once referred to a group or individuals that went against a King which was known as high treason and treason against a lesser superior was petty treason. In law a person who commits treason is known as a "TRAITOR" and a traitor is one who betrays their own political party, nation or President. President Barack Obama is Not a King as you might find in England, Spain, or Saudi Arabia; however, his position as President of the United States holds the highest position in the Executive Office of Government in a Political Democracy within the culture of the American People.

They want to make President Obama a one term President because of his views on change which has already taken place. The Republican Party and many Democrats does not want change, they are members of the "Good Old Boy" network that never wanted change, they want to live by the old traditional standards of keeping the SLAVES in their place. Just take a real good look at what the Republican Party is doing with the 1% Rich population, the Republicans don't want them to contribute any money not one dime to help the middle class or the poor. They have not created one job since they have been in power. The Rich and Wealthy Slave Masters of today is pushing the American People backward into slavery.

We have said this a thousand times but it appears that it still falls on deaf ears; "When we referring to both some Democrats and Republicans "There is no difference between the Wolf and the Fox for one exception, the Wolf is an outright animal, he will aggressively pounce and attack his prey, where as the Fox is keen and slick, he will stalk his prey before he attacks, nevertheless, these two animals have one thing in common, they both are members of the "DOG" family and they both like lamb meat.

Thank You Sincerely,
Charles Fletcher

The Willie Lynch Speech

This writing is still true to this very day, However, we as a people blacks, whites, Hispanics etc. have been transformed from a chattel slave into a mental institution of psychological misfits. many are mis- educated,totally ignorant of self and, refusing to want to think for themselves and has become religious zealots. Many are still waiting on God and Jesus to save the country and the world. Nevertheless, this same thinking of God and Jesus has annihilated the effort for the human mind to think for itself. For example, God has refused to stop the bickering in the United States Congress. President Barack Obama has done his best to to bring together stability to all America and this was done from his own thinking and energy. Not from God or Jesus,all knowledge and intelligence comes from energy, "Energy" is the storage facility and keeper of all knowledge and wisdom in creation. Our Presidents accomplishments comes from the *"ENERGY"* within his own mind, soul, spirit and this is not a miracle or magic but from his own intelligence.

Thank You Sincerely,
Charles Fletcher

Please read the writings below

This speech was delivered by Willie Lynch on the bank of the James River in the colony of Virginia in 1712. Lynch was a British slave owner in the West Indies. He was invited to the colony of Virginia in 1712 to teach his methods to slave owners there. The term **"lynching"** is derived from his last name.

[beginning of the Willie Lynch Letter] Greetings,

Gentlemen. I greet you here on the bank of the James River in the year of our Lord one thousand seven hundred and twelve. First, I shall thank you, the gentlemen of the Colony of Virginia, for bringing me here. I am here to help you solve some of your problems with slaves. Your invitation reached me on my modest plantation in the West Indies, where I have experimented with some of the newest, and still the oldest, methods for control of slaves. Ancient Rome would envy us if my program is implemented. As our boat sailed south on the James River, named for our illustrious King, whose version of the Bible we cherish, I saw enough to know that your problem is not unique. While Rome used cords of wood as crosses for standing human bodies along its highways in great numbers, you are here using the tree and the rope on occasions. I caught the whiff of a dead slave hanging from a tree, a couple miles back. You are not only losing valuable stock by hangings, you are having uprisings, slaves are running away, your crops are sometimes left in the fields too long for maximum profit, you suffer occasional fires, your animals are killed. Gentlemen, you know what your problems are; I do not need to elaborate. I am not here to enumerate your problems; I am here to introduce you to a method of solving them. In my bag here, **I HAVE A FULL PROOF METHOD FOR CONTROLLING YOUR BLACK SLAVES.** I guarantee every one of you that, if installed correctly, **IT WILL CONTROL THE SLAVES FOR AT LEAST 300 HUNDRED YEARS**. My method is simple. Any member of your family or your overseer can use it. **I HAVE OUTLINED A NUMBER OF DIFFERENCES AMONG THE SLAVES; AND I TAKE THESE DIFFERENCES AND MAKE THEM BIGGER. I USE FEAR, DISTRUST AND ENVY FOR CONTROL PURPOSES**. These methods have worked on my modest plantation in the West Indies, and it will work throughout the South. Take this simple little list of differences and think about them. On top of my list is "AGE," but it's there only because it starts with an "a." The second is "COLOR" or shade. There is **INTELLIGENCE, SIZE, SEX, SIZES OF PLANTATIONS, STATUS** on plantations, **ATTITUDE** of owners, whether the slaves live in the valley, on a hill, East, West, North, South, have fine hair, course hair, or is tall or short. Now that you have a list of differences, I shall give you an outline of action, but before that, I shall assure you that **DISTRUST IS STRONGER THAN TRUST AND ENVY STRONGER THAN ADULATION, RESPECT OR ADMIRATION**. The Black slaves after receiving this indoctrination shall carry on and will become self-refueling and self-generating for **HUNDREDS** of years, maybe **THOUSANDS**. Don't forget, you must pitch the **OLD** black male vs. the **YOUNG** black male, and the **YOUNG** black male against the **OLD** black male. You must use the **DARK** skin slaves vs. the **LIGHT** skin slaves, and the **LIGHT** skin slaves vs. the **DARK** skin slaves. You must use the **FEMALE** vs. the **MALE**, and the **MALE** vs. the **FEMALE**.

You must also have white servants and overseers [who] distrust all Blacks. But it is **NECESSARY THAT YOUR SLAVES TRUST AND DEPEND ON US. THEY MUST LOVE, RESPECT AND TRUST ONLY US**. Gentlemen, these kits are your keys to control. Use them. Have your wives and children use them, never miss an opportunity. **IF USED INTENSELY FOR ONE YEAR, THE SLAVES THEMSELVES WILL REMAIN PERPETUALLY DISTRUSTFUL**. Thank you gentlemen."

LET'S MAKE A SLAVE

It was the interest and business of slave holders to study human nature, and the slave nature in particular, with a view to practical results. I and many of them attained astonishing proficiency in this direction. They had to deal not with earth, wood and stone, but with men and, by every regard, they had for their own safety and prosperity they needed to know the material on which they were to work, conscious of the injustice and wrong they were every hour perpetuating and knowing what they themselves would do. Were they the victims of such wrongs? They were constantly looking for the first signs of the dreaded retribution. They watched therefore with skilled and practiced eyes, and learned to read with great accuracy, the state of mind and heart of the slave, through his sable face. Unusual sobriety, apparent abstractions, sullenness and indifference indeed, any mood out of the common was afforded ground for suspicion and inquiry. Frederick Douglas LET'S MAKE A SLAVE is a study of the scientific process of man-breaking and slave-making. It describes the rationale and results of the Anglo Saxons' ideas and methods of insuring the master/slave relationship. **LET'S MAKE A SLAVE** "The Original and Development of a Social Being Called 'The Negro.'" Let us make a slave. What do we need? First of all, we need a black nigger man, a pregnant nigger woman and her baby nigger boy. Second, we will use the same basic principle that we use in breaking a horse, combined with some more sustaining factors. What we do with horses is that we break them from one form of life to another; that is, we reduce them from their natural state in nature. Whereas nature provides them with the natural capacity to take care of their offspring, we break that natural string of independence from them and thereby create a dependency status, so that we may be able to get from them useful production for our business and pleasure.

CARDINAL PRINCIPLES FOR MAKING A NEGRO

For fear that our future generations may not understand the principles of breaking both of the beast together, the nigger and the horse. We understand that short range planning economics results in periodic economic chaos; so that to avoid turmoil in the economy, it requires us to have breadth and depth in long range comprehensive planning, articulating both skill sharp perceptions. We lay down the following principles for long range comprehensive economic planning. Both horse and niggers [are] no good to the economy in the wild or natural state. Both must be **BROKEN** and **TIED** together for orderly production. For orderly future, special and particular attention must be paid to the **FEMALE** and the **YOUNGEST** offspring. Both must be **CROSSBRED** to produce a variety and division of labor. Both must be taught to respond to a peculiar new **LANGUAGE**. Psychological and physical instruction of **CONTAINMENT** must be created for both. We hold the six cardinal principles as truth to be self-evident, based upon following the discourse concerning the economics of breaking and tying the horse and the nigger together, all inclusive of the six principles laid down above. NOTE: Neither principle alone will suffice for good economics. All principles must be employed for orderly good of the nation. Accordingly, both a wild horse and a wild or natural nigger is dangerous even if captured, for they will have the tendency to seek their customary freedom and, in doing so, might kill you in your sleep. You cannot rest. They sleep while you are awake, and are awake while you are asleep. They are **DANGEROUS** near the family house, and it requires too much labor to watch them away from the house. Above all, you cannot get them to work in this natural state. Hence, both the horse and the nigger must be broken; that is breaking them from one form of mental life to another. **KEEP THE BODY, TAKE THE MIND!** In other words, break the will to resist. Now the breaking process is the same for both the horse and the nigger, only slightly varying in degrees. But, as we said before, there is an art in long range economic planning. **YOU MUST KEEP YOUR EYE AND THOUGHTS ON THE FEMALE and the OFFSPRING** of the horse and the nigger. A brief discourse in offspring development will shed light on the key to sound economic principles. Pay little attention to the generation of original breaking but **CONCENTRATE ON FUTURE GENERATION**. Therefore, if you break the **FEMALE** mother, she will **BREAK** the offspring in its early years of development; and when the offspring is old enough to work, she will deliver it up to you, for her normal female protective tendencies will have been lost in the original breaking process. For example, take the case of the wild stud horse, a female horse and an already infant horse and compare the breaking process with two captured nigger males in their natural state, a pregnant nigger woman with her infant offspring. Take the stud horse, break him for limited containment. Completely break the female horse until she becomes very gentle, whereas you or anybody can ride her in her comfort. Breed the mare and the stud until you have the desired offspring. Then, you can turn the stud to freedom until you need him again. Train the female horse whereby she will eat out of your hand, and she will in turn train the infant horse to eat out of your hand, also. When it comes to breaking the uncivilized nigger, use the same process, but vary the degree and step up the pressure, so as to do a complete reversal of the mind.

Take the meanest and most restless nigger, strip him of his clothes in front of the remaining male niggers, the female, and the nigger infant, tar and feather him, tie each leg to a different horse faced in opposite directions, set him afire and beat both horses to pull him apart in front of the remaining niggers. The next step is to take a bullwhip and beat the remaining nigger males to the point of death, in front of the female and the infant. Don't kill him, but **PUT THE FEAR OF GOD IN HIM**, for he can be useful for future breeding.

THE BREAKING PROCESS OF THE AFRICAN WOMAN

Take the female and run a series of tests on her to see if she will submit to your desires willingly. Test her in every way, because she is the most important factor for good economics. If she shows any sign of resistance in submitting completely to your will, do not hesitate to use the bullwhip on her to extract that last bit of [b—] out of her. Take care not to kill her, for in doing so, you spoil good economics. When in complete submission, she will train her off-springs in the early years to submit to labor when they become of age. Understanding is the best thing. Therefore, we shall go deeper into this area of the subject matter concerning what we have produced here in this breaking process of the female nigger. We have reversed the relationship; in her natural uncivilized state, she would have a strong dependency on the uncivilized nigger male, and she would have a limited protective tendency toward her independent male offspring and would raise male off-springs to be dependent like her. Nature had provided for this type of balance. We reversed nature by burning and pulling a civilized nigger apart and bullwhipping the other to the point of death, all in her presence. By her being left alone, unprotected, with the **MALE IMAGE DESTROYED**, the ordeal caused her to move from her psychologically dependent state to a frozen, independent state. In this frozen, psychological state of independence, she will raise her **MALE** and female offspring in reversed roles. For**FEAR** of the young male's life, she will psychologically train him to be **MENTALLY WEAK** and **DEPENDENT**, but **PHYSICALLY STRONG**. Because she has become psychologically independent, she will train her **FEMALE** offsprings to be psychologically independent. What have you got? You've got the nigger **WOMAN OUT FRONT AND THE** nigger **MAN BEHIND AND SCARED**. This is a perfect situation of sound sleep and economics. Before the breaking process, we had to be alertly on guard at all times. Now, we can sleep soundly, for out of frozen fear his woman stands guard for us. He cannot get past her early slave-molding process. He is a good tool, now ready to be tied to the horse at a tender age. By the time a nigger boy reaches the age of sixteen, he is soundly broken in and ready for a long life of sound and efficient work and the reproduction of a unit of good labor force. Continually through the breaking of uncivilized savage niggers, by throwing the nigger female savage into a frozen psychological state of independence, by killing the protective male image, and by creating a submissive dependent mind of the nigger male slave, we have created an orbiting cycle that turns on its own axis forever, unless a phenomenon occurs and re-shifts the position of the male and female slaves. We show what we mean by example. Take the case of the two economic slave units and examine them close.

THE NEGRO MARRIAGE

We breed two nigger males with two nigger females. Then, we take the nigger male away from them and keep them moving and working. Say one nigger female bears a nigger female and the other bears a nigger male; both nigger females—being without influence of the nigger male image, frozen with a independent psychology—will raise their offspring into reverse positions. The one with the female offspring will teach her to be like herself, independent and negotiable (we negotiate with her, through her, by her, negotiates her at will). The one with the nigger male offspring, she being frozen subconscious fear for his life, will raise him to be mentally dependent and weak, but physically strong; in other words, body over mind. Now, in a few years when these two off springs become fertile for early reproduction, we will mate and breed them and continue the cycle. That is good, sound and long range comprehensive planning.

WARNING: POSSIBLE INTERLOPING NEGATIVES

Earlier, we talked about the non-economic good of the horse and the nigger in their wild or natural state; we talked out the principle of breaking and tying them together for orderly production. Furthermore, we talked about paying particular attention to the female savage and her offspring for orderly future planning, then more recently we stated that, by reversing the positions of the male and female savages, we created an orbiting cycle that turns on its own axis forever unless a phenomenon occurred and shifts positions of the male and female savages. Our experts warned us about the possibility of this phenomenon occurring, for they say that the mind has a strong drive to correct and re-correct itself over a period of time if it can touch some substantial original historical base; and they advised us that the best way to deal with the phenomenon is to shave off the brute's mental history and create a multiplicity of phenomena of illusions, so that each illusion will twirl in its own orbit, something similar to floating balls in a vacuum. This creation of multiplicity of phenomena of illusions entails the principle of crossbreeding the nigger and the horse as we stated above, the purpose of which is to create a diversified division of labor; thereby creating different levels of labor and different values of illusion at each connecting level of labor. The results of which is the severance of the points of original beginnings for each sphere illusion. Since we feel that the subject matter may get more complicated as we proceed in laying down our economic plan concerning the purpose, reason and effect of crossbreeding horses and niggers, we shall lay down the following definition terms for future generations. Orbiting cycle means a thing turning in a given path. Axis means upon which or around which a body turns. Phenomenon means something beyond ordinary conception and inspires awe and wonder. Multiplicity means a great number. Means a globe. Crossbreeding a horse means taking a horse and breeding it with an ass and you get a dumb, backward, ass long-headed mule that is not reproductive nor productive by itself.

Crossbreeding niggers mean taking so many drops of good white blood and putting them into as many nigger women as possible, varying the drops by the various tone that you want, and then letting them breed with each other until another circle of color appears as you desire. What this means is this: Put the niggers and the horse in a breeding pot, mix some asses and some good white blood and what do you get? You got a multiplicity of colors of ass backward, unusual niggers, running, tied to backward ass long-headed mules, the one productive of itself, the other sterile. (The one constant, the other dying, we keep the nigger constant for we may replace the mules for another tool) both mule and nigger tied to each other, neither knowing where the other came from and neither productive for itself, nor without each other.

CONTROLLED LANGUAGE

Crossbreeding completed, for further severance from their original beginning, **WE MUST COMPLETELY ANNIHILATE THE MOTHER TONGUE** of both the new nigger and the new mule, and institute a new language that involves the new life's work of both. You know language is a peculiar institution. It leads to the heart of a people. The more a foreigner knows about the language of another country the more he is able to move through all levels of that society. Therefore, if the foreigner is an enemy of the country, to the extent that he knows the body of the language, to that extent is the country vulnerable to attack or invasion of a foreign culture. For example, if you take a slave, if you teach him all about your language, he will know all your secrets, and he is then no more a slave, for you can't fool him any longer, and **BEING A FOOL IS ONE OF THE BASIC INGREDIENTS OF ANY INCIDENTS TO THE MAINTENANCE OF THE SLAVERY SYSTEM**. For example, if you told a slave that he must perform in getting out "our crops" and he knows the language well, he would know that "our crops" didn't mean "our crops" and the slavery system would break down, for he would relate on the basis of what "our crops" really meant. So, you have to be careful in setting up the new language; for the slaves would soon be in your house, talking to you as "man to man" and that is death to our economic system. In addition, the definitions of words or terms are only a minute part of the process. Values are created and transported by communication through the body of the language. A total society has many interconnected value systems. All the values in the society have bridges of language to connect them for orderly working in the society. But for these language bridges, these many value systems would sharply clash and cause internal strife or civil war, the degree of the conflict being determined by the magnitude of the issues or relative opposing strength in whatever form. For example, if you put a slave in a hog pen and train him to live there and incorporate in him to value it as a way of life completely, the biggest problem you would have out of him is that he would worry you about provisions to keep the hog pen clean, or the same hog pen and make a slip and incorporate something in his language whereby he comes to value a house more than he does his hog pen, you got a problem. He will soon be in your house.

Power of the Vagina: Power of the Penis

I truly hope that next year 2012 will fine us in a better state of mind than 2011. For great starters we must learn to think for ourselves. To think for oneself is to recognize that our own individual mind, individual soul, individual spirit is all controlled by individual thought and by the individual brain. Nothing, absolutely nothing can think for you. Not Jesus, Not God, nothing has the power to think for you but you. When you allow something other than your true self to think for you, that thing or something has taken control over your mind. You have become a slave to that entity. Sex, drugs, money, religion, politics all have taken control of the minds of our children, and the adults that grew up during the 60's and gave birth to the sexual revolution has totally neglected those children that was born during that era. Today our children are influence by the sexual lyrics of rap and hip-hop music, church goers are influence by gospel music, money influence everything, politics enforces these influential beliefs and has pushed our children off a cliff where there is a bottomless pit, our children continues to fall into this pit of sex, violence, mayhem, rape, robbery. *The Vagina and Penis has taken control of our children's mind, soul, spirit and it does not matter rather the children are straight, lesbians, or homosexual. It is the Rich and Wealthy Slave Masters that keep this scenario on going, they know that money will influence our children to do any and everything money will buy with no holds barred.* I heard a woman say that she is a slave for Jesus. *Why would someone want to be a slave for anything?* When we look at the terminology of slave you will fine that its meaning is akin to addictive behavior. Why would you want to be a slave for Jesus or God when in truth you don't even know what either of them mean? *You read the Bibles, Qurans, Torah etc that was written by some other men utilizing their own individual brain power long before you arrive, you truly think that their individual thoughts will help you learn more about yourself and your thoughts which are not your own and you think that this will help you gain knowledge of who you really are. We are to lazy to even think for ourselves.* We want to depend on some one other than our own self.? If there was ever a God why would God want you to be a slave? Religion has taken control over 95% of the world population, and to think that a whole generation or two will have to pass through this world without ever understanding their own true power. Animation creates the illusion and a false impression an representation of reality that give the individual the idea that animation is the truth.

Marlin The Magician

In February of 2011 we discuss the use of the **Media and Politics** , and for many we did not go deep enough to better understand what is truly happening today. We talked about the Pope of Rome and the hidden knowledge stored at the Vatican. The Pope and his position as the head of the Church is an understatement. Many Catholic believers think the Pope is the true representative of Jesus Christ, the robes he ware signifies the cloak that Jesus wore during his life time. and many clergies throughout the world still ware these elaborate robes as the head of their Church. However, the real reason for these garments was to poetry the role of *"Marlin the Magician"* in the motion picture *"King Author"* and if you ever watched the movie *"Excalibur"* you would find "Marlin" the Magician who signifies *"Magic"* and *"Witch Craft"*. For the benefit of those who have truly studied religion knows that (all religions) was born out of "Witch Craft" and if you have ever studied the beginning of religion your research will take you to "Witch Craft". The Pope represents Marlin the Magician and is endowed with Magic, he can make the dead come to life, he can cause miracles and before he dies he must perform three miracles to become a Saint. This idea of magic teaches that most clergy ware the same robe as do the Pope and as did Marlin and most all clergy in their respective religious beliefs also represent Marlin the Magician. *This is why the vast majority of the world's population that believes in religion have a hard time believing in anything else other than their own religious beliefs. they are lovers of magic and mythology.*

The First Lady

Dear Colleagues:

Many of us have totally dismissed the fact President Obama is still the President of the United States for all the people within the boundaries of the United States of America and to all allies. It does not matter what your occupation is, the President is for all the people. However, must we forget that his wife Michelle Obama is the *"True Power" in the White House.* The White House and its white occupants have been a dominant force since it was built, they called it the White House not because Black Slaves built it, but because *"White Males"* Dominated this structure from the time it was built. Let us not get it twisted, that there has been many mix blooded white males that have sat in the white house that passed the test as pure white males but was never ever identified as a Negro with one drop of black blood during the 17th, 18th, 19th Century because if they did, they would have been lynched by the so-call Aron Angelo Sextons during that time period. Many of the Good Old Boy network still hate the fact that a Black President has taken up the occupancy of the White House. This among other reasons is why the GOP wants to get Obama out of the White House so that they bring back the Good Old Boy practices in the White House. They don't want to change that good Old tradition of white controlling blacks. When a Black male of African decent impregnates a white female, many times the child might come out of the womb looking like President Obama, on the other side of the spectrum if a white male impregnates a black female, at birth that child could come out of the womb looking like Vanessa William. All pregnancies are not the same with mix races, there are some tribes in Africa that have given birth to Albino Children and there are yet other tribes that have given birth to blond hair blue eyed children and their parents were jet black. The First Lady Michelle Obama is a real gem, a jewel, she is graceful, with the stature of a True Goddess, her mother knew that Michelle was going to be something great for the world and she protected Michelle. Everything you see in Michelle you can see those same principles coming from her Mother. It must be truly gratifying to watch your own child display the real power of true womanhood and hold the reigns of a Goddess in action. Many white males that work in the white house detest the First Lady because of her sound judgment. They thought that Michelle was going to sit around and do nothing just as the other First Ladies had done. They didn't see Michelle coming. The White males in the White House has tried everything in the book to trick Michelle, but she has held her ground as a mother and true devoted wife to her husband and children. Michelle knows that if she should slip during anything negative, they would eat her alive.

Stay strong First Lady.

Human Sexual Appetite

As a rule we never pay attention to what we think about, we do things without really thinking about it, we eat fast food because of conveyance, the food is already prepared to our taste and liking. Our appetite for sex has the same connotations. The vagina is already a finished product for our children and many adults and they do not understand the process by which the vagina was created and for what purpose. We never take the time to truly understand and look at what we are doing when it comes to sexual intercourse or as the hip-hop generation calls; *"getting your freak on"*. This behavior has produced real insidious problems among or children and adult population. We must take a serious look at what the vagina was created for. Because this organ is the birth canal for human delivery, something happens along the way and the sexual revolution took off at supersonic speed. Today sexual intercourse has been found with adults and toddler babies. How can the mind stoop so low? Sex education in public schools is truly a joke and public education has constantly help influence our children by giving them condoms thinking that this will protect our children from sexual diseases. Today sex is a past time sport just as basketball, football, horse racing etc. At a time in our history sex was only allowed in our late ages of life and something reversed that trend of thinking. Today our children are having babies as young 10 years old and the human population has increased seven fold where as in many cases they are starving to death.

As we examine the female anatomy we as a human species have not come close to truly understanding the purpose and function of the vagina known by many names, Pussy, Cunt, kitty cat, beaver, monkey, funky stuff just to name a few. Today even the specialist in Gynecology still has not fully understood the true purpose of this organ. Slavery has taken away the high expectations as to what the Vagina was meant to convey. We have mis-used, abused this organ as a past time sport, each level of this organ has a long history of itself, long before it was developed as the female Urethral uterus, each level of the Vulva has a history of its own. The Right & Left Ovary=Histology, the Ilia Artery, the clitoral hood, clitoris, labia menorah, urethral opening, vaginal opening, perineum, cervix, ovary, urinary bladder, G-spot=erogenous zone-orgasm. Many women do not know what these functions are used for. The same with male. The Penis a Latin word for tail or the Indo-European Greek word Pesos=Phallus. From Spectroscopy Acronym has the Proton- enhanced nuclear. The Penis produces the spermatozoa and under a microscope looking at one drop of human sperm there are numerous thought patterns that we must consider before having a sexual intercourse. The head of the sperm drop=Acrosome, plasma membrane, Nucleus, centriole, mitochondria, terminal disc, mid (connecting) piece, Axial filament, the tail and end piece just to name a few.

Zombism: Religion

No matter how hard we raise the issues of religion, we can't seem to raise the consciousness of those in the church that truly believe that God and Jesus is the proper venues in religion as a true state of mind in all religious denominations. *We must now take a serious look at how churches, mosques, synagogues in all religions have taken full control of the minds of the people that practice these religious beliefs.* Moreover, we cannot throw the baby out with the bath water in all religions, because of the many quotes from different scriptural texts that are meaningful to those beliefs. It never fails that the end results of understanding religion always boils down to mind control thoughts of God and Jesus. These unorthodox religious beliefs are the same mind controlling teachings that put the peoples in a zombie mind state. These same practices today are still in our church, mosques, and synagogues and among our religious leaders, reverends, rabbi, imams, ministers, priest, etc.

Carl West is a prolific writer and friend. In December 2011 he wrote an article talking about people walking around like *"Zombie's"*. Not like the portrayal of the undead in the Michael Jackson's Thriller video looking like something coming out of the grave. *It is this religious mindset that put people in a zombie trance.* The term Zombie and Vodou or (Voodoo) originated in West Africa and later used in rituals in Jamaican West Indies and Haitian Communities as a religious practice. It was moved to places like New Orleans in the early 19th Century as a Creole tradition called Zonbi meaning: "Toxoplasmosa", Gondii, as an *animated* corpse. In the Voodoo (Vodou) cultural ritual tradition, it is the *"Bokor"* or Witch Doctor as in ("Witch Craft") is the one controlling the Zombie; this Bokor is tantamount to Ministers, Imams, Rabbis, Reverends, Preachers etc. The term Vodou or (Voodoo) is akin to Kikongo the word Nzambi meaning: "God".

What is a PhD

What happens when a person graduates with a Doctorates Degree? Does this raise the consciousness of the individual? Or does it put him among the real money makers of the world? The book **"Rich Dad Poor Dad"** really addresses this phenomenon and brings the idea home. Material wealth has nothing to do with academic education. People can sale water at a bus stop and get rich, a teacher can teach in public schools and never make ends meet. Most educators are satisfied with the little knowledge they have acquired since leaving the University they graduated from. Many have this feeling that they have made it and they have completed the curriculum that gave them a PhD. The next step is, how can they utilize this knowledge to make a living. This required money. Money becomes the operative word once you complete college. *But what about the knowledge itself?* Education was never mean to find employment or a better job, in fact education has never meant to acquire financial wealth. The Slave masters thought that if they utilized education as a means to control the masses, they would be able to further control the slaves from a high-powered analogy. Today, nine out ten that graduates are extremely poor from spending every dime to acquire their PhD. Then they must pay back all those loans they acquired over the years trying to get that PhD.

The soul purpose for going to school is to learn how to think intelligently. To think intelligently one needs to understand the basic principles of thought and the process by which a thought takes place. *This is true education*, because by the time you learn how to think intelligently, you will have learned how "Energy" created this entire system we call education.

We've talked about the Noosphere,or mind, soul, spirit and the whole parts which connects us to a high level of thinking we never engaged in before, because many with the PhD think that they are fully prepared for the understanding of creation and the universe. But you know they are not because it was the State Education Department that wrote the curriculum for the PhD program by which each and every University must adhere to. Many of those at the state level did not even have a PhD when passing the students in the PhD program. There are many schools of thought that have these same principle. When we confronted the Illinois Department of Professional Regulations requesting that they tell us why environmental education was not required for medical physicians and nurses? They said: "because environmental education was never a part of their medical practice". Why wouldn't a doctor or nurse be required to have a environmental education when all illness and disease are directly associated with environmental factors? The Rich and Wealthy Slave Masters love to keep the population blind to facts that need immediate investigation. But, like Donald Trump, most Graduates think that they are smart because they have a PhD.

Internal vs. External

Here is a serious question for all those that truly believe in religion and that God is real and Jesus being the Son of God. When the One percent Rich Slave Masters of the world decided to expand their Power in the world, they needed to be 100% sure that they had absolute power over the masses of slaves they owned. ***To do this the Slave Masters knew that money was the great influence that would bring the slaves to them on their knees begging for the crumbs off the Rich Mans table.*** They truly wanted the lower class of people to worship them at all cost. Today, the clergies in every religion always ask their following to pray to God and ask for forgiveness in fear that they would not gain God's blessings. Then the Rich Slave Masters added an additional requirement, they had many men to write manuals, Constitutions and scriptures that the slaves would have to follow. *The Slave Masters are the true God that all religious believers worship and the Sons of these Rich Slave Masters is the Jesus that is talked about in the scriptures, the one that is to come, that many follow and it does not matter what religion you belong to, there is always a prophet or some messiah that's coming back in the last days and you must go through this Son before you can reach God.* The Rich and Wealthy Slave Masters know that all Slaves worldwide have no power to do anything but except what the Slave Masters put before them. ***They have missionaries all over the world to continue this assault on the human Physic knowing that the slaves must come to them for the Slaves substance or (money) that is need for the Slaves to survive.*** There is a verse from the Bible that said: ***"It is easier for a camel to walk through the eye of a needle than for a Rich Man to enter the Kingdom of Heaven".*** This is the dumbest founded statement you could ever say to a human being especially if you are already Rich and living in heaven. But the Slave will never enter the kingdom of heaven because he has no material wealth like the Slave Master and will always be materially poor unless God the Slave Masters gives him the wealth to enter his heaven. These Rich Slave Master will give some of the slaves a little wealth like third world countries, U.S. Congress, entertainers, sport celebrities and some so call educators.

We as human beings we place more emphases on external things than we do internal things, what keeps us in this state of mind is material wealth, games of chance, politics, religion etc. The internal things are reflective of the entire external world. *If you look at the veins in the human body, it is reflective of the streets and roads in the external world we live. If you look at the blood cells that runs through our veins you will reflect the automobile, and the workings of each cell in reflective of the workings of the human, body, mind, soul, spirit.* **Looking at the internal workings of the human body, there is this hollowness that we see when we close our eyes; we see sunspots and darkness. This hollowness is the "Energy" within.** We cannot see energy otherwise, if we search for it in the external world, *only* when there are natural disasters, weather phenomena like storms, earthquakes or catastrophes in and around this material world. We call this the: **"OUT-OF-SIGHT, OUT-OF-MIND, and SYNDROME".** Within the internal workings of the body, mind, soul, spirit Energy is the controlling factor of our existence. Energy does not require us to worship it, Energy created each and every thing we can see or image, Energy is not Jealous of anything in its creation. Energy does not have a Son to follow it, and When it is time for you to depart from your body and this earth all of your energy will depart from your body and return to that awesome Energy Grid that awaits your return. It is there where Energy created you from the beginning. the power that gives you the energy to see from the eyes in your body, you will still see once you depart from your body. What is so hard about this to understand?

Slavery of Our Forefathers

When President Barack Obama said that he would bring about change that you could believe in, what did you think he meant by this statement? Surely change means different things to all people. for most of us we think change is just for the few and not for the many. Consequently, many all cultures do not want change, just look at the GOP they want things to remain the same. Let us look at this from another perspective. An individual who can quote bible verses from a passage that was written by people years before their time is all well and good, but ask that person to quote something the individual have said on their own and from their own thinking, their mind goes blank. They cannot quote any analogy from their own creative mind. *"Energy" is within each and every living creature and you were created with this energy inside of you so that you can think for yourself.* This is why the majority of the world's population is at the mercy of the Rich and Wealthy one percent and at a total stand still because they have not been taught to think for themselves, and because other people have been doing the thinking for them. It does not matter what kind of job you have, where you live you still have to follow the laws and rules of that company that hired you and you still depend on that company to pay you, but you are not aware that those in power like Wall Street, Big Banks are controlled by the Rich and Wealthy Slave Masters of today. This is truly sad. It was said by Carl West, Publisher and CEO of ***"Truth B Told"***, They are nothing more than program Zombies who has no original thoughts of their own. When you speak of Energy as the Controlling source, they point to biblical verses to justify their point of view. This should prove the point that the one percent is still in control and has complete power over the slaves of today in 2012. *The slaves of today are not just those in the Churches, Mosques, Synagogues and those living in poor neighborhoods, the slaves are in the United States Congress, third world countries, Kings and Queens, slavery is not limited to any race culture or class or belief. A slave is one that is subservient to a power above that persons own individual thinking, in mind, soul, spirit, and aspirations.* The Rich and Wealthy Slave Masters of today still controls the slave and what the slave will thinks about. We can never forget what the Slave Masters done to our forefathers of all races because it is still reflective today.

Peter Love; is a correspondent among the thousands of emails I receive and he asked a profound question (below) that I was more than glad to respond.

Charles,

At some point in time, and if you have the time, I would like to hear your views on why people fear death; yes, even religious folks.

In our society it seems we, as a whole, are afraid of growing old and dying. Keep your opinions coming. I find them very interesting.

Peace,
Peter Love

Thank you for your comment. This is really a great question and I am more than glad to respond. **Peter, death is only an horizon that appear to be too complex for human understanding.** However, *death is not complex, but it has been made to appear that way.* For example, "Energy has two components that we use continuously in our lives over and over and over again in many different ways. These components are *Positive Energy* and *Negative Energy*, love and hate is another, fear is another component of "Energy". We will use Slavery as a jumping off point. *During slavery, the Slave master would dramatize the other slaves by killing a slave in front of other slaves, they would tie one halve of the slaves body to two horses and have those horse pulling the slave in two different directions which would pull the slave physical body apart while the other slaves watched. or tar and feather the slave and sat the slave afire, or take a pregnant slave of nine months, tie her hands in a tree naked and take a machete and split her belly open and the fetus would fall on the ground and the slave masters would take that same machete and split the fetus wide open where all the slaves could see.* This kind of mascare and fear tactics put extreme fear into the slave and other white families that watched this kind of mayhem, then on top of that they gave the slave the teachings of the King James version of the

Bible and told the slave that they should never question the word of God. The God of the slaves was the White Slave Master and the slave would bow to his master just as any dog or animal. The slave feared the white slave master.

Peter, there is no reason for anyone to fear death, death is an extension of your own life as "Energy has created it to be. Because your body dies, it is the "Energy" within you that continues to live long after your body has decade or cremated, your body is only a vessel to carry energy until it is time for you to depart from that body. *However, because we have never been taught about the environment and what the environment does, we fall prey to religious beliefs as this is what the slave masters taught, and we continue psychologically to believe in the teachings of the slave masters up into this very day.* I just answered a letter from a young woman that sent me quotations from the Bible, I know that her mind is totally locked up in her religious beliefs and it is very hard to penetrate these religious beliefs because the Slave Masters did a superb job en-stealing fear into the slaves mind. Because she has allowed the Jesus, God mentality to control her mind, she is now totally OUT-OF-HER—MIND.

Oosphere=Ovum

We have discussed many of the SPHERES in Physics such as Quantum Jumping, moving into multiple universes, and there are other phenomenon's we have not even touched the surface, What does it mean to become a human Reptilian Shape shifter? We have discussed the Biosphere components but have not talked about the "OOSPHERE" meaning: "Ovum" and must not be confused with the "NOOSPHERE" meaning: "Mind" but there is an association, and we will discuss these terms in future articles. This is what has been missing from our entire environmental educational system and why wouldn't each and every human being want to know what their body consist of and capable of. Why it exists in this form? If you were never taught what your body is capable of doing you will live your entire life not even wanting to know what your body could really do.

The knowledge of the Oosphere is only given to Gynecologist and Medical physicians in their practice, and as we have indicated in previous articles to inform our readers; according to the ***"State of Illinois Office of Professional Regulations"*** and those from other State License Bureaus, environmental education was never a part of the medical curriculum. So ***why was "Environmental Education" omitted from medical practice when the human body was created from the physical environment? We eat food which is an environmental necessity, all medication comes from herbs that grows in the environment, Illness, disease, behavior, death and the effects of magnetic energy fields are all associated with environmental factors. So why was environmental education omitted from the medical curriculum?*** *There is so much knowledge being denied to the public until it is shocking to understand why. Today our children have to pay to enter public schools, and then pay again to go to college, and then pay again when they complete college.* ***It is the One percent that has capitalized off these basic educational needs.*** This is truly greed and sadistic on the part of the Rich and Wealthy Slave Masters of the Global Economy.

The Oosphere=Ovum also has many layers of knowledge that we fail to reflect. The Oosphere is associated with the Spermatozoa in as much as one drop of sperm from the male reproductive system has to enter the Ovum to impregnate the female. There is the Vitelline Layer, Protein Recepttors; inside the Ovum are the egg cytoplasm and membrane, the Perivitelline Space, Cortical Grande, and Cortical Content, the gametophyte=Egg Cell, oogonia develop into the Ova the primary oocytes. The ooplasm=yolk germinal Vesicle Nucleolus, the Corpus, Cavernosum, Cowper Gland, Testis made up of three layers. We truly hope that each of our readers will research what we share in these articles; we know that these are the true facts, and we challenge anyone to prove otherwise.

The Kingdom=Energy

What do we know and understand about the terminology of "Kingdom"? In Biology, Kingdom=Biology, Taxonomic Rank, a three domain system. The complete sequence of rank is life, domain, kingdom, phylum, class, order, family, genus and species. The United States use a system of six kingdoms, animalia, Plantae, fungi, protista, archaea and bacteria. All six are driven by "Energy". There are also two words in the one word King-Dom, King meaning Monarch, Dome=Hollow upper half of a sphere. Now as we progress to another level or dimension within the internal world of Biology, there is another kingdom and like all things in creation, "Energy" is the absolute power. Within the internal world of thought Kingdom has another meaning at a higher level of understanding and consciousness. Many of us have been in a situation where we lose all control of our thoughts, this is because thought moves at such a high rate of speed until we can lose focus of what we are trying to say or express either in conversation or just thinking about an idea. **Thought moves faster than light.** When we indulge in the thought of sex or sexual intercourse there is a point at which we reach a feeling of utopian pleasure, just by thinking of sex, when the mind is in this state, the individual tries to prolong this feeling as long as they can until the overpowering sense of ejaculation or either just before the time of ejaculation for the male and the G-spot orgasm in the female. These are only the physical body exercise by which "energy plays a direct part in this act of copulation. The massaging of the organs (Penis and Vagina) in many cases causing extreme ecstasy. *In this state of sexual awareness, something else is happening but we do not acknowledge what it is*, Energy at the height of our ecstasy issues the command to release the spermatozoa and at this point the ejaculations becomes so overpowering until the release of the spermatozoa becomes necessary and because of the release of the sperm the penis in many men lose its erection and the blood flow deflates. *In this state we are entering the Kingdom and many will attest, it makes you feel like you are in heaven. The fact of the matters is, you are in heaven during this act, heaven has always been in the mind, soul,* *spirit of the human being and the act of sex moves the thought process into the kingdom of heaven.* Most people actually think that heaven is in the external world somewhere beyond the blackness in space, but they fail to realize that each and everything in creation is also within the internal world of each individual mind, soul, spirit, otherwise, how would you have ever known how heaven truly felt?

Believe in Yourself

When President Obama asked our Young People; *"to believe in yourself"*, here is what he meant; our very first question is: ***"What is your true self"?*** Your true self is the "Energy" within you. Your "Energy" control each and every part of your body from the time you were born on into your adult life today. "Energy" controls all of your senses and there are quite a few other than the five that most have come to learn, sight, smell, taste, feel, hear, within your body, ***your body does not control any part of itself, all is done by and through "Energy".*** Your senses and nervous system is controlled by "Energy". (An automobile battery operates on the same principle). You feel pain because of the nervous system, You need to know how pain feels when it happens, it is "Energy" that truly sense the pain, not the body. ***The body can become num and not feel pain or Like Senator Mark Kirk, the body may have a stroke because Energy has stop serving that part of the brain which causes the body not to respond to those commands that controls the left or right side functions of the brain in your body.*** You are energized to respond to the commands and controls of the "Energy" within, it appears in each and every human being that you are in control of your body which is a natural feeling of all human beings and rightly so.

But you must look a little deeper into what is really controlling the body since the body is only a vessel to serve the "Energy" within you. At the time of your individual death all "Energy leaves the body by leaving the body dead just as a blade of grass or a leaf from a tree. The body began to decade and your "Energy is drawn in by that Awesome Power of the *"Magnetic Energy Field"*. If you have ever seen a magnet that attracts metal or a group of nails this is the same principle that happens when "Energy leaves the body, the Magnet Energy Fields draws Energy from the body and pulls that Energy into itself the *"Energy Grid"*. At that point your Energy unites with other "Energies" that you might have not seen for thousands of years. Energy is the life within and has always been the life within, Energy is the entity that gave the body sight to see because energy is the sight that see, "Energy" is the ears that hear, the nose that smell, the tongue that taste and the body that feels.

Thank You Sincerely, Charles Fletcher

Dunamis-Woman=Power

Dear Colleagues:

We have said in previous articles that religion is an unnatural phenomenon because it was not created by the elements in the environment. However, we cannot throw the baby out with the bath water. Meaning this: Because religion is a worldwide practice of many denominations, the knowledge in religion is also *"Energy Driven"*, the development of religion has caused a cataclysmic assault on the human Psychic, causing a monumental illusion as to what God really mean and what Jesus really stood for as an icon of worship. All knowledge is created by "Energy" and cannot be destroyed except by "Energy".

Therefore, religious knowledge has to be re-defined in a way that all believers will take a second look at what they truly believe. To do this, one must have a thorough knowledge of the scriptures and is able to utilize the scripture to address the mind, soul, spirit of today. Most religious believers know that the scriptures should not be taken literally and the illusion that the scriptures were written by God is a fallacy. ***All scriptural writings are written by men.*** Today, women have taken the lead in addressing religion from a whole new perspective and DaVetta "Dee" Collins Founder, Publisher and CEO of *"Dunamis-Woman Magazine"* and *"Real Awesome Men"* publications, is one of those women. On Monday nights at 9:30PM she has her own TV show on WJYS channel 62 in Chicago. Watching her in action is truly an experience not to be denied.

Thank You Sincerely,
Charles Fletcher

Dunamis-Woman=Power

We have said in previous articles that religion is an unnatural phenomenon because it was not created by the elements in the environment. However, we cannot throw the baby out with the bath water. Meaning this: Because religion is a worldwide practice of many denominations, the knowledge in religion is also *"Energy Driven"*, the development of religion has caused a cataclysmic assault on the human Psychic, causing a monumental illusion as to what God really mean and what Jesus really stood for as an icon of worship. All knowledge is created by "Energy" and cannot be destroyed except by "Energy".

Therefore, religious knowledge has to be re-defined in a way that all believers will take a second look at what they truly believe. To do this, one must have a thorough knowledge of the scriptures and is able to utilize the scripture to address the mind, soul, spirit of today. Most religious believers know that the scriptures should not be taken literally and the illusion that the scriptures were written by God is a fallacy. *All scriptural writings are written by men.* Today, women have taken the lead in addressing religion from a whole new perspective and DaVetta "Dee" Collins Founder, Publisher and CEO of *"Dunamis-Woman Magazine"* and *"Real Awesome Men"* publications, is one of those women. On Monday nights at 9:30PM she has her own TV show on WJYS channel 62 in Chicago. Watching her in action is truly an experiance not to be denied.

Thank You Sincerely,
Charles Fletcher

Death of Whitney Elizabeth Houston

We all were created for different reasons, we might not like the position that was assigned to us, but we can choose to either except the assignment or abort it, Suicide is a choice or option that's given to us and it has come to the mind for many. We are not sure what caused Whitney's death. But what we do know is that when her time was up, she left as she had chosen to leave. She done her job well with a few bumps in the road, but she left a legacy for generations to come. Here is something that each and every one should think about and pay close attention to every word, *"**each of us have died many times before and was resurrected in other lives**".* We were brought back to earth under different circumstances and situations many times before, and many of us can not and never will remember our past because of deep psychological hypnosis by many forms of slavery, illusions and trickery being implemented deep into the super sub consciousness of our memory. Death is nothing to be afraid of and how can a person fear death when it is inevitable that death will find you? Here is what religion will never teach you unless you can look really deep into the meaning of scripture. The teachings in many scriptures suggest that Jesus was tormented on the cross, died and was buried in a cave or Tome and was resurrected in three days. Days in scriptural language mean years and centuries because once you leave earth among the humankind, time has no meaning. *You have passed through the death thresh whole thousands and thousands of time but your mind cannot recognize any past events in human memory.* **Most of us truly think that we have never died and this life here on earth was the first and only life as we know it.** This is why it is extremely important that we go within our mind, soul, spirit and meditate on who we really are, **we are much more than what we see in the mirro**r. Our life does not stop at death. Death is the vehicle by which we make the transition from this living organism to our next assignment. Our next assignment is predicated on what you acquired here on earth. This is why we need to understand what "Energy" truly mean and what it does. "Energy" moves and controls the entire creation and it advance the creation by leaps and bounds at will.

Thank You Sincerely,
Charles Fletcher

Religion and Politics

If we have learned anything from the recent escapades with our Political Leaders on religion it is to pull away from religion all together, religion is nothing more than a political scam to control the masses. Just look at what is being said about the Presidents faith. *Even if the President did not succumb to any religion at all, this does not have anything to do with the issues on the economy, health care,and job opportunities.* *At this juncture, religion has no place in politics.* **We understand why President Barack Obama embrace the Christian doctrine prior to entering politics and becoming President.** *Religion in America has a grip on the political system and our leaders want the power to control the flow of knowledge among the masses.* Should you not believe in the Christan philosophies you are cast out as a dis-believer, and you do not qualify for the highest office in the land. This is the same problem the Greeks had when they embraced the Mythology of Zeus. Today, if you do not believe in God or the Lord and Savior of Jesus Christ, you are not only a disbeliever but you are condemned by the people of the church, synagogue or mosque and this type of mind set has nothing what so ever to do with the economic values of our existence. **If you do not follow the Christian, Mormon, Muslim, Jewish, Buddha, or Hindu beliefs you are among the infidels, and the irony of this is that all of these religions are saying the same thing, not one religion is different from the other except for the language and culture.** At what point do they stop this charade? *It does not matter what President Obama does it will never be enough for the Republican Party, they continue to say his birth was not in the United States, his birth certificate is not authentic, he is a threat to the United States, and this goes on and on and on, they have treated the President as if he was a criminal and the United States Justice Department has not tried to intervene to stop these attacks on the President.* **My question is where is the Attorney General of the United States? Eric Holder has allowed these attacks to go on without no intervention. Why has the Attorney General allowed all of these attacks on our President? Is Eric Holder a member of the GOP?** What's going on? We need answers immediately.

Why Should We Think?

I get emails all the time from people far and wide, they ask me how do I know what I know? No matter how many times I tell them, they continue to ask the same question over and over again. I meant with Hermene Hartman, Publisher and CEO of N'DIGO last week, and I asked her, :what is wrong with the people that they cannot see what is happening and whats going on? Mrs. Hartman said: *"they do not want to think for themselves"*. It was astonishing to hear these words coming from such an articulate woman. She said what I've been saying for years. So, it was not just me. many religious zealous don't want to hear the real truth about religion because it makes that individual look like a fool and they will defend their religious beliefs at any cost. They became a slave to their own beliefs. Then they say: *"a person can believe whatever they want to believe it is their prerogative"*. *this is a fact of life in America, but the truth of the matter is that religion is not a truth, but a fact based on the writers analogy at the time of scriptural writings.* I can give you many facts however, if you do not believe these facts they will leave you hunting for the truth. A fact can become a witness, but that witness may not be the credible truth or vice versa," *all truth is created by the natural environment". **There is no way of getting around the truth. Let me give you another example, all scriptural knowledge is based on allegorical speeches of many facts, but what is it that makes that individual believe that those facts are the truth**?* They rely upon what they read instead of researching the truth of what they have read. Most people want the truth but are afraid to look for it, they would rather stick to their own superstitious beliefs or take the word of a friend because research requires in depth study and intelligence, this would put forth a challenge to their own mind, soul, spirit. *This would require an incredible amount of time, concentration and confirmation, but who do you confirm your finding with? The scripture do not teach the believer to worship the environment nor the elements in the environment according to II Peter.* To the contrary, the believers, believe that the elements in the environment are the works of Satan. **Did it ever occur to you that if you never talked about things** *other than God you would never want to know anything else other than God?* The creation was already here long before there was ever mention the word God. Most people actually believe that God created the havens and earth and they do not want to believe otherwise. *If people would learn to think for themselves* outside of their religious beliefs, there is a whole new world waiting for your discovery. *But they are so afraid of denouncing the word God until the very thought of denouncing God send trimmers of fear up and down their spine. This is what slavery produced, slavery introduced the fear tactics into the minds of the slaves so that even if they thought about denouncing religion, fear would come over them like a raincoat on a stormy day.* Slavery is a powerful antidote against religion. As we look upon religion and politics, we can see the tug of war that our political leaders are having with President Obama, instead of them helping the President, they think they can do a better job than what he has already done. But we already know what the real reason is. President Obama is a black African-American and racism is the God given rights to the White America.

The Contraception Controversy

We have discussed the the true power of the "Woman" and how her power will subdue man and take over the world, we also spoke of of how men came into the ruler ship over the woman. *We said: "That there was a time when men were the slaves of women and for centuries on end.* The woman has always had the controlling power over men, but most men have always felt that they were the real power because the woman had allowed the man to take control and dominion over the earth. The male species has always wanted the power of the female gender, to secure this point, we only have to look at the **"CONTRACEPTIVE"** legislation that is now before the many Congressional Representative all over the Country. Rowe vs. Wade was just the beginning of the abortion saga. *When President Barack Obama said that he would bring about change that you could believe in, what did you think he meant by this statement? Surely change means different things to all people. for most of us we think change is just for the few and not for the many.* The Woman just began to vote in the past 100 years or so. The bigger question is: *"Why are Congressional Leaders so bent on controlling the reproductive organs of women they are seriously afraid of her power"?* It is like the woman can't control her own body and it is up to the man to decide this fact for her. This suggest that the woman is still a slave under Man Ruler ship and man has the power to develop laws to keep her in check. Man has always talked about the "Big Bang" Theory when the separation of the earth and the moon created a blast. but the true separation of the power was from the female gender to male, Now we must get ready for the real Big Bang as this is not a theory. The "Woman will take back the power from the male gender, the earth must be returned to its natural power. "The Woman".

Thank You Sincerely,
Charles Fletcher

Psychology of Money

Originally "Money" was design to take the place of bartering, People would trade just about anything to make payments to the people they owed a debt. prostitution was one of the greatest way of paying a debt, by which slavery became even more popular because the male gender thought that sex would nullify the debt. For centuries livestock and other agricultural items were bartered for sale or trade. Just before the advent of Julius Caesar the Emperor of Rome who first start putting his picture on coins, money was being used for payments and it became more popular and convenient for trade and exchange. Today the practice of bartering has a whole new meaning, but the ideas and principles remain the same. *The Rich and Wealthy Slave Masters of the world like the Koch Brothers can pick and choose any derelict that has the propensity to be lead by negative reasoning and a docile slave mentality that worships the addictive behavior of money will always have a partner in crime.*

Let us take this a step further, Mitt Romney the front runner for the GOP has bragged about how much wealth he has obtained and has demonstrated how he can use his wealth to win the nomination as a Republican for President of the United States. Today he has spent over $44.4 Million dollars trying to buy the office of the President. His opponent Rick Santurm has only spent about $3 million in his campaign and he has demonstrated that you really don't need a lot of money to win the votes of the American People. Most people believe if you have enough money, you are successful and you have made it in life. This is the most elusive of all thinking, Millionaires, Billionaire and Trillionaires have been chosen to guide the world in economic parity, But many who have this wealth has chosen other wise and have cause many to become homeless,hunger, death, suicide and destruction. We thought that the Church would bring about stability in communities of color, but have ascertained that the church is the root cause of violence and destruction in communities,the money collected after the church sermons are placed in the church volt or a bank for the Ministers use. In Chicago a lone there are so many stores front churches many as ten churches in a one block area and what are these churches doing for the community??????????? ....

NOTHING, not one thing. yet they open their doors every Sunday morning to make another collection as another profit for the clergy. *Where and when does it stop?*

Health Care Bill & The United States Supreme Court

Dear Mr. President:

Whatever the Supreme Court's decision is on The Health Care Bill, please know that the entire Bill will not be discarded, This could be a good thing, as this puts you even in a better position to "AMEND" the Bill to be inclusive of what the GOP is looking for (with reason) and put your Own analogy where it is needed in the Bill as an enforcement policy for health care. It only proves once again that the GOP want the Insurance Companies back at the table. Rather the Supreme Court act for the Bill or against the Bill this once again puts the President back in the driver's seat to give further directions for the implementation of the Bill.

Addiction in Human Behavior

The human body has many additive personalities, here are a few of these additions, money, drugs, sex, politics, religion, food, fabrication, mayhem, robbery, thievery, alcoholism etc. This is a short list for starters. *"Today additive personalities is the most serious of all psychological behaviors"*. Most people actually think that this is a natural phenomenon of human behavior. I beg to differ and would not subscribe to such behavioral conduct. *"Money"* appears to be the dominant addiction of the day., the more money you have the more you want, and once you find a way to multiply your wealth the more of the addition you pursuit, the more your personality become addictive to the method of obtaining more money. Money can only buy you so much, and after acquiring a house, automobile, airplane, boat, jewelry, clothing, investment for your children if you have any. etc. After that the individual began to indulge in another form of addition *"hoarding"* Money. The wealth acquired by the Rich and Wealthy Slave Masters of the world has hoarder this wealth and utilize this wealth to lord it over the masses. *"Drug*s" is a cultural past time rather the drugs are illegal or prescription, drugs help relieve the pains of reality and gives pleasure differently from a clear healthy mind respectively. There is plenty of money to be made from the sale and use of drugs rather legal or illegal. *"Politics"* like *"Religion"* has a behavior that has the ability to influence fabricated ideas to the masses, which translate into *Positive and Negative* behaviors of the people. To utilize a document call the United States Constitution that was written over 246 years ago, that is not conducive for the people in 2012 creates an analogy that places the American People thousands of years behind the times. As Americans, we only give the appearance that we are ahead of the times, however, in reality we are so far behind the times until the Baby Boomers generation is late in coming of age. Those who wrote the Constitution all had slaves and this document has never been amended to eradicate the racism content that it is protecting. *It is for this reason that racism still exist within America.* The United States Congress is quick to say that the Amendments of the Constitution had protected the American people from the pit falls of racism, but to which people were they speaking, the blacks of whites?. I beg the differ, **look at how they treat the President of the United States?** *You would think that President Obama was still a slave to the Rich and Wealthy Slave Masters of the World and in many ways he is.* "**Religion**" has been the culprit for retrograding the culture of human behavior, sending our intelligence backwards some 15,000 to 20,000 years. There was a time when religion was never mentioned in the history of the earth and the people were extremely talented and more progressive than they are today. There are certain men of wealth and power that pushes the agenda that American culture is the best in the world today. "**Food**" is a necessity to maintain life in the human body, it does not take a lot of food to fill the stomach but gluttony has increased the appetite of most human beings and this has become a past time for most people who are overweight. Food is an addictive behavior that is extremely hard to overcome and as we age it becomes even harder to bring our food intake under control. "**Fabrication**" is something that every human being has uttered at some point in their life, lying comes in the form of jokes, laughter, protecting a person's life and as a form of deceptive practices. "**Mayhem,**" today the murder rate has increased at 75% nationwide and will continue as we look upon our youth engaging in gang related activity as casualties of war in gang violence. "**Robbery**" is a behavior by which many factors are considered, poverty is one of the main reasons for robbery and greed is the ultimate desire for more money or financial gain and "**Thievery**" falls into that same category. and "**Alcoholism**" is also looked upon as a drug of choice. How can we reduce our addiction to these behaviors? "Energy" controls all of our body functions and Energy can cure us from all of these additive behaviors. Yes, it is hard but we must began to utilize the "Energy" within to overcome our addictions by simply turning our attention inward and contemplating on our own individual behaviors.

The Woman-Part III

Women are the true creators of all human life, they are "Female of The First Power in Human Creation", They are so ancient that the ancestors forever bow to their incredible power. They are truly a force to be reckon with.

Today we have encountered an attack on the woman's principles and values, they want to deny women birth control, over turn Obama care and send the health care system back to the wealthy insurance companies so much so that the Republican Party has developed an agenda to demonize women as a means to control her every move. Should they want to have an abortion, she would have to have a vaginal prob prior to any abortion. this is to say that women do not have control of their own bodies. This is also saying that the United States Congress has the authority as to what a woman can do to their own body and it does not matter rather the woman had been raped, sexual abused or otherwise. The whole premise of the GOP is to secure life when it is the womb. This is a prime indication that women are still nothing more than chattel slaves for the rich and wealthy slave masters of the world. This is no difference than how women are treated in Iraq, Iran, Afghanistan, Africa, Saudi Arabia, China etc. But when asked the same questions concerning men they have rejected any and all comments concerning men sexuality. Here is what most men will never understand, When the women began to unify their own thoughts of taking full control of the world, men will step up their assault on women, there will be unprecedented assaults on women physically, mentally, spiritually because men fear the power of the woman more so than the power of black and Latino America. White men do not want to see the woman making more money, taking over the health care system and believe me, they will do anything to keep the woman from obtaining their true natural power. But it is inevitable, and it is coming rather they like it or not and she will take the power boldly. Women that are aware of who they really are is waiting for the right time and moment to take this power back. As we look at the United States Congress and the so call Constitution which has given white

America the power to keep the masses enslave to a system that subvert the human consciousness to that lower than an animal. This is why when the President and members of Congress are sworn in to UPHOLD the United States Constitution, they have refused to Amend the document because that would take away the power of enslavement by which the United States Constitution supports the true nature of slavery. President Obama knows this and so does the Republican Party know and this is why they want to get President Obama out of the White House and turn the clock back to the good old boy network.

Part IV-The Woman

We have always said consistently that; if a person wants to better understand a thing, it is prudent that you go to the root cause. When you look at "Religion" you cannot help but wonder its meaning as to what it was trying to convey. In the Bible, Geneses talks about the creation of the woman, it said: ***"that the the woman was created from the rib of Adam"***. This teaches us just how ill-informed the male species really was and still is. They said that God created man and then created woman from the rib of the man, this could be this reason why God is always inferred to as He, HIM always manly or male dominate focus. It also demonstrates just how franc the male species was to harness the power from the woman. *Real power has always been with the Female Human Species.* **We have said that the entire creation is a scientific project in a living active motion,** as we meditate and travel to the Super-Subconscious state we can see that the woman is *the true scientist in creation*. The male species has always envied the woman and her awesome powers and wanted to emulate her skills but could never encounter the power of the woman. ***It was the woman that created the male species through a scientific project.*** It was the woman that understood the "X" and "Y" chromosomes that she harness inside her body, she has always known how the two chromosome could be separated and produced the male species. After she created the male species, she completed her task and allowed him to rule, She created him for her own pleasure. Through her tireless efforts after creating the male species she fell asleep and remain asleep for thousands of years, and dreamed of the havoc that we are experiencing today. She is now awakening from this deep sleep and she is about to call on the Four winds of "Energy", who has always bowed to her power. Today we call this power "Mother Nature". To further understand what the Old Testament was trying to convey, we now turn our attention to the New Testament where Jesus Mother, Mary gave a virgin birth to a child without the aid of a man, this gives reference to the true power of the woman. We have always said that we should not throw the baby out with the bath water when looking at world religion which is manmade.

Part V-The Woman

As we examine the Book of Genesis in the Bible we can conclude that the writers had written these saying in a way that would disturb the consciousness of those who read it. ***Today we must now unravel the secret mysteries of knowledge as it relates to the biblical references***. Many of us are so root ground in the literal meeting of the Bible until they don't know anything else and truly don't want to know anything else. For example, in Genesis, it said: "In the beginning God created the heavens and earth". My question would be how could God create the heavens and earth without naming all the other planets that were already formed long before the earth was formed? After the earth was formed and he seen that it was good, God said "Let ***"US"*** make man in our image and after our likeness and give him dominion over the heaven and earth, {*This dominion would also include the eating of the fruit on the tree of good and evil}*. The word US is plural, meaning that there was more than one God or persons at the time of man's creation. This also suggest that God could not nor did not create man by himself and that there were others around him to help at the time of man's deliverance. When reading the Bible, it skips over mountains of questions that is never brought to the reality of the conscious mind. Then there is the creation of the "Woman", The Bible never go into detail as to how the man or woman was created, It said man was created from dust, but how was he created from the dust? Additionally, since the image of God was that of another man, how is it that the woman was created from the rib bones of the man? ***This is so illogical until the writers of religious theology have made the analogy that man should never question the word of God"***. When speaking of the woman it said that the woman was made from the rib bone of man, just how can God create a woman from the rib of a man? *The writers did not want the readers to know that the real creators were the* ***"WOMEN"*** of that time period. Here is the giveaway, ***there was the serpent snake or reptile that spoke to the woman***, this serpent could have been a reptile of any kind, maybe even a shape shiftier as the high developed science was very extraordinary during the time of the creation of man. In the garden of good and evil, the serpent said to the woman that God told her not to eat of the tree and she thought that to eat of the tree she would surely die, the serpent said that God did not want her to eat of the tree because her eyes would become open to the true realities of life and death. So the woman ate of the fruit and shared the fruit with her husband after God had told him not to eat of that tree, this suggest *that the woman had great influence over the man and the man did eat of the fruit, he did what the woman suggested or told him to do.* but what kind of fruit was eaten? Most people thought that it was an apple. It does not say what kind of fruit was eaten. There are many missing pieces to the story in Genesis that was not told, but why? Where is the missing information? If we knew where the missing information was this could help unravel the mystery but the powers that be do not want the masses to ever know the real true science of the creation of man. The Vatican in Rome Italy is the keeper of all historical knowledge on the earth, and they guard it with high security and this knowledge is kept in a vault with highly sensitive electronics. The rich and wealthy male slave masters of the world does not want the real truth to be known or told to the masses. This would give away the true intent of the male species.

Women Will Never Ever Become Priests

It is true that there really is a "WAR ON WOMEN"

Please read the article below

Is there anything about this article that women do not understand?

In Part IV & V "The Woman" we shared with you where most of the world knowledge is kept as it relates to "The Woman" and it is for good reason, It is in Rome Italy at the Vatican among well-guarded security. If you have ever witnessed the dressing of the Pope, it is he that is emulating the female dress from his under garments to the crown on his head. The Catholic Church has good reason for not wanting the woman as a Priest. *It would be the end and conclusion of the male dominate rule as we know it worldwide.* We said in previous articles that the male dominance will come to an end, we can see this among the Rich and Wealty leaders of the world and the way they treat the women all over the world and especially in America. *Astrology has played a role in all human life as it was astrology that started the beginning of religion.* The High Priestess was always the "Woman" of high statute, the term Goddess originated from the readings in Astrology and the term God or the oneness of God was taken from the terminology meaning of the Goddess they wanted the Goddess looked upon as a lower statue than the male species. The Woman was always look upon as the one with true power until the rise of the male species, The Greek God Zeus submitted to her power. This was the beginning of the rise of the male species. Today Astrology is looked upon as a animated past time with no rooted beginnings just as the male dominance looks upon the woman as a past time sexual slave. Most women in the executive position are still less of a consequence to the male species because of the amount of money they were allowed to earn as a means to keep her quiet. *Today the executive woman has limited privileges when it comes to the real power of the male species as stated below* This is because the conscious and the sub-conscious mind, soul, spirit has been dialated with the ignorance of religion and has made the average religious believer reject any once of positive thought otherwise against religious beliefs. *It was first the Catholic Church that was responsible for the slavery of women, this was past own to other religions, and they rightfully are fearful of the woman coming into her true and rightful power, it is for this reason that the Pope and the Catholic Church truly fear the rise of all women.* When you look back in history you will find the "Goddess of Wisdom" was always a women of high statue, Nevertheless, the true history of the woman has been locked away from public scrutiny and the consequences are astonishing and astounding to the consciousness of a thinking person.

Enjoy!

Part II-Addiction In Human Behavior

In our last articles on *"Addiction In Human Behavior"* we did not address Guns, Sex, or Music addiction. All three of these addictions influence each other, Music can influence both sex and guns, as a person listen to the lyrics in a song or rap music along with the beat and sound of the music. Today our young artist and music entertainers knows that sexual lyrics in song or rap lyrics *sales,* and has the propensity to influence gun violence among gang members, drug dealers and prostitution throughout America. How can we reduce the recidivism rate in America? The first thing we need to understand is that sexual behaviors are induced on the surface of the conscious mind, especially with many adults and young teen age children. The sub-conscious mind, soul, spirit generally does not influence the sex drive, sex is always at the conscious level and not at the sub- conscious. *The sub-conscious will influence you not to do negative things but the conscious mind will over rule the sub- conscious and the individual will carry out what ever act the conscious mind tells it to do.* It is the sub-conscious that acts as the equilibrium for conscious behavior. It is the sub-conscious that always give the individual the option to either reject a negative act prior to the execution of the act. As we have said countless of times, an individual only has two choices to choose from, it is either *"positive or negative",* these are the only two choices you have and you do this at such a high rate of speed and we do this in a matter of a few seconds. Remember, the positive and negative also act just like a car battery, that has both a positive post and a negative post and it takes both positive and negative to start the automobile and to keep it running. We as human beings also utilize both the positive influences and the negative influences as we choose the directions we wish to go. Please don't get this twisted, these are the facts of everyday life.

Part II-Addiction In Human Behavior

In our last articles on **"Addiction In Human Behavior"** we did not address Guns, Sex, or Music addiction. All three of these addictions influence each other, Music can influence both sex and guns, as a person listen to the lyrics in a song or rap music along with the beat and sound of the music. Today our young artist and music entertainers knows that sexual lyrics in song or rap lyrics *sales,* and has the propensity to influence gun violence among gang members, drug dealers and prostitution throughout America. How can we reduce the recidivism rate in America? The first thing we need to understand is that sexual behaviors are induced on the surface of the conscious mind, especially with many adults and young teen age children. The sub-conscious mind, soul, spirit generally does not influence the sex drive, sex is always at the conscious level and not at the sub- conscious. ***The sub-conscious will influence you not to do negative things, but the conscious mind will over rule the sub- conscious and the individual will carry out what ever act the conscious mind tells it to do***. It is the sub-conscious that acts as the equilibrium for conscious behavior. It is the sub-conscious that always give the individual the option to either reject a negative act prior to the execution of the act. As we have said countless of times, an individual only has two choices to choose from, it is either ***"positive or negative"***, these are the only two choices you have and you do this at such a high rate of speed and we do this in a matter of a few seconds. Remember, the positive and negative also act just like a car battery, that has both a positive post and a negative post and it takes both positive and negative to start the automobile and to keep it running. We as human beings also utilize both the positive influences and the negative influences as we choose the directions we wish to go. Please don't get this twisted, these are the facts of everyday life.

Prayer Is The Acknowledgement Of The Power Within You

Many of us are totally baffled as to what "Prayer" actually means. Prayer is not a religious function as most people would associate with worship to a deity. The institution of "Prayer" dates back millions and millions of years long before religion was ever thought of. When we see the fetus inside the womb of the mother, that fetus is in a submission posture in the womb "Energy" has caused that fetus to develop, the brain and organs all have been formed and ready for birth, moreover, as we look at the fetus in the womb of the mother, it gives the impression that the fetus is in prayer. When a person prepare for a catastrophe either on a plane or tornado etc. they ask the person to get into the "FETUS" position. This is the body submission, ***but there is something more that is going on in the mind of the fetus.*** Most people don't even believe that the fetus is thinking while it is in the womb, many actually think that a child doesn't even have memory while it is in the womb, but the fetus hears what the mother hear, see what the mother see, and is feed what the mother eats. ***Remember, "Energy" controls the flow of all knowlege at all times.*** However, after the child is born the doctor in most cases will slap the fetus on the butt to hear the voice or sound of the infant. We don't give our children much credit for having intelligence while they are in the womb. ***The fetus is always in a stay of "Pray" while in the womb.*** When that child arrives in the world, the infant brings with them knowledge unbeknowing to its parents. All Infant are born to many different races of people, and they remain silent until they have learned how to speak the language of that people by which they were born to. In reality, when an individual prays, they turn their attention and focus inward to the power within. when you hear people talking to themselves, they are praying which is very healthy for the functioning of the brain. When you see children playing by themselves, they are actually praying and this help to develop their brain power and expand their intelligence. Then at certain ages the child might say something so profound that you would ask, how could that child know that at such a young age? When you Pray you are acknowledging the power thats within you, it does not matter which deity that you are praying too. Many people pray for bad and negative things just as people pray for good and positive things. There is an old cliche' that reads: *"Be very careful of what you pray and ask for"*.

Jealousy Can Be A Dangerous Behavior

Below is an email I received from a friend seeking advice on Jealousy, and I thought his questions were worthy to be shared with all.

I really admire your writings. At some point would you write your thoughts on Jealousy? Whether it be jealous between siblings, a mate, a friend having more materially or a higher job status, etc., people seem to harbor jealous feeling towards others that they perceive to have more. One person I know hates anyone that has achieved more than he and harbors hate within as a result. Sad, but true.

Thanks again Charles. Peace.

Hi Peter:

Jealousy is a very dangerous emotion when left unchecked. When a person is jealous that person does not measure up to the standards of positive emotions. remember "Energy" controls both positive and negative emotions, everyone will not show positive emotions or vice versa. Nevertheless, many can display negative emotions but out of that negativity some positive influence could arise and vice versa. balance or equilibrium has to be shared when negative emotions are present, meaning this, when you become aware of the negative influence you should wait until that person is alone and share with him some understanding and try to steer that person in a positive direction, However, you must be aware that they may not really want any understanding concerning their emotions. Their whole life could be based on negativity, this is why many times you can walk in a room and feel the negative vibrations all around you. *These people are insecure, fearful with anger, resentment and helplessness, many have deep sexual differences mostly in the male species.* There are many men that are jealous of their best friends, wives or girlfriends or another man's woman, or a friend of a jealous person would tell him how he had a long sexual intercourse with other women and men with deep jealousy feels anger either because the jealous person had bad experiences with women for reasons he would never admit. Premature ejaculation is one, small penis is another, unattractive girlfriend another, financially incompetent, not having an automobile, equal education to his friend and a whole host of things that brings on jealousy. We must as men overcome these bigotry ideas and thoughts. We are much more than the reflection we see in a mirror. As we stated in our article :" Our Greatest Struggle in Life is to Understand Who We Are". *Ben Jealous is the head of the NAACP, What a last name.*

Peter's answer to the email:

"What advice would you have to help a person to free oneself from the vicious grips of jealousy? Is this an intrinsic behavior or a bad emotion learned as a child or what"? Any suggestions would be greatly appreciated.

Thanks once again and have a great day.

Peter

Yes Peter:

Much of these behaviors are intrinsic and could have adolescent influence and has grown up within that person, my advice is this; *That individual needs to go within themselves into a deep meditation as to what their true interest are and what holds their attention spend on what is more important in their life, especially in addressing their own behavior.* Meditation is something that most people will find it hard to do, but once you start meditating you will began to see things you never seen before within your own personality. *There are many stages to mental development.* You must learn how to do this just as you learn how to do other things in your life. This is an area that most people find extremely challenging, because you are entering the conscious mind (the everyday stuff), then the Sub-conscious (you began to enter the deep meditation of Sub-Conscious Thought) many Yogis may call this the search for the *Kundalini* (the flickering light within) then the Super-Subconscious, (in this state of mental awareness, it will take you into a quantum trance of awareness, your soul began to see and hear other spirits around you). The next level is the *Mega Super Sub-consciousness*; this is an extremely rare entrance into mental awareness.

Power Speaks

We must get away from language that defend religion as a law, religion is not a law, and it has nothing to do with politics. The law and Justice are political concepts and has nothing what so ever to do with religious beliefs. When we look at the United States Constitution the language in the Constitution has nothing to do with religious concepts, this is why the First Amendment give the power of religion as an independent belief of the Constitution itself. We have a right to practice it, but it is not a law that governs. A person that does not believe in God has a right to practice their beliefs, just as those that believe in the God concept. We cannot force our beliefs on others, but we do have the right to criticize other beliefs. As we review a couple of the above biblical verses, we must have a clear understanding as to what these biblical verses truly mean., the question is ***do we accept the language of what is said literally or allegorically?*** Let us examine the first Biblical verse Isaiah 55:8 it reads "For My Thoughts are not your thoughts nor are your ways My ways, says the Lord. How do we look at this statement?

First, all human thoughts are implemented and controlled by "Energy" and there is no way of getting around this fact no matter how hard we try to make this something other than what is being said rather Positive or Negative, our thoughts are controlled by "Energy, you can debate rather "Energy" is the LORD, GOD. even Jesus. "Energy" does not limit your mind, soul, spirit to address the power and functions rather you call it "Energy", Lord or God. However, the proper thinking is to recognize that nothing in creation can move, or exist without "Energy" This includes God, Lord, Jesus or anything in a religious context or conscious thought, it must have "Energy" to survive. NOT ONE SINGLE THING IN CREATION can exist without "Energy" to be politically correct, rather you are honest in your convictions, right in your philosophy or whatever your thinking is, it is "Energy" that controls all thoughts and thinking of all created things.

I Corinthians 11:11, Nevertheless, neither is man independent of woman, nor woman independent of man in the Lord. This is an extreme contradiction, unless the thinking is in reference to impregnating the woman because the woman is totally independent of the man when you look at the very nature of the woman who has a monthly period, carry as child nine months before she gives birth to the child, a man cannot do either one of these things in the Lord or otherwise. The woman's physical body is totally independent of the man or male species. This is the problem when people start reading the bible, they can't seem to see the forest for the trees.

Thank You Sincerely,
Charles Fletcher

The Willie Lynch Concept

In my meditation time this morning, I had to be true to myself. I said, "Self, what is wrong with you? Why are you so angry? This is not your true self, or is it?" Selah. I had to really sit back and do an evaluation of my own soul. I needed to know how I could channel these feelings. Often times, we spend our time of prayer and meditation talking to Our Creator, however there are times that we need to talk to ourselves and then wait for him to talk to us. In my spirit man, I kept hearing the word "knew." Such a small word yet, a word full of power! I had to spend additional time in meditation and self-reflection to gain an understanding of such a small but powerful word. As I moved beyond my reasoning, I looked up the term knew from the English and Greek language. Knew in the English Webster Dictionary is defined as the past of know. Knew in Strong's Greek Concordance is defined as the term "ginosko", which means "to know" in a great variety of applications and with many implications [as follows] be aware, perceive, be resolved, can speak. I am aware that the term ginosko is defined in the Greek as an aspect or part of the mind however, in laments terms it is when you really know something deep down within, but without tangible proof. It is beyond your human intellect of reasoning and rationalization. As I correlated the two terms, along with my feelings, I began to come into a greater understanding of myself. Anger is an emotion given to us by God, our Creator. However, the strategic formula to being angry is knowing the root cause without your angry feelings being channeled in a destructive manner. Anger channeled the wrong way will cause you to miss the mark of purpose (Ephesians 4). In being true to myself, I had to admit that I am really sick and tired of being sick and tired of seeing us as Black people living beyond our privileges, gleaning from those who we deem to be great, but losing ourselves and dreams in the process. It is beyond my comprehension of how the trauma of slavery and victimization is holding us hostage. For many of us, our bodies are free, but our minds remain enslaved. As women, no longer can we continue to allow mistrust to permeate our souls, causing us to backbite and betray one another. No longer can powerful men and women call each other the "B" word. No longer can we continue the process of breaking each other down with the power of our tongue as opposed to building each other up. Many dispute the facts regarding the Willie Lynch training of the slave masters. Many dispute the fact that Satan is real. Many dispute the fact that God is real. I am tired of us debating and disputing the history of time through human intellect and reasoning only to abort our ginosko. Debating certain facts can be a waste of time, especially when we witness on a daily basis the damaging and destructive affects inhibiting us from excelling as a people at large. It is time to know that you know that you know that you know. It is time to put our hands to war in order to make wholesome changes occur in our homes, communities, churches, etc. Time is not waiting on you or me to figure things out within ourselves. All men know in pieces and in part. However, if we come together as dunamis women and real awesome men, especially in our black communities and put all our pieces together, then our power will be exuberated in the earth. Men and women will begin to ignite change for true wealth and prosperity, because change occurred in our minds. Make a decision today to lay your opinions and facts aside in aim to embrace the truth. The truth is we are perishing. Let's rise above ourselves in aim to stop the violence within our own souls, which is causing us to take advantage of others in order for us to succeed. Let's stop the violence within our own souls, which is causing us to assassinate the character of fellowman in order for us to look good in the eyes of others. Let's stop shifting the blame on others and take responsibility for our own actions and behaviors. I hope that this article made you angry, because I learned today that anger is good. My righteous anger comes to stir up yours so we can come together and stand united in aim to make a change, not just for ourselves, but for our future generations. In 1712, Willie Lynch taught the slave owners on how to treat a black man and woman in aim to break their souls (mind, will, and emotions) down, greatly diminishing our power. He admonished the slave owners to implement the teachings and strategies for a year, and by doing this, the breakdown of the black man and woman would last a minimum of 300 years. Well, we have embarked upon 300 years (2012) and NOW it's time to prove Satan, the devil, to be the liar that he is. Power Speaks… !

Ephesians 4:

Matthew 7:23

Hosea 4:6 Contributing Writer Charles Fletcher

As we reflect on the name Willie Lynch as mentioned above, the term Lynching was derived, and we should not confuse the picture of the slave with whelp marks on his back as Willie Lynch. Mr. Lynch was a slave owner and he was teaching other slave owners how to keep the slaves in a slave mentality and should that slave disobey the master, these owners had the right to lynch any slave at any time in front of all the other slaves so that the slaves would fear the slave owners. But more important than that, Mr. Lynch method was so antagonizing that he predicted that this method would last for another 300 years or more. Additionally, this mentality has lasted even unto this very day. It was these slave masters that introduced the slaves to Christianity and it's concept to the slave an d gave the bible as an alternative to save the soul of the slave should they disobeyed their master. Today the slave still uses the bible as the source that will save him from the hell fire of the slave master. When you ask the slave who wrote the Bible, he will say GOD and his son Jesus. The fear of the slave master is embedded in the weak-minded slave that still fears the white slave master even as we witness this embellishment today. It doesn't matter what religion a person practice, the teaching of Willie Lynch would still apply. *BECAUSE THE SLAVES HAD NOTHING TO HELP THEM, RELIGION WAS THE ONLY FORCE OR SPIRITUALITY THAT WOULD SAVE THEM FROM THE SATONIC MENTALITY OF THE SLAVE OWNERS. THE SLAVES WANTED SOMETHING TO* BELIEVE IN AND IT WAS THE SLAVE MASTERS THAT INTRODUCED THE SLAVE TO THE GOD CONCEPT. However, the real focus of the slave owners was to be looked upon as the God of the slaves and was and is the slave masters of today. Today the church has refused to disassociate itself from the white slave masters of today. We have all heard of the old cliché' *"If the white man does not say it, you can't believe it".*

Recognizing Change

I'm sure that every body at one time or another have had some kind of calamity of some sort, it may have been a money situation whereas you could not obtain the resources needed to get what every it was you needed, it could have been money to pay a bill, your mortgage, car note etc. Or it could have been that you had money to do all of these things, but you did not have the courage to tell your spouse that there was a co-worker that had feelings for you and you were afraid to tell that person that you truly love your spouse and you did not want to cheat on your spouse or start a relationship. Or it could have been that your boss gave a position to another co-worker that you thought it should have been given to you. These are just a few scenarios that we all face each and every day. *These feelings or emotions stems from negative and positive behaviors, none of us will maintain positive or negative behaviors all the time, nature does not require that you maintain positive or negative behaviors all the time, creation commands that you maintain balance throughout your entire life as hard as it is to do.* *You began to trade one issue for the next in your mind continuously.* Although these type of thoughts centers on both positive and negative behaviors, most of the time, this could be a warning to you of an upcoming change in your life. Many of us really do not want to change when these behaviors arise. Many want to remain in the same state of mind because of the enjoyment of their present state of mind. The whole objective in understanding Creation is to **RECOGNIZE CHANGE** when it approaches and be willing to change our state of mind to a higher level of consciousness or an altered state of mind. Many of us actually think that because we are living in luxury and content in the pleasures of life, we will never want to add anything else to this state of mind for the rest of our life. *Creation allows us to experience high levels of pleasure and for many their whole life will center on maintaining the simple pleasures of life. and there are many that live and die in poverty, however, even in this level of consciousness, there are pleasures in life that are never experienced by those who are rich and wealthy. The point here is this, we must all* *recognize change when it approaches our consciousness, and we must not be afraid to make the change when these emotions appear.* Life is an alternating current and much time there is a direct current. For many the change might make the person rich and the rich might become poor, but it is the change in creation that we must recognize. Many people that work on Wall Street, they see this change each and every day, so those that have the wealth to invest, they pay the knobbiest to keep the investment moving in their direction in more lucrative investments and higher dividends to remain in that rich and wealthy state of mind until the day they die should they make the right investments. On Wall Street the rich are made richer, and the poor are made worst.

Cutting the Salaries of The United States Congress

Dear Mr. President:

You have encouraged the American People to do more with less, how does this apply to the The United States Congress? Although the Congress is bent on cutting necessary programs that the majority of the American People actually depends on. Mr. President, not one time have the American People **heard you talk about cutting the salaries of your administration, or the United States Congress especially the House of Representatives and The United States Senate**. Please tell me Mr. President, is it true that a person should lead by example or is this all rederic and talk just for show? How can the American People depend on the Leadership in Congress when most of them are financially rich and they keep cutting the programs of the poor to make them even more richer? **If Congress does not care about the middle class, how can they possibly care about the underserved communities? They really do not care how the poor can progress or how poverty makes them feel, their main concern is how can they aquire and add another million to their bank account**. Mr. President this is an election year, and the people want to know and see that you are true to what you say. Please keep in mind that money does not make you the person you have become, it is your upbringing in poverty and your intellectual development that makes you who you are. You are constantly trying to prove who you are, you don't have anything to prove to Congress other than you are still the President of The United States.

As A Father, What Should you Be Thinking About On FATHER'S DAY?

Dear Fathers:

Let us put this in true perspective, a great percentage of men today are thinking about how they will acquire their next dollar and for many their next meal. We arrived here in this world alone, it does not matter rather you are a twin or sextuplets, you came out of the womb one at a time alone in your own body. *You arrived on the Planet Earth freely and everything you do on earth should be done freely.* The *"Energy"* in creation allowed you to come to this planet for specific reasons and to share your intelligence with others who were already here when you arrived. It does not matter what your intelligence is, rather it is negative or positive it has to be shared with the masses starting with your parents as an infant. We are the care takers of the planet Earth. Each and every single thing on this planet is under our authority to do as we please. However, we developed laws of attraction to stabilize the environment and economic clarity, this implies laws against violence, domestic violence, laws to protect wildlife, plants, water, air, etc. Today as a parent and father we should look real deep into our psychological being and ask our self, *"What happen to the Freedom in America"? "We are not free today and have never been free from the tyranny of slavery".* The Rich and Wealthy seems to glorify themselves in their wealth and care less about those that do not have. Please remember that: *"Work does not stop after you die and pass away".* It takes "energy" to live, it takes "energy" to work, it takes "energy" to die although energy is being extracted from your lifeless body. *That same "Energy" that was in your body moves on from your lifeless body to another dimension and given another assignment within this vast Creation, your work never stops but travels on into infinity.* Happy Fathers Day.

We Are The True Time Travelers

We are indeed **"True Time Travelers,"** we are forever traveling through the many dimensions of time, death being the transporter of this transformation. "Energy" is what cause the mind, soul, spirit to move from one dimension to the next. *Time merely suggests that our stay within a dimension is for a short, limited time period only.* **We can travel forward or backwards once we learn to quantum jump from our present state of consciousness into an altered state of consciousness.** The images of your physical body can remain in tack because of our thought patterns in behavior, controlled by "Energy". **We constantly create new images of ourselves as we advance in our intelligence and build upon our positive and negative images**. Example, just look at the clothing we wear, we dress ourselves from dead plants and animals, it is these living organisms in plants and animals that keeps the images colorful in ourvision and thoughts. It is the elements in the environment that keeps our images alive. **We see these images in our dreams and our everyday thoughts and we cannot deny the fact that it is "Energy" that keeps all of this alive and in motion.** *This is basic elementary education that should have been taught at every level of our educational system.* We need to understand the real reason why we are here and what our true purpose is for being here. **The pursuit of financial gain and religious beliefs has crippled the peoples thinking and has hindered many from understanding the true mission and purpose for being here on the planet earth**. Money and material pursuits has undermined our true purpose. *This type of mind enslavement has caused a serious illness and rif among the people, a diabolical, crippling disease of ignorance, docility and servitude among the masses.* Should we continue this focus on acquiring vast sums of money just to look like we are financially rich and stabile, we will never climb out of this state of mind, we will continue to think that money is the only salvation for our children and their generations to come, we will remain lost in this world of continuous political confusion.

The Office of the President od the United States of America is not for sale

Mr. President:

It was never the intent of the Founding Fathers that the President of the United States and that Office should be an auction for the highest bidder. The Office of the President can not be bought, only one vote from each person or individual, by the people of the United States that are born on it's shores. The First President of the United States was George Washington and was elected by a majority vote and no identification was necessary, no money was involved during that selection. Today the Republican Party has used money as the bargaining chip for the Office of the President. This was done because the United States Supreme Court Ruled in favor of CPAC money and big Corporations could give as much money as they like to any candidate of their choice. *This has caused an influx of donor contributions to those who will bow and do anything for the sake of money as we have seen with Republican Mitt Romney. Justice Roberts and the Republican Court made this ruling, and should Mitt Romney be elected as President, this would turn the principles of the United States Constitution on its head and violate the true principles of that document.* Justice Roberts recently made another Ruling on the Health-care Bill giving the Majority Ruling to the President Obama and the Democratic Party knowing that had he and the Republican Majority Court Overturned this Bill, that the Rich and Wealthy donors and big corporations would have had a field day with the Office of the President. *Justice Roberts is very much aware that he could not allow a Ruling to tilt the balance of power and allow the rich and wealthy donors to utilize their power and influence to subjugate the Office of the President of the United States. We strongly suggest that you President Obama go before the American People and make it crystal clear that the Office of the President of the United States is not for sale period and will never be for sale.* This was never the intent Mr. President. *You and the United States Congress has taken an oath to uphold the United States Constitution and today you and the Congress have made this document useless and a laughing stock in the eyes of the American People and the world.*

Particle Higgs Boson

Dear Colleagues:

The Particle Higgs Boson was discovered by the Hadron Collider in Switzerland, this finding raises serious questions about Scientist in general. When funding is needed for high profiled Physicist, the rule of thumb is to come up with a plan or finding that will look promising to investors and believable to the masses. Remember the original name for the Higgs Boson was *("The God Particle")* this suggests that the Higgs Boson was a religious connotation in search for the beginning of creation. Common since should tell the average thinker that *"there is no beginning of creation".* Creation was here when you arrived and will be here when you leave. ***No one, absolutely no one will ever, ever, ever find the beginning of creation.*** There will always be liars and fabricators that will pretend to think that they have found the beginning of creation or when the earth was formed, they can only guest at these questions not ever knowing when this ever happens utilizing the term *"THEORY"* as a matter of fact. The Particle Higgs Boson is one of many particles that are found, and scientist will continue to find other particles even greater than the Higgs Boson. The Universe is full of particles greater than the ones that have already been found. Many scientists have finally suggested that there might be other universes outside of our own universe. We wrote about this last year. Here is what common sense should tell the average thinker, *("of course common sense is not common any more")* if creation has created everything on this planet, all the other planets, stars, galaxies, atoms, protons, neutrons, electrons etc. and all in between as far as the mind's eye can see and understand, why should not creation expand to other universes outside of our own? When we study creation, we can see that each and everything in creation is multiplied and creation is constantly creating as we continue to move forward in our own lives., we all die and advance our Energy even farther than we are now. ***We continue to travel forward and sometimes backward in our experiences in other forms of creation in another dimension.*** This is why we "Time Travel". Our scientist are thousands of years behind in research as supported by our own educational system in the United States. Many of us refuse to travel inward to the energy within our own body in search for higher knowledge of self.

Most of us think that going to college will prepare us for the future, but how can we prepare our children for the future when we can't even understand the basic knowledge of our enter self? Education begins with your enter self, and your enter self is the working "Energy" with you. If you seek that knowledge of your enter self, you will find it. But remember, everybody's energy is not the same, some are extremely negative and others are extremely positive with a little of both in between.

Reality Challenge

The *"Greatest"* challenge in life is to understand *"Energy"* the source of all creation and the real reality of its use within our own human body. *which will require an enormous amount of discipline and foresight within our own soul, mind, spirit,* {all interchangeable}. Like all "Technology" it was created by Energy, and we must learn how it works. With technology, there is always something new coming down the pipeline. *"Energy "is that "God" that all religions worship.* Energy is what gives each and every single thing life. Your life Energy within your body does not die but leaves your body just as a leaf on a tree must depart in the fall. You cannot build a building without energy being the soul source of the brick and mortar. *All Universes, Planets, stars, gases, elements are all created by Energy.* There is no beginning of Energy which causes Creation, they both are one of the same and have always existed, it has been here and has no beginning and there is no end to creation.

Terrorist Threats against the First Lady?

Since President Obama became President, there has been continuous racist threats against his life simply because he is African American. But this new low is to attack his wife "The First Lady" by a police officer that was a part of her motor cad. When top officials ascertained this Officers intent, he was later taken off security for the First Lady and place on desk duty. President Obama needs to give another public address on race relations and conflict resolutions. *For someone of any race, color or creed who issues a terrorist threat against the wife of the President of the United States and later given a desk job, opposed to 'immediate termination of employment, placed in a jail cell in solitary confinement just as any other terrorist are confine with no bond, is the most outrageous of insurrections ever imposed on the life and wife of a setting President in American History.* We know and understand that our President is very patient when taking action, but for someone to give a terrorist threat against the life of your spouse, patients can be thrown out the window. Why would anyone want to harm Michele Obama? *She has done what no other First Lady has ever done in the History of any Presidential First Lady. Race hatred is one of the most diabolical behaviors in human development.* Here is what is central to all human life and those things that has life, it has no color and it is shared with each and everything that has life, even those objects that are said not to have life. It is the "Energy" within each one of us. *So why do we continue to practice racism when we all are connected to the same power that created us all?* Our skin color is design to show diversity, Charles Darwin wanted to show diversity in evolution, for many others there is diversity in psychology, science, math, technology etc. This is the real RACE and this has nothing to do with skin color nor does this make a difference in how much money a person have. Money is not the key to success. *Success is based upon the understanding of knowledge and how the wisdom should be used.* Energy created money as a means to border and trade, it was the negative and greedy slave masters that utilized money as the peniacal of success, and today more people place emphasis on acquiring as much money as they can as a means for financial success. This kind of thinking and understanding of knowledge is past on to their children and their Children's children and the consequences is what we are witnessing today in the personage of Mitt Willard Romney. ***As a person, it is imperative that we change our way of thinking about Race, the power of racism and its implications.***

To Heaven and Back

Dr. Mary C. Neal a Spinal Surgeon wrote a book entitle *"To Heaven and Back"* where she talks about her death experience while kayaking in a river in Chile. Her kayak tilt over and she was emerged under water, she remains under water until someone rescued her, *she was pronounced dead after about 15-25 minutes of resuscitation, she also said during her out of body experience that she felt herself pulling away from her lifeless body.* However, during those moments of unconsciousness she claim that she saw God, then later she said it was Jesus that came to her aid and said: "It was not her time and she had to return because there is something more she has to do, he also said the person in question told her that her son was going to die". About ten years later her son did pass away. Dr. Neal also said in her interview with Matt Laura on NBC Today Show indicated that she felt that she was at home and did not want to leave this serine place. As we closely analyzes Dr. Neal's statements, we must conclude and ask the pressing question,; *"what was it that was pulling away from her lifeless body"?* Most religious believers would say; *"that was her spirit, soul pulling away from her body".* Well, if that is true then *"Energy"* is the sole source of that spirit of mind, which all of these senses are interchangeable and produced by *"Energy"*. If a medical doctor has no formal education in environmental studies which was not required at the time of his training in medical school as stated by the *"Illinois Department of Professional Regulation"*, they will never know that Energy is the sole source of all life in creation. So, why wasn't environmental education a part of the basic curriculum in grammar schools, high schools, colleges and universities? *Why was this imperative knowledge omitted from the educational system? The rich and wealthy slave masters wanted the masses to remain ignorant of creation so that they could manipulate their mind by introducing religion as the controlling source of their existence. Consequently, when a person departs from this dimension, all that he has learned will come to light, this is done because "Energy" allows the thought process of that individual to continue as it did all of its life while inside that individuals body.* All of any person's thoughts and the process are created by "Energy". *Energy is the only true transparent entity in creation.*

Colorado Massacre

The Colorado Massacre has planted fear in the minds of most Americans and our children are devastated at the very thought of being murdered by any one like the gun man James Holmes. Today all across America like in Chicago, there has been numerous of murders of young children by gang bangers as many would expect by that kind of mind set. But the hoopla around the mayhem in Colorado was never expected by a student aspiring to acquire his PHD. ***Here is what has been missing from our human thoughts. as we ponder over why this happen at the time and place it happen.*** Prior to us arriving here on earth by way of our mother's womb. There were many souls gathered to discuss who would take the mission or assignment to act out this mission. James Holmes could have refused the mission, but he excepted the mission. In a sense we as human beings go through the same process prior to us coming to earth on our particular assignments. We actually choose our mission prior to our departure to earth or any other place in the Universe and beyond. We chose by seniority and our next assignment after we return back to the "Energy Grid" or if you will HEAVEN. ***At each and every funeral most clergy always describe the person who has just passed away as he has returned HOME***, and he will say; "you will see him or meet him again". The bigger question should be, why are there so many murders and so much death? Each and every time a person dies, there is always a teachable moment for those who are witnessing this turn of events. We have said time and again that we need to go within ourselves and take a serious observation as to what is truly happening with that Energy within us. Let us take a closer look at what we do when we pray. In religion, we claim that we pray to God and ask God to favor us and keep us safe from sin death and destruction, right? The reality is that you turn your attention to that "Energy" within you. ***You do this because your human body depends on that "Energy" for its sustenance, you know you must eat the nutrients in food, drink water for nourishment to sustain that life for your body.*** That "Energy within you does not require any of those physical things by which your body craves. ***The "Energy"*** *within you is the same "Energy" that cause the earth to spin, gravity to pull the magnetic energy to the earth, lightning to strike, thunder to roar, rain, hurricane, tornado's, earthquake, tsunami, fire, wind, ice, creation of planets, galaxies, stars etc. That same "Energy within you is totally independent of your physical body functions, yet it controls each and every function of your body. Therefore, at the time of your death, that "Energy" within your physical body will exist and return to its original home.* Your physical body is placed in the earth or cremated as it was only a vessel or vehicle for the use of "Energy".

Energy is the Architect & Archives
of all History and Memory

For the sake of understanding the history of "Energy" you must know that "Energy" has no beginning and no end, to take this a step further, if you could live the many lives in search for the beginning of "Energy you could never ever find it. *It would be like taking the tallest building on earth stacking it a top of the highest mountain then multiplying that height by the circumference of the universes one thousand trillion times, and of course that would be a number unreachable and once that could be attainable there would be another number even larger than that one.* Energy has always been here, the earth has transformed over the many years trillions and billions and millions of times, nothing, absolutely nothing stays atop of the earth forever, because evolution always bring about the change on the earth. Just look at the climate change. *"Energy is in each and every single thing on and inside the earth, it allows many things to exist for thousands of years to allow the elements in creation, man, animals, insects, fish etc.to learn and grow from these objects of life. Having said this, there is another level that all life must enter, when we say life we must understand that all life is nothing more than "Energy" in a living active motion*. This energy is in the atoms, neutrons, protons etc. this same "Energy is in insects, fish, animals, and humans just as it is in bowels of the earth and all other planets, stars, and moons, etc. If we continue to focus our attention on the material things in our life and not recognize the preparation for our next transformation, we are neglecting the real purpose of our mission here on earth and in this dimension. *Every one will not adhere to the reality of this life because of the hoodwink, bamboozles and criminology imposed upon the masses by the slave masters of the world. Politics and religion has taken our eye off the ball of reality, because of that belief system it has trapped many in wars of deceptive behaviors.* Has it ever accrued to you that "Energy" as we know it today has created other dimensions far greater than this one with more wealth than the present? *Many have become so in love with this creation that they would want reincarnation just to return to this lifestyle with all of its deceptions and that is also possible as part of your own belief system,* however, for many more, they want to advance to greater dimensions that will impel them to higher levels of consciousness in creation. In closing, the next time you walk out of your home into this wide-open outer space, just look around you and tell yourself; *"all of this creation is all mine". In truth it is yours* because of the "Energy" within you is also connected with the "Energy" that is all around the external life of you.

Implications of Change

When President Barack Obama talked about *"change"*, most Americans did not and still do not understand the implications of *{CHANGE}*. The word *ignorance* is taken from the word *ignore*. When we ignore a truth or fact, for whatever reason we place ourselves in the state of ignorance. Change on the other hand provides the opportunity for us to address our ignorance by changing the way we think about things. *If a person is religious, CHANGE also means that we must change the way we see religion and its implications.* Most religious believers are satisfied with their religion and refuse to change the way they see life because of the FEAR of God. *They hate to think about objecting God and the bibile from their religion. That is because this is all they know it is like being imprisoned as a slave and it is the slave masters who wrote the bible and they wanted the slaves to take on this fear in their hearts.* So even if they thought about rejecting God that fear would cease them by an over whelming sense that would embrace them like a coat on an cold day. They become *"EXTREMIST"* in religion. This was the intent when the bible was written. *These religious people become extremely superstitious, and they fear change and reject change and the consequences are staggering.* When we look at the many wars worldwide, domestic violence in America, death of young children, people will take to the streets in protest by marching but want lift a finger to stop the violence and the only thing most people will say is that: *"God works in mysterious ways".* When you start talking about ignoring their religion they do not want to change their beliefs. Otherwise, whats the purpose of change? *Change means we must take a total change in the way we think about each and everything we do. Creation is changing every fraction of a second and sooner so why are we not changing?* We remain on the same page doing the same thing over and over and over again for our total life. It is the rich and wealthy slave masters that keep their feet on the necks of the poor and middle class because they are the leaders in religion. It is as simple as looking at how the religious right is treating President Obama. The President cannot bring about the necessary change we need by himself, he is in need of every body's help. *We must stop believing in religion and start believing in that "Energy" within us. It is that "Energy" within us that will bring about the necessary change in our life. That is the real so call God that all religions worship.* "ENERGY" is the ultimate change in all life in this world and the next.

Who will climb the Mountain
That is Steep?

What is a Mountain that is Steep? It is a mountain that is perpendicular in nature, it is vertical (straight up and down) however, most mountains are not perpendicular, they have horizontal steps and crevices which would make the climb very difficult. Many men have climb high Mountains like *"Kilimanjaro"* many have died trying to get to the top, some have succeeded, and many have not. *To climb a physical mountain is very difficult on one hand and for many it's like child's play comparing to a mounting that is steep, because after you have climb the mountain and reach the top, that is as far as you can go.* A mountain that is steep is of high intellect, for example, *all knowledge is always descending and ascending simultaneously. It is "Energy" that causes this to happen. "Energy" is the only entity that can pierce the skull with direct contact to the brain when needed, this is done because of the "Energy" within the human body is always in contact with the external "Energy" outside the body, this operates as a "Magnetic "Energy" Field." It is the "Energy Grid" that has the power to call all individual energies within the human body at will, at any time or place.* Most scientist are still struggling to ascertain how knowledge is formed in the brain but neglecting the fact of high intelligence that knowledge is formed in the "(*Ooosphere of the mind*).and *what is the mind, soul, spirit but the "Energy" within us?* Nevertheless, it is "Energy" that controls all knowledge, wisdom and understanding of all things created.

Energy is the true Olympian of Life

The 2012 Olympics is a reminder of the "Energy" within the human body and how the human body can expand it's cartilage in acrobatic movements with enormous discipline to be used and become a champion in the games of choice. We should acknowledge the Greeks for originating these games in the beginning. *These Olympic Champions are in these arenas that was once a place to challenge an opponent to the death and many contenders lost their life in these arenas until Emperor Theodosius decreed in 393 A.D. that these religious cults be banned.* These cults were linked to to the Cult of Zeus, the first ancient Olympic was traced as far back to 776 B.C., it was dedicated to the Olympian god's and was staged on the ancient plains of Olympia. The importance of these games today was and still is a religious ritual and the participants owe homage to the religious Olympic gods of yesterday. *It really boggles the mind to know and think that most people cannot recognize the "Energy" of life within their own human body and not recognize the same "Energy" that is found in each and every single thing in creation and beyond.* It is utterly impossible to point to anything in creation and not recognize that "Energy" created each and every single thing we can imagine on earth, in the universe, and beyond. *The Olympic Games should open the doors to the human psychic how important the use of "Energy" is to everything around us.* However, most Christan's would believe that God created Energy, but any person of sound mind and intelligent thought knows that God could never exist unless God had Energy as a life source, nothing can move in creation without "Energy" being its source of its existence. Secondly, you would have to say which came first 'the chicken or the egg', God or "Energy"? *The entire creation is "ENERGIZED" meaning this, that each and Everything has to have "Energy" before it can come to life this would include the so-call God. If there was ever a God in creation it would have to be "ENERGY."* When a person goes to pray, what is it that the person turns their attention to within themselves? You close your eyes, and you pray to WHAT? You pray to that "Energy within you as the only source of your own existence. Your personal "Energy" is separate from your physical body, yet it controls everything within your body. *"Now that is a true Olympian."*

"Jezebel the Spirit of Manipulation and Witch Craft"

Audley Redwood has sent you a message.

Dear Friends, our books called, Jezebel the spirit of manipulation and witchcraft and The Crucified Seed is in Barnes and Nobles Bookstores. As esteemed friends we were hoping that you would purchase copies. Thank you kindly,

Dear Audley:

I do not believe in any religion, and I have read portions of your book *"Jezebel the Spirit of Manipulation and Witchcraft"* As quoted; *"Some people talk about The Jezebel spirit because this is the kind of spirit that was working powerfully through the Queen Jezebel a Sidonian princesses who married King Ahab of Israel. (See Revelations 17.6)*. As quoted; *"There are serious problems with Jezebel spirit in many churches (See christian faith.com."* The *"Crucified Seed"* also deals with the religious concept of the cross of Jesus, *"So there we are again on the top of the mountain with God"*. In my article we talked about what happens after a person reaches the top of a mountain. There is no place else to go but to descend down the mountain from which you climbed. That is if you are not over taken by calamity. Audley, "Energy" is the only entity that cause the human body to move, live and die. *Nothing in creation can move without "Energy." ABSOLUTELY NOTHING!*

   God cannot exist without Energy giving it life. All Religion is totally unnatural and like many religious books it always focus on what someone else has said and not about what you as an individual have said. Religious people will quot biblical verses until the cows come home but cannot quot anything from their own mind. As you read the bible you are reading what someone else wrote from the influence of rich and wealthy slave owners. Please remember that Black people were not the only chattel slaves. Slavery has been here for centuries on end with all races. Please keep this in mind when you write your next book, many write books for money and to keep the minds of the masses in ignorance, many write to keep food on their table but how many can re-write a bible that will quot the knowledge of today. This is why there is so much ignorance in the world. You must learn to write about this time you are living in, this dimension, this time of created "Energy". Jezebel was a time in past history as was the so-call Jesus. *If you do not understand your past, you can never know your future.* All those who wrote the bible was murdered afterward so that the people in the future would never understand the real truth behind these writings. We all have the right to believe what we want to believe and I will support you on this issue. Nevertheless, you should go within your own mind, soul and spirit and search for the real truth within you, the "Energy" within you is the key to a higher knowledge than what you have already written. Thank you for sharing.

Jezebel the Spirit of Manipulation and Witch Craft-II

I was in the middle of writing my next article, but you have raised an issue that I need to address, and that is this: Most people do not realize that slavery has place a lock and Key upon our children through the educational system, meaning this; *"today our schools are teaching our children how to become better slaves to a system that has polarized our country. **When the slave masters allowed African American to read and attend public schools, it was the slave masters that controlled the curriculum of all the educational institutions nationwide with the idea and intent that white children would have more of the access to higher education than Blacks**.* and furthermore, Blacks would be taught the same education, but it had to be separate but equal. That scenario was false because white children would receive the better books to educate them and Blacks would get literature that was about five to ten years behind white children. This is the same system today only it is more technological than it was a few years ago, we call this "high tech lynching". ***Audley, "Environmental education was never taught in public schools until just recently, about several years ago with help of Chicago State University. I have personally worked with quite a few Universities across the Country with a focus on illness, disease, behavior, death and the effects of magnetic energy fields".*** The reason why environmental education was omitted from our educational system was because most educators really did not understand what the environment is and what it does. Audley, I truly understand where you are coming from when you say:*" **Your faith is in the Lord Jesus Christ and your "Energy" is the Holy Spirit".*** However, you must look deeper into your own psychic mind as to what is really happening around you. Just look around you and tell me what you see? ***There is not one single thing you can point to on earth or in the universes that was not created by "Energy" in the environment***, **NOT ONE**. Let us take this a step further, take a look at your own physical body, your blood, veins, organs, brain etc. all is controlled by the "Energy" within you. That "Energy" within you is separate from your physical body, and when you die, that "Energy" within you will separate itself from your body leaving it lifeless. Your body will be buried in the earth or cremated, and your "Energy" will return to the all-powerful "Energy" Grid. *That spirit, mind or soul you call holy is nothing more than the "Energy" that you experience each and every day, through wind, rain, earthquakes, hurricane, tornado's trauma, snow all created and controlled by "Energy". Most religions refer to God, Allah, Jehovah, YWAY etc. as HE, yet they deny women the right to become Preist, Cardnals in the churches and mosques.* This was totally discrimination against women. *But Energy is "Translucent" meaning that it is not male or female, black or white, "Energy" is all transparent.*

The Transparent Power of Energy

Charles, all this points to the greatness of God that he would create someone like himself that is full of power to overcome much and achieve dynamic results.

Someone that just doesn't have the ability to think but also to create by simply using words.

Someone that because they know who they are and who he is, can call things into existence that the world have never seen and yet they are only finite beings?

God has put this tremendous glory in man (human) and he wants to give you, Charles, a heavier weight of his glory.

God bless you, Audley

Remember Audley:

That words are created and energized by "Energy". the words on this email is generated by "Energy". To think that God created anything in creation is a misnomer, *it is like saying that God came from nowhere without "Energy" and that God is above the Energy that created the God?* This kind of thinking puts the mind on the level of Houdini or David Copperfield. Audley.\, Magic is produced by the slick of the hand, the magician can always explain how the trick is done, *if I understand you correctly, you are saying that God can't even explain how his own energy and power is obtained and used? Audley,* Absolutely Nothing in creation can be created without "Energy" **NOTHING!** Try checking this out for yourself. The word God was invented in Africa and later the Greeks immortalized this terminology. It was originally referred to as the ruler in the skies in Astronomy and Astrology. They later began to tell fables about the Zodiac that was design by the elder physicist, later the God Zeus was invented to illustrate the power of Astronomy and Astrology for the formation of the Zodiac. Religion became predominate among those who practiced Astrology and today we can see that this religious practice still exists. Like yourself and millions like you they still believe in the power of Zeus.

Balance=A State of Equilibrium

We can never talk enough about *"Balance." NEVER!*. Counterpoise or Equipoise is shifted from one side to the other. *Also it means a mental steadiness or emotional stability, habit or calm behavior, judgment.* We can ask the personal question to ourselves. *"Am I balanced in my thinking, my work, play, sex, behavior, judgmen't? etc.* Today we see an imbalance in our politics, religion, economy, war, wealth,etc.The rich and wealthy feeds on an imbalanced economy, look at the Republican Party a good example is watching the amount of money that is used to elect Mitt Romney as President. *"Balance"* would suggest that those with wealth should share their wealth with the masses of people that are in need. However, today *"Balance"* is irrelevant to those who have abundance of wealth. When looking at things that are *negative* and *positive* we can see how *"Balance"* plays a unique part in stabilizing these two entities. To be honest the whole world is out of *Balance* and this practice of imbalance has put a struggle hold on the economy and the masses worldwide. When the mind of the rich and wealthy began to pool their resources to take control of the Office of the President not knowing what the Office really stand for, only that if their wealth could control this office, it could push the masses backward to the good old boy days. This is a prime example and indication that the rich and wealthy does not care about those who have less. Their whole objective is to acquire and maintain as much wealth as they can muster. Where is the *"Balance"?* Here is the pressing Question without ambiguity: *"How can we the poor take back our wealth from the rich?*

Images in Dreams

There are positive and negative influences of "Energies" that are constantly moving within your body and if they are not properly "Balanced as we have discussed, that person or individual will become imbalance and select negative or positive behavior as a result of their own thinking. When we are asleep and began to dream, many times the images in our dreams might place us in a remote place that you might have seen before and you might not, maybe you are being chased by someone, or something, an animal (a real nightmare) and it is close on your heels. "Energy" might intervene and awaken your body before you are captured, or you might get consumed by that thing that over powered you and this could lead to a heart attack and you never awaken again or you become the thing that was chasing you. You awaken as though you had been running and out of breath. This is an indication that your "Energy" had been in a chase while your body was sleeping. "Energy" is a very illusive entity and has direct contact with the "Energy" that surrounds you at all times. At this level of thinking you have moved to a higher level of consciousness.

Here is something to add to the article *"Complexity of Dreams"* that we did not say. As common people we have so much going on in our mind that we just do not think about the real things that keeps us alive. Our bodies gives us the sensation that we are breathing but all the while it is the "Energy" within us that keeps our body in an active living motion. The greatest thinkers in the world does the exact same thing that we are doing each and every day. That person could be the greatest professor, at the greatest university, yet to address a point of view to his challenging students, that professor must do research and go *within him/herself to search for answers* that the student needs to move them from point A to point B of any given assignment. There is a power in each and every individual that can rise up at any commanding thought and advance that individual to a higher level of intelligence by challenging your own thoughts and the way you think about things. If you believe in yourself. However, *you must examine the process by which you think about things and that is the "Energy" that gives your whole body the imaginary thought and power to act as if you are in total control. "Energy" gives you the impression that it is you that is doing the thinking but it is "Energy" that does all your thinking for your physical body. Your body is being energized by "Energy" to function as it does.* Nevertheless, it is that "Energy" within you that controls your physical body. *The lack of knowledge feeds the ignorance within those who cannot an refuse to think for themselves.*

2012 Election

This is the year for the people of the United States of America to elect the right person to Lead our Country to a more prosperity in the 21st century. *I have received literally hundreds of emails from both political parties requesting donations because one party has raised more money than the other. Many have utilize money as the pivoting point to outspend their opponent. Using money to make more money and to high light how the rich and wealthy has prospered by using money to make more money.* **Debt over powering equity.** President Obama must use dramatic illustrations and demonstration as to how He intends to jump start the economy and develop new employment for the unemployed, negative campaigning can overpower the positive if there is no aggressive focus on change and how that change can and will help the economy. Nevertheless, those who are wide awake will support President Obama because they know what the President is trying to achieve. ***This election is not about who has the most money***, it is about rising to the challenges of change by solving immediate problems. The change to remake America is to recognize the opposition and its failures, it taken George W. Bush 8 years to bankrupt the economy, yet the opposition want the American people to think that the President must turn the economy around in four years. ***President Obama stated in his inauguration speech that it would take more than four years to correct the bankrupt American economy.*** That is not a proper balance. If the distribution of wealth is unbalance, just how can a balance in job creation would change within four years? From the beginning, Racism has dictated the posture as to the progress of President Obama. ***From the onset of the Obama Administration Senator Mitch McConnell has indicated that he wanted to make President Obama a one term President and for sure, the Republican Party like Rush Limbaugh has agreed that they wanted President Obama to fail.*** But the President has an open record of his achievements and accomplishments he has done over 75% of what he had promised the American people rather you agree or disagree. ***Because "Energy" is the*** *controlling life source of all change and achievements, "Energy" will* *always work with the power to change rather we like it or not this is* *what "Energy" does.* "Energy" will always bring about change to all things *in life,* *"Energy" is Life Abundantly.*

Keep It Moving

Frank Schaeffer is a New York Times best-selling author. Obama Will Triumph—So Will America

By Frank Schaeffer

Before he'd served even one year President Obama lost the support of the easily distracted left and engendered the white hot rage of the hate-filled right. But some of us, from all walks of life and ideological backgrounds—including this white, straight, 57- year-old, former religious right wing agitator, now progressive writer and (given my background as the son of a famous evangelical leader) this unlikely Obama supporter—are sticking with our President.

Why?—because he is succeeding.

We faithful Obama supporters still trust our initial impression of him as a great, good and uniquely qualified man to lead us.

Obama's steady supporters will be proved right. Obama's critics will be remembered as easily panicked and prematurely discouraged at best and shriveled hate mongers at worst.

The Context of the Obama Presidency

Not since the days of the rise of fascism in Europe, the Second World War and the Depression has any president faced more adversity. Not since the Civil War has any president led a more bitterly divided country. Not since the introduction of racial integration has any president faced a more consistently short- sighted and willfully ignorant opposition—from both the right and left. As the President's poll numbers have fallen so has his support from some on the left that were hailing him as a Messiah not long ago; all those lefty website's and commentators that were falling all over themselves on behalf of our first black president during the 2008 election.

The left's lack of faith has become a self-fulfilling "prophecy"— snipe at the President and then watch the poll numbers fall and then pretend you didn't have anything to do with it!

Here is what Obama faced when he took office—none of which was his fault:

An ideologically divided country to the point that America was really two countries

Two wars; one that was mishandled from the start, the other that was unnecessary and immoral

The worst economic crisis since the depression

America's standing in the world at the lowest point in history

A country that had been misled into accepting the use of torture of prisoners of war

A health care system in free fall

An educational system in free fall

A global environmental crisis of history-altering proportions (about which the Bush administration and the Republicans has done nothing)

An impasse between culture warriors from the right and left

A huge financial deficit inherited from the terminally irresponsible Bush administration.

And those were only some of the problems sitting on the President's desk! "Help" from the Right?

What did the Republicans and the religious right, libertarians and half-baked conspiracy theorists—that is what the Republicans were reduced to by the time Obama took office—do to "help" our new president (and our country) succeed?

They claimed that he wasn't a real American, didn't have an American birth certificate, wasn't born here, was secretly a Muslim, was white-hating "racist", was secretly a communist, was actually the Anti-Christ, (!) and was a reincarnation of Hitler and wanted "death panels" to kill the elderly!

They not-so-subtly called for his assassination through the not-so-subtle use of vile signs held at their rallies and even a bumper sticker quoting Psalm 109:8.

They organized "tea parties" to sound off against imagined insults and all government in general and gathered to howl at the moon.

They were led by insurance industry lobbyists and deranged (but well financed) "commentators" from Glenn Beck to Rush Limbaugh.

The utterly discredited Roman Catholic bishops teamed up with the utterly discredited evangelical leaders to denounce a president who was trying to actually do something about the poor, the environment, to diminish the number of abortions through compassionate programs to help women and to care for the sick! And in Congress the Republican leadership only knew one word: "No!"

In other words the reactionary white, rube, uneducated, crazy American far right, combined with the educated but obtuse neoconservative war mongers, religious right shills for big business, libertarian Fed Reserve-hating gold bug, gun-loving crazies, child-molesting acquiescent "bishops", frontier loons and evangelical gay-hating flakes found one thing to briefly unite them: their desire to stop an uppity black man from succeeding at all costs!

"Help" from the Left?

What did the left do to help their newly elected president? Some of them excoriated the President because they disagreed with the bad choices he was being forced to make regarding a war in Afghanistan that he'd inherited from the worst president in modern history!

Others stood up and bravely proclaimed that the President's economic policies had "failed" before the President even instituted them! Others said that since all gay rights battles had not been fully won within virtually minutes of the President taking office, they'd been "betrayed"! (Never mind that Obama's vocal support to the gay community is stronger than any other president's has been. Never mind that he signed a new hate crimes law!)

Those that had stood in transfixed legions weeping with beatific emotion on election night turned into an angry mob saying how "disappointed" they were that they'd not all immediately been translated to heaven the moment Obama stepped into the White

House! Where was the "change"? Contrary to their expectations they were still mere mortals!

And the legion of young new supporters was too busy texting to pay attention for longer than a nanosecond. "Governing"?! What the hell does that word, uh, like mean?"

The President's critics left and right all had one thing in common: impatience laced with little-to-no sense of history (let alone reality) thrown in for good measure. Then of course there were the white, snide know-it—all commentators/talking heads who just couldn't imagine that maybe, just maybe they weren't as smart as they thought they were and certainly not as smart as their president. He hadn't consulted them, had he? So he must be wrong!

The Obama critics' ideological ideas defined their idea of reality rather than reality defining their ideas-say, about what is possible in one year in office after the hand that the President had been dealt by fate, or to be exact by the American idiot nation that voted Bush into office. Twice!

Meanwhile back in the reality-based community—in just 12 short months—President Obama:

\# Continued to draw down the misbegotten war in Iraq (But that wasn't good enough for his critics)

\# Thoughtfully and decisively picked the best of several bad choices regarding the war in Afghanistan (But that wasn't good enough for his critics)

\# Gave a major precedent-setting speech supporting gay rights (But that wasn't good enough for his critics)

\# Restored America 's image around the globe (But that wasn't good enough for his critics)

\# Banned torture of American prisoners (But that wasn't good enough for his critics)

\# Stopped the free fall of the American economy (But that wasn't good enough for his critics)

\# Put the USA squarely back in the bilateral international community (But that wasn't good enough for his critics)

Put the USA squarely into the middle of the international effort to halt global warming (But that wasn't good enough for his critics) #Stood up for educational reform (But that wasn't good enough for his critics)

Won a Nobel peace prize (But that wasn't good enough for his critics)

Moved the trial of terrorists back into the American judicial system of checks and balances (But that wasn't good enough for his critics)

Did what had to be done to start the slow, torturous and almost impossible process of health care reform that 7 presidents had failed to even beginv(But that wasn't good enough for his critics)

Responded to hatred from the right and left with measured good humor and patience (But that wasn't good enough for his critics)

Stopped the free fall of job losses (But that wasn't good enough for his critics)

Showed immense personal courage in the face of an armed and dangerous far right opposition that included the sort of disgusting people that show up at public meetings carrying loaded weapons and carrying Timothy McVeigh-inspired signs about the "blood of tyrants" needing to "water the tree of liberty". (But that wasn't good enough for his critics)

Showed that he could not only make the tough military choices but explain and defend them brilliantly (But that wasn't good enough for his critics)

Other than those "disappointing" accomplishments—IN ONE YEAR—President Obama "failed"! Other than that he didn't "live up to expectations"!

Who actually has failed ... are the Americans that can't see the beginning of a miracle of national rebirth right under their jaded noses. Who failed are the smart ass ideologues of the left and right who began rooting for this President to fail so that they could be proved right in their dire and morbid predictions. Who failed are the movers and shakers behind our obscenely dumb news cycles that have turned "news" into just more stupid entertainment for an entertainment-besotted infantile country.

Here's the good news: President Obama is succeeding without the help of his lefty "supporters" or hate-filled Republican detractors!

The Future Looks Good!

After Obama has served two full terms,(and he will), after his wisdom in moving deliberately and cautiously with great subtlety on all fronts—with a canny and calculating eye to the possible succeeds, (it will), after the economy is booming and new industries are burgeoning, (they will be), after the doomsayers are all proved not just wrong but silly: let the record show that not all Americans were panicked into thinking the sky was/is falling!!!!!

Just because we didn't get everything we wanted in the first short and fraught year Obama was in office not all of us gave up. Some of us stayed the course. And we will be proved right.

PS. If you agree that Obama is shaping up to be a great president, please pass this on and hang in there! Pass it on anyway to ensure that his "report card" gets the attention it deserves.

Understanding Sexual Behavior

Sex is Extremely pleasurable yet it is totally out of control as an e-motion. *Do we really and truly understand the purpose of sex and the many acts of sex with a partner, other than what we have been taught?* Let us take a closer look at sex and its implications. Today we see the pleasures of sex as a goal to be achieved, it is a physical energy that will drag the conscious and the subconscious to a mental break down. The greater world population indulge in the sex acts on a daily basis some time five and six times a day, their mind is consumed with sexual thoughts. This promotes rape, child abuse, mayhem, violence and many dysfunctional behaviors. *The value system for proper sexual behavior and relationships has been turned upside down. Most people look at sex as a past time with nothing else to substain their consciousness. We have understood that women after a certain age develop menopause and just recently, scientist has discovered that men also will develop menopause at a certain age.* So they came up with a medication that will stimulate blood flow in the male penis to give him an erection, medication like Viagra, Cielis and other paraphernalia, there are all kinds of sexual enhancement drugs such as marijuana cocain etc. What science is saying, is that mother nature can take a back seat to human sexuality. Many women always ask the question to men: *"Can you get it up"?* There are many men that can get up with a little help but there is a bigger question: *"Are men afraid to except the fate that menopause is a fact of life for all men and that sex will become a thing of the past in their life."?*. Let us look at this another way, the youth at the early ages of one years old to puberty they are celibate even into later years unless peer pressure get the best of them, or if they watch their parents engage in the sexual act. However, there are also youth that obtain menopause at a much early age. A urologist once said that: "no one have to have sex if they do not want it. Sex is not a thing that adults or young people has to have just look at the monks and some Catholics, it is only necessary for reproductive growth. Slavery was and is the culprit for promiscuous behavior. and slavery has been around for hundred of thousands of years, it is older than prostitution, because the prostitute becomes the slave of sexual encounters. To understand change is to except your natural human development. ***Proper communication and understanding is the highest of all knowledge, wisdom and intelligence.***

Religion in a Time Warp

We have said many times in the past that America has offered its freedom to all people around the world along with many third world countries. But are we truly looking at the religious component in America and looking at other religious beliefs around the world in comparison? Let us take a closer look. In America we brought the Christian Religion as our principle beliefs from as far back as the birth of Jesus. *This analogy places the religious concept backward some three thousand years. It is understood that the American people of today supports those ancient times as to what those people believed during their time period.* To take this a step further, the politics in America still utilize the United States Constitution as a document written in the 17th Century as a guding law with Amendments that has no place with the people of our own times. We have the power to write our own laws that are applicable to our own daily times. We should not be utilising an out dated documents and other religious writings thinking that the ancient writing are applicable to our own time.

This same example is seen with those that believe in Islam around the world. They are bent on utilizing a belief that was formulated some thousands of years ago as the ultimate religious belief. *Consequently, we are dealing with a mass of religious be livers that are stuck in a time warp of religious beliefs. It is like we don't have the courage to write our own bible if needed or re-write the Quran if you are still bent on religion.* To days issues are much more difficult than those thousands of years ago. Creation is the advancement of new ideas and change. It does not wait around for you to adjust your beliefs to advance forward to your own time in history. This is why the people are so lost in their religious beliefs, many think that the ancient beliefs are better than the present beliefs. *Religion is a mind control drug just like any other addiction.* It is very difficult to walk away from these beliefs due to the label of hypocrisy and superstition. *We must began to develop religious rehabilitation programs because most believers do not think that religion is addictive, they actually think that God of their religion control their every thought and they are right because the word God never existed, it was invented by the same people that invented Zeus.*" It was the Rich and Wealthy Slave Masters of that time". We cannot continue to utilize ancient beliefs for the time we are now living in. History is exactly what it is *"HIS-STORY"* Now what is your story? We are a different people, in a different time, with many different beliefs and ideas.

Music—The Great Communicator

Music is no doubt a great communicator, "Energy" created music for its own pleasure. When humans or animals and all those things that hear the melody of music, they will respond to the sound of music, even if it is nothing more than rhythmic tap on hollow wood that will make the sound. It can give the individual the mood and motion to dance, soothing mental telepathy or just the pleasure of listening. Music is all sound created by "Energy". It is Energy that gives the physical body the ability to dance and that depends on how much energy you have to dance, meaning this: "At a certain age music becomes a soothing antidote for relaxation". Today there are many types of music such as Jazz, Rock, Gospel, Country, Opera,Rap, Hip- Hop etc. Music can become a leak to physical violence, sex, educational drama, work etc. Nevertheless, we would hope that you take away from this article how the "Energy", within you utilize sound as a Great Communicator. It is very difficult for many individuals to set in a total quit, silent room with no sound or noise only listening to your own heartbeat. This takes a highly discipline person to set in a totally quit, silent room with no noise, at this level you can hear the many sounds of Energy moving within your head and body. You will start to hear a buzzing sound within you and if you are attentive to the quit silents you might even start to hear voices. This is because you have started to attune your thinking to what is really going on within you. Many people will lose their mind for fear of this kind of thinking because they have never set in a totally quit and silent room, some people will tremble at the very thought of this kind of setting.

Obtrusive Behaviors

We have said time and time again that the whole of Creation is a chemistry in a science project in a living active motion, many people will never understand how "Energy" have been used to energize the entire Universe. *There are many that love the life and system of life here on earth and have no sense of understanding that nothing stays here on earth forever. NOTHING!* Additionally, Did you think that this entire Universe operated without your input? Most people want to believe that after death that is the end of your life. In reality the only time many of us will recognize the separation of the body and the "Energy" within us is at the time of death. *We can't phantom how "Energy" began to emerge into a sperm drop mixed with ovum. Without environmental Education the people are lost in a obtuse state of mind* The knowledge of our Creation is all around us and we just look at daily life and birth as something from an invented God not trying to understand the real purpose of our own existence. After death, there is another life that began, the "Energy" that departed from you travels to another assignment in another dimension that is also part of this massive universe and many scientists believe that there are more than one massive Universe. *This suggest that "Energy" has the authority to send you not only within this vast Universe but to the many other universes and not past through the same life twice.*

Your body is the object of death, that life within you never dies because you are connected to the same "Energy" that created this vast Universes. Let us look at this from another angle, take the dinosaurs and giant reptiles that existed millions of years ago, they died true enough, but they also had that same "Energy that we have today and because of their size they had more. Additionally, this would suggest that the life of the dinosaurs had to return to that all powerful "Energy Grid and "Energy" has the power to move those Dinosaur images anywhere in the universe it choose. All of these movement are under the explicit control of "Energy". *Most People cannot phantom the human body being separate from the "Energy" that resides within them. The human body and the "Energy" within us seemed inseparable like semis twins.* Therefore, when we look at the people in the Christan religion here in America and those in third world countries supporting their ideology of Islam and their Prophet, we can see both religions that has same level ignorance and that has devastated our own economy and their own economy with the practice of tribalism. Both of these communities are so steep into ancient religious conviction, they are backwards in their ideology until many still live like ancient peasants right here in America. In retrospect, many Americans have adopted many of those same antics. You can still hear many Christians singing that same old song, *"Give me that old time religion, it is good enough for me".*

Redistribution of Wealth

Taking wealth from the poor and giving it to the rich and wealthy, is a true definition of redistribution of wealth according to Mitt Romney and the Republican Party and they do not think that this is applicable to them. In his statements to a group of investors, he quoted President Obama statement when he was a State Senator 14 years ago, indicating that he would support a redistribution of wealth so that every one is afforded a fair shot. In past articles we ask the question: *"How do we take back our wealth from the rich"?* Redistribution of wealth is just one way to recover the wealth that the rich has taken from the poor. *President Obama statements still stands true today, a redistribution of wealth would provide and equal shot at the American dream and would give individual families the opportunity to secure the necessary economical resources need for their survival.*

Republicans like Mitt Romney do not want redistribution of wealth because they feel that all the wealth that they accumulated belongs to them and no one help them acquire their wealth although they stole, manipulated companies and the economy to acquire that wealth. If you have been watching the news concerning how Romney acquire his wealth, anyone can see that Mitt Romney manipulated his own company Bain Capital to acquire his wealth causing many companies to close and people to lose their jobs and health care insurance. Mitt Romney does not want to give back the wealth that he swindle the American people out of. *This is what greed does to the ignorant mind.* You must ask the question: "Why do people like the Republican Party like to see others suffer when they are the real culprit that cause many people to suffer extreme loses? *It's like they get great pleasure out of watching the people suffer.*

Manipulation and Ignorance
of Mitt Romney

It is apparent that a person do not need intelligence to run for the highest office in the land, President of the United Stated. You only have to be rich and wealthy with many funders and investors in your midst. Here is a politician in the personage of Willard Mitt Romney that has refused to share the many years of his own tax returns that is required by any candidate running for President. In a newly released video tape Mr. Romney stated that 47 percent of Americans pay no taxes and depend on the Federal Government for assistance. ***Among that 47% also include many of the rich and wealthy investors that also depends on corporate welfare that is used to support Mitt Romney's campaign.*** *So who is fooling who?* The masses are the real victims of greedy, rich and wealthy men. *Romney truly believes that he made his wealth and success all by himself and no one helped him achieve his success.* ***No one, absolutely no one can acquire any wealth on their own, NO ONE.*** It takes "Energy" to create any kind of wealth and Energy utilize its own resources and power to give wealth to those that use manipulation to acquire it. This is called the negative influences of "Energy". ***How can Mitt Romney create jobs all by himself without the help of other people? Utterly imposable! How can he reduce the role of Government when it is the Government that is creating the so call jobs he insist that he will create if he is elected?*** If he creates more jobs as President, this would automatically increase more Government spending for the rich and wealthy contractors, the government would make tax breaks for the rich causing more government spending that would benefit the rich. ***Romney is a great manipulator of resources and his investors are aware of his manipulation skills and this is why he can raise millions of dollars the way he does.*** Mitt Romney is truly the Great Wizard of Oz until the coveres are pulled back and revile who he really is.

Stop, Put The Breaks On, The Nfl Refferees Make More Money Than Our School Teachers?

Is America just totally backwards or what? This is something we must stop and change immediately, In Chicago, Illinois we just had a teachers Strike which most teacher with today's economy make less than $50,000. A year. The referees for the *[NFL] National Football League* went on Strike and was given over $200,000 dollar salaries, this suggest that a ball game has more preference and seniority with the rich and wealthy media than the education of our children. *You do not have to go to school to learn how to play a ball game. However, it is imperative that you must go to school to learn how the game is played.*

Expansion of Education & Growing Power

I watched Education Nation over the weekend and some profound students said some things that we might want to give thought. For starters, what we have done over the years to educate communities around the Chicago area with Growing Power should be expanded to the Chicago Public Schools as well. *What one student had suggested was that students could participate in a growing power program by growing their own food at their school to help cut cost in the public school system. Additionally, these students could be taught how to grow the different food groups while in class and right on the school grounds providing that the school has the grounds to grow the food. Newt Gingrich said something during his primary election that is worth noting. he said: "We could engage janitorial learning with the students and pay the student a stipend to clean the schools under supervision". Nevertheless, this could lead the student into learning to achieve and hopefully a degree in engineering.* We must start working in these communities by teaching our children early from kinder *gardening* on into the 12th grade into college levels. With this type of curriculum funding for this program it is inevitable that funding would be available because the teachers are taking the students out of the classrooms into the communities. to see how the agricultural system truly benefits families in their own home and communities. The Agricultural school on 111th street would be a great expansion for all public schools. Professor Block, this might be something you could discus at the next meeting. we need to look at a new evaluation for student learning and how teachers evaluate their students fairly. Many students will not go to college many will learn early but agricultural growth is a necessity for human development.

Part II—Money Influences

Money and material wealth has influence the people for ages and has escalated in the pass few years, The Rich and Wealthy Super Slave Masters has utilize this method of slavery for thousands of years and it is more obvious today than in any time in history. The people have been massively deceived, they have been hoodwinked, bamboozled, tricked, lead astray as if Houdini or David Copperfield had played a masterful trick on the human brain and the people has excepted it as true. Money, politics, religion, and the American education system are all influences of a mass deception. Let us look at the Money and how money influences the other three. Our President has raised over three quarters of a billion dollars for his re-election campaign, his opponent Mitt Romney and his donors like the Koch Brothers are willing to offer Mr. Romney and the Republican Party over $400 million and more to help unseat the President and there is one Billionaire that can out spend all of the Republican donors combine.

The whole argument in this election is to show case WHO CAN SPEND THE MOST MONEY giving rise to the voters that the Republican Party has the money and power to put America back to work and buy the Office of The President. Here is what's missing from this scenario, The Rich and Wealthy Super Slave Masters has a long standing Worldwide to utilize money to influence politics, religion, third world Countries and the entire educational system worldwide. Religions also part of the trick-nology the Super Slave Masters has used to further keep the masses enslaved to the idea that if you believe in God and the Lord Savior Jesus Christ, you will be saved from the torments of Hell. Today The whole Country is leaving in the so call Hell, Look at what is happening today in our political system. In reality, there is no such thing as a hell, there is only **Negative** and **Positive** behaviors that is triggered by the "Energies" within your body, Hell is the negative impulses that you experience each and every single day of your life on an hourly daily bases. It is so sad that the masses cannot see what is going on in the Churches after they have placed their hard-earned money into the coffers of the Church.Our educational system is controlled by the super Rich Slave Masters of the world. today our elementary Schools are now paying fees to enter into public schools, these are the same people that writes the curricula for the public schools and all schools worldwide.

Advancing Forward in Creation

Dear Colleagues:

It is time to take another step forward, to spring forward mentally we must look at where we are today in this dimension and where we would like to go in the future. This is not complex at all, the reason for this is to better understand the power of "Energy" within you. As we have pointed out to you that after your death your "Energy" will past through your body and separate itself from your physical body, in religion they call this your soul or spirit but it is nothing more than the "Energy" that has kept your body alive. If people would take a closer look at what is really happening within them they would never be fearful of death but would welcome death as a powerful friend waiting and ready to transport that enter "Energy" to all powerful Grid that awaits you at the time of death. Your "Energy" is the real life that gives your body movements that it does, your "Energy" is like sitting in the cock pit or an airplane.

This might suggest that there are many other bodies that "Energy" takes control, just look at the animals, the insects etc. "Energy" is in every single thing we can imagine, to prove this point, if you have every walked into a drug store or supermarket and see all the products, and each of those products are individually packaged and their contents are also individually produced. but they all are developed by "Energy" and each and every item has become "Energized". This is also why when things are destroyed, "Energy" can sweep up everything on the planet and cause it to dissolve in the earth or in the air. That what "Energy" does. Now, let us take this a step further. As we look at our massive universe, we see stars but we also understand that there are Planets all around this universe, "Energy" multiplies each and everything it creates this include this massive universe, creation does not stop at one thing, it multiplies any and all things it creates. We can see this by looking at the stars and our own human race, sand pebbles, water etc.

So, we have many options upon our return to the all powerful Grid. The creation is so huge you can choose billions of forms that you might want to enter. "Energy" is so powerful that it can send you leap years ahead or retrograde to years gone by. It is more beneficial for many to advance foreword to see the many universes "Energy" has created. We must always learn to utilize Negative and Positive "Energies" as two halves of the same coin.

Was The Human Body Created In A Laboratory?

We have said in the past that this entire creation is a science project in a living active motion. The chief Scientist that created this Universe is "Energy". *All of our intelligence is provided by "Energy" Our thoughts are "Energized" by and though "Energy" our physical body was created in a whole different universe and was placed here by "Energy".* Many of us do not want to believe that our human body was "Energized" by "Energy", although your body is constantly craving for a new breath of fresh air to "Energized" your own body. After the human was created, it was place on a planet that was conducive to human habitation where it would survive for a period of time, then it would die, and that energy that controlled that body would eventually return to the "Energy" Grid were all things were created from its basic inception. *The human individual "Energy" is the real true life of the body human, this life within the human body never,ever,never,ever, dies, it is transported from one dimension to another dimension on into infinity.* This is why whatever "Energy" creates, it always multiply meaning that "Energy" is everywhere at all times and controls this entire creation from the past to the future.

As we look at science today and observe how animals have been cloned and now the body human, we can clearly see that science has raised serious questions as to how the physical body was created. Let us take a closer look. *To clone a human is to take the spermatozoa and mix it with ovum and incubate these two with a human body temperature for the same way a pregnant woman incubates the fetus in the womb. However, we need to look at this a little deeper, the human organs were created under a microscopic vision prior to its growth and development. Additionally, we must keep in mind that the human body was created in stages long before the body was complete, the organs, brain, limbs, blood etc. all was created in stages long before the body was complete. "Energy" seen that after the whole body was developed and complete, it develop a seed within the body that would multiply human growth while in the womb, this was done by microscopic development so that when "Energy" was inserted into the embryo that embryo would retain "Energy" from both male sperm and female ovum that would "Energize the fetus. "Energy" is transmitted from the male and female at the time of pregnancy it is the sperm that enters the egg ovum and at this point life Begin in the womb.,*

Hurricane Sandy: The Many Arsenals of "Energy"

Hurricane Sandy is one for the record, the wingspan of this enormous hurricane is approximately 900 miles wide with high winds of about 90 miles an hour and on the north west end of the Hurricane there will be snow and ice which will impair approximately 50 million people. The whole airlines, bus services, on the East Coast has been shut down even the railroads has been shut down. and the temperature dropping as the nor'easter moves in with freezing rain and snow in areas like New York City. *Yet we still have those doubter about climate change. Let us just count the arsenals that "Energy" is using with Hurricane Sandy, wind, rain, snow, ice, water, oceans, lakes, the Full-Moon and its magnetic influence it has on the water ways on the earth, especially in this geographical area.* It is very imperative that we recognize the power of "Energy" and its arsenals. Our religious Brethren would quickly assert that this is Gods Curse on the Wicked. *Nothing could be farther from the Truth, when these type of weather-related incidents happen, "Energy" is telling the people that it is time to Change again and (make changes in one's own behavior), because this massive hurricane will bring about changes in that area and around the world.* It does not matter how the destruction accrue, rather it is hurricanes, snow, rain, wind, ice, earthquakes, volcanic eruption, tsunami, tornadoes, meteors, asteroids etc. The destruction behind this massive Hurricane will cost billions of dollars and might go will into the trillions. The cleanup could be catastrophic in many areas and the sustain winds could increase or decrease its assault after it makes land fall, hopefully. *"Energy" is the most Powerful entity in all of creation.*

What's The Difference Between The Taliban and The Republican Party?

The Taliban and the Alqida network have terrorized their women and young girls with the threat of death if they continue to seek education for themselves. *They want to keep the women and girls enslaved under a ancient Islamic doctrine that prohibits women from getting a true education. A case in point was when a young 14-year-old girl in Afghanistan was shot at close range in the head because she refuse to allow the Taliban Islamic practices to stop her from acquiring an education. She is now getting treatment is a hospital in London. However, here in the United States the Republican Party has issue statements that they believe in life begins at conception without exception even if a woman was raped by incest, or criminal intent they believe that a woman should bare the child if she became pregnant.* The most heinous of all these assertions is that these men are married to women that except what these politicians are saying. *How can a woman allow her husband to make such allegations and not be offended? Are these women living in fear like those woman in Afghanistan, Syria, Iran?* This suggest that the Republican Party wants the same thing as the Taliban, they want to keep the woman enslaved to the idea that the male has total control over the woman's physical body as his own personal property and she has nothing to say about it. *The difference between American Women and those in the Middle East is that the women in America is allowed to get an education with freedom of speech.* Nevertheless, we can see similarities in both countries, among a certain group of men with money and wealth.

Psychology In Dysfunctional Behavior

Psychology and Psychiatry are the treatments for mental and abnormalities in behavioral disorders, we found that the fathers of Psychology were individuals like Wilhelm Wundt, of the University of Heidelberg, Hermann Von Helmholtz, Jean Piaget, William James of Harvard University *These men are known as the Master of Psychology, but today we live in a circular society and our life time is quite different from the times in the 18Th century*. However, we can barrow a passage from Jean Piaget who once said : *"The principal goal of education in schools should be developing or creating within men and women who are capable of doing new things, not simply repeating what other generations have done"*. This speaks volumes in understanding the true purpose of life. We should always be seeking new ways and means for obtaining new knowledge and not repeating the same things that past generations have done or mastered. *This includes the practice of religion, politics, and things that causes the human mind to retrograde into the past by thinking that those people that wrote the bible had the knowledge and understanding to control the people in the future. In retrospect this has indeed happen and the masses truly believe in a book that has nothing to do with our future, it is imperative that we create our own books of knowledge and develop our own future by utilizing our own enter mind.* **For many religious believers this is the exact cause as to why so many people are still living in the past as they keep believing that the bible is telling them the truth about life.** We must be proud of our President because he understands how religion has hoodwinked and bamboozled the minds of the people worldwide. Nevertheless, he must maintain his own religious views so that the American people will continue moving forward on the high knowledge for change. Just look at how they have treated scowled President Obama, yet he never wavered nor stooped to the low life ideas of the Republican Party. You got to tip your hat his patience.

Conclusion

There are issues within this book that is undeniable and there is no argument that could change the facts. That is the status of "Energy", there is nothing in creation that is equal to the power of "Energy" absolutely nothing. There is no science, no religion, no politics, no educational philosophy that can mis—interpret the use of energy in this book. Nothing in creation can exist without "Energy". NOTHING!

It does not matter what religion a person believes in, the terminology of the word God is a word that was invented by the Rich and Wealthy Slave Masters of the world and they were successful in getting the majority of the world population to believe that the word God is the true power of creation and that terminology of God truly exist. This has been done by the utilization of money and its influence.

"Energy" has allowed the human thought to indulge in senseless behavior s due to the negative and positive influences that "Energy" controls and will bring about a change in the total creation at will. The ***change has come*** with the appearance and presence of President Barack Hussein Obama.